THE BELFAST
COOKERY BOOK

A Dish of Champ

THE BELFAST COOKERY BOOK

for students in the
*Belfast College of Domestic Science
and others interested in food with
an Ulster flavour*

BY

MARGARET BATES
*in association with
the Principal and some Members of the Staff*

LINE DRAWINGS BY
KENNETH GILBERT

PHOTOGRAPHS BY
ROBERT J. ANDERSON

PERGAMON PRESS
OXFORD · NEW YORK · TORONTO · SYDNEY
PARIS · FRANKFURT

U.K.	Pergamon Press Ltd., Headington Hill Hall, Oxford OX3 0BW, England
U.S.A.	Pergamon Press Inc., Maxwell House, Fairview Park, Elmsford, New York 10523, U.S.A.
CANADA	Pergamon of Canada Ltd., 75 The East Mall, Toronto, Ontario, Canada
AUSTRALIA	Pergamon Press (Aust.) Pty. Ltd., 19a Boundary Street, Rushcutters Bay, N.S.W. 2011, Australia
FRANCE	Pergamon Press SARL, 24 rue des Ecoles, 75240 Paris, Cedex 05, France
WEST GERMANY	Pergamon Press GmbH, 6242 Kronberg-Taunus, Pferdstrasse 1, West Germany

First edition 1967

Reprinted 1968, 1974, 1977

Library of Congress Catalog Card No. 65–28095

Printed in Great Britain by Biddles Ltd., Guildford, Surrey

ISBN 0 08 018952 0

CONTENTS

FOREWORD

THIS is a book which should give pleasure to all who enjoy good food. It is practical and comprehensive in its mingling of recipes, classical and local, with social history. The value which was placed on local produce, such as the potato, Lough Neagh eel and shell fish, is part of the history of Ireland and illustrates how food habits and patterns reveal the type of culture of a people.

Many classical recipes are included in the section dealing with foreign food. There is a delightful French Christening Cake, instructions for the famous Fritto Misto Mare from Italy, Kebabs from Turkey and advice on the making and serving of curries.

Recipes for old national dishes are reproduced. Yellow Man, a traditional Irish sweet-meat, and Brotchan Roy, a broth made with leeks, are typical examples which should prove to be of more than local interest.

The first chapter sets out the philosophy of the book, that while first class ingredients are necessary, flavour and texture are vital to the production of good food. To achieve this, detailed information is given on seasonings and flavourings and on the use of herbs and wine.

The thanks of the staff and students of College are due to the Vice-Principal, Miss Bates. Many students and a wide section of the public, both here and abroad, will benefit by her research and be grateful for this work.

February 1965

JOYCE STEWART
Principal,
Belfast College of Domestic Science

ACKNOWLEDGEMENTS

WHILE writing this book I received much help. An especial debt is owed to the Principal, Miss Joyce Stewart. It was she who initiated the book and she has given generously both of her time and of her wide culinary knowledge.

Sincere thanks are due to my colleagues Mollie McVeigh, Kitty Pennington, Kathleen Jones, Sadie Harrison, Margaret Bambrick and Margaret McDermott for discussions and for providing recipes which they themselves had tested; and to Elizabeth Boyle and Renee Coffey for their constructive criticism of the text.

MARGARET BATES

RELISHES, DRESSINGS AND AUXILIARIES

SEASONINGS

Good seasoning is fundamental to good cooking, and in the art of seasoning and flavouring food lies much of the skill of the cook.

Seasoning cooked with the food is more effective than when it is used as an addition at table. Indeed some dishes can never be adequately seasoned once they are served. This applies to many everyday things such as creamed potatoes and stews.

Salt and pepper are the two common seasonings, but anything which gives food a greater relish can be claimed to be one. Sugar is of value in some savoury dishes, particularly peas and those containing tomatoes. Curry powder may be used discreetly in a number of dishes, while cheese is sometimes treated as a seasoning rather than a distinctive ingredient.

Mustard, too, is important, particularly in dishes made with cheese and beef.

It is interesting to note that stuffing is sometimes referred to as a seasoning.

SALT: The best salt to use for cooking is coarse kitchen salt. Unfortunately, this is being superseded by a refined salt which contains other additions to keep it free from lumps but which detract from its flavour.

Most salt is distilled from the sea, but some is found in the earth in a crystalline form called rock salt. Our own Maldon salt is of this latter variety and it and what the French call "gros sel" have an excellent flavour which is appreciated by all who enjoy fine food. Such salt is best used in a salt mill. PEPPER is much used as a condiment and it may be obtained in the form of a powder or as whole peppercorns — a type of spice. Since the ground pepper quickly loses its aroma and flavour and also because it is open to adulteration, it is better to use freshly-ground pepper from a peppermill. The peppercorns are of two types — black and white. The white is the same seed freed of the outer skin. It is less pungent than black pepper and is more suitable for use in white sauces and all light-coloured dishes.

PAPRIKA pepper is ground from the sweet red pepper. It is not hot and may be used as a seasoning in sauces, some cheese dishes and dishes of Hungarian origin notably goulash. Comparatively large quantities may be added. It is also valued in the kitchen as a decoration for savoury food.

CAYENNE pepper is ground from red chillies. It is red and very hot and not to be confused with paprika pepper which is mild in flavour.

Cayenne is used in small quantities as a condiment, particularly in cheese dishes and in mayonnaise. It is, of course, used in curries.

MUSTARD: It is the seeds of the plant which are ground to give mustard and there are a variety of forms, the best known being white and black. In this country mustard is usually sold as a powder to be mixed with water, milk or vinegar. French mustards, on the other hand, are sold as a paste with herbs added and mixed with the juice of unripe grapes as in Dijon mustard, or an unfermented wine as in Bordeaux mustard.

SALTPETRE is used in pickle for meat because it gives it an attractive red colour. It must be measured carefully and used in small quantities as it also has a toughening effect.

FLAVOURINGS

VANILLA is a valuable flavouring obtained from the pod of a type of tropical orchid. It may be used in cooking in various forms:

The vanilla pod — when buying a pod the best to choose is one of 8-12 in. in length. The surface should be black, smooth and frosted. It is sold in a glass tube, but in the kitchen it is generally kept in a covered jar of sugar. The sugar which absorbs the flavour is used in cooking, fresh sugar replacing it as necessary. Vanilla sugar with a stronger flavour can be made as follows:

Cut a $1/_4$ oz vanilla pod into small pieces and place in a mortar with $1/_4$ lb castor sugar. Pound until fine. Sieve and store in an airtight container.

Vanilla sugar may also be purchased from a good grocer, and it is best bought by the $1/_2$-1 lb rather than in small packets.

Vanilla essence has the advantage that it is convenient to use. A good quality should always be purchased.

ORANGE or LEMON SUGAR is a useful kitchen store. It may easily be made by adding the finely-grated rind of 1-2 oranges or lemons to $1/_4$ lb castor sugar. Work the two together with a knife until a uniform colour. Dry and store in a covered jar. Use within a reasonable time for adding to any dish in which these flavours are required, such as cakes and puddings.

CARAWAY SEEDS are a form of aromatic spice used as a flavouring in bread and cakes and for scattering over savoury biscuits. They are also used in certain savoury dishes and in the making of some cheeses.

POPPY SEEDS are also aromatic and because of their flavour and attractive appearance they have been used since ancient times for sprinkling on bread, biscuits and cakes. They are occasionally used as an intrinsic part of a dish.

With age they lose their aromatic quality.

SESAME SEEDS are used as a food grain and for their oil. Industrially, they are used in the making of some margarines, cosmetics and soap. In the kitchen their attractive appearance and nutty flavour when toasted make them useful to sprinkle on bread and savoury biscuits. Their use is of very ancient origin.

SAFFRON is prepared from the dried stamens of the autumn flowering saffron crocus. It is usually purchased as a powder but may also be obtained as dried stamens, which are steeped before use. As it is expensive, the powder is open to adulteration. It is used as a flavouring and colouring in savoury dishes as well as in some breads and cakes.

HERBS

The discreet use of herbs in cooking does much to lift the flavour of food from dull and conventional levels to higher planes. In recipes it is difficult to do more than give guidance in their use and much must be left to the skill of the cook in using them wisely and with imagination.

Dried herbs are easily purchased, but their use is often disappointing as they become stale and lose their fragrance. Some herbs dry and store better than others, notably sage, thyme and basil.

Fresh herbs are much more satisfactory, but it must be realised that their flavour is pungent and that they should be used with discernment.

BASIL is a spicy and aromatic herb and it is important in any dish made with tomatoes such as tomato soup, sauce, drinks and tomato dishes in general.

BAY-LEAVES are one of the ingredients of the classic bouquet garni and come from a species of laurel. They are also used in flavouring potted herrings, liver paté and sometimes in custards, cornflour mould and rice pudding. They are easily dried in a warm atmosphere and their flavour preserved for a long time. It used to be the custom to grow a bay tree near the kitchen door for the convenience of the cook.

CHERVIL is a pretty plant suitable for using as a garnish. It is also a favourite flavouring in potato soup.

CHIVES are a member of the onion family with many uses in savoury dishes. The grass of the chives may be clipped finely with scissors and used as a garnish for soup or in French dressing, salad, sandwich fillings and champ among other things.

DILL is a feathery plant, the leaves and seed heads being much used as a garnish in Scandinavian cooking. Dill is also used in sauces to accompany fish.

FENNEL is also a feathery plant used in flavouring fish and the sauces to accompany fish. The stems of Florence fennel are eaten raw and have a flavour reminiscent of aniseed.

GARLIC is another member of the onion family. The bulb is easily broken into "cloves" and, after the papery skin is removed, is ready for use. The clove of garlic is generally crushed with the flat blade of the knife or finely chopped with salt for adding to savoury dishes of all types.

The diffident, who only wish a trace of flavour, prefer to rub a cut clove of garlic round the inside of the dish or pan. Garlic imparts a very savoury flavour to food and, especially when cooked, is not nearly so strong as many believe.

MARJORAM is used generally for flavouring purposes. It has a lovely scent and is valued in pot-pourri.

MINT is greatly used in this country for mint sauce to accompany roast lamb. A spray of mint may also be added to the water when boiling new potatoes or peas. Sometimes the tip of the spray is used as a garnish and looks effective when crystallised.

ORIGANO is wild marjoram and it is greatly used in Italy and in Greece where it is used as a flavouring for kebabs.

PARSLEY is widely used in this country both as a garnish and as a flavouring. The stems rather than the leaves have the flavour and it is in this form that it is used in a bouquet garni.

ROSEMARY is a herb much used in Italian cookery. It is pungent and so must be used with discernment. In cooking it is associated with roast lamb, pork, chicken and duck, often in a simple way by placing a spray under the joint of bird in the roasting tin.

SAGE is also pungent and must be used with discrimination. It is used in flavouring the stuffing for roast pork, 'duck and goose.

TARRAGON is the herb favoured by the French and the best variety is called French tarragon. It is widely used in flavouring savoury dishes, but particularly vinegar, mustard and roast chicken.

THYME and LEMON THYME are excellent and may be widely used where herbs are required in savoury dishes. They are sometimes made into a jelly.

BOUQUET GARNI

A bouquet garni, bunch of herbs or fagot is called for in many recipes for sauces, soups, stews and other savoury dishes. The classic bouquet is made up of a piece of bay-leaf, 4-5 stalks of parsley and a spray of thyme. Other herbs may be added according to the recipe and may include a strip of lemon or orange peel. The items for the bouquet garni should be tied together with a thread to facilitate their removal after use. Sometimes they are tied loosely in a piece of muslin, but this is generally unnecessary except when dried herbs or whole spices are included.

SIMPLE GARNISHES AND DECORATIONS

The presentation of food is important and well cut suitable garnishes and decorations add greatly to the smart appearance of a dish. A garnish should, of course, contribute to the eating qualities of the food.

LEMON is used to garnish pancakes, fish dishes and some meat dishes. For this purpose the most satisfactory method is to cut it into wedges. These are easy to squeeze over the food at table and there is no waste involved. The pieces should be trimmed free of white pith and seeds and may be decorated with parsley.

Lemons and oranges are frequently sliced for floating in drinks.

CRESS: In cooking, two types of cress are important:

Watercress—used to garnish grilled and roast meat or in salads. The young leaves are bright green, but many prefer

4

the bronzed foliage of the older plant. It has a slightly bitter hot flavour reminiscent of mustard and is a good accompaniment to mild summer cheeses, in the same way that celery is a foil for the mature blue cheeses of winter.

Watercress should be well washed and picked over. It is better dressed with oil and vinegar before serving.

Garden Cress — usually grown in conjunction with mustard. It should be carefully washed and system used to avoid tossing the fine stems irrevocably. It is a useful garnish, particularly for cold dishes. It is also used for salads, sandwiches and hors-d'oeuvres.

CURLED CELERY makes an attractive garnish and decoration. Preferably use the end of the stick of celery nearest the root and cut into lengths of approximately 2 inches. Then, using a sharp knife or potato peeler, cut into slivers. Put these into iced water and put aside for a time to curl. Drain and use as required.

Sometimes one or both ends of a length of celery are fringed and put into iced water to curl.

RADISHES may be used whole, sliced or made into radish flowers for garnishing hors d'oeuvres and salads. If the radishes are young and crisp their texture and flavour are enjoyed best if they are served whole, with a little of the green top remaining to add to their appearance and act as a handle. Radish flowers, while attractive if neatly cut, are better used in a limited way as a decoration. After cutting put them in iced water to open out.

CHOPPED JELLY: Jelly for chopping should be rather stiff.

Turn it on to a sheet of wet greaseproof paper and, using a sharp wet knife, chop it quickly and lightly. Sweet or savoury chopped jelly may be used to decorate cold dishes and, if a very neat appearance is required, it should be piped from a paper bag—no actual pipe being necessary.

ANGELICA is an aromatic plant not unlike rhubarb. The stems are candied and are recognised by their fresh green colour. Chopped angelica may be used in cakes for its flavour, while it is useful for ornamental purposes when cut into diamonds of varying sizes. The candied surface should be washed in hot water before cutting.

COLOURED SUGAR makes an inexpensive decoration. It looks particularly well dredged over a spiced apple cake, or sprinkled discreetly on a mountain iced cake. To make it, add a drop or two of colouring to a little castor sugar. Work the two together until the desired shade is obtained. Dry and store for use.

COCO-NUT may be moistened and coloured in the same way.

THE USE OF WINE IN COOKING

Wine may be added to stews, sauces and gravies, to give them a rich aromatic flavour which is obtainable in no other way. Its use has also a tenderising effect on meat, but this is really a secondary consideration.

The wine in such dishes should always be cooked and in cooking it changes flavour. It is not really necessary to use more than a glassful to a dish and a cheap wine will prove adequate. As a rule, but a rule with exceptions, it is usual to use a white wine with fish, chicken and veal dishes and a red wine with beef and mutton dishes. Dry cider may be substituted for a white wine if economy is necessary, though cider is also used in its own right.

WINE for GRAVY and other dishes where it will only be briefly cooked should be bubbled quickly so that it reduces and combines with the other ingredients to form an essence full of flavour.

A MARINADE: Meat is frequently marinaded in wine with the addition of a few vegetables, spices and herbs before it is cooked. This gives it flavour and tenderness. The time for marinading depends on the quality of the meat, but might be anything from a few hours to 2-3 days.

If the cut of meat is a joint for roasting, it should be dried after removal from the marinade before putting it in the oven. The vegetables should be strained from the wine and discarded. While the wine itself is usually reduced and used as the basis for a sauce or gravy, red-currant jelly, for example, may be added to it if it is to accompany mutton or roast saddle of hare.

If the marinaded meat is to be stewed, the strained wine will be used as part of the liquid for the stew. The vegetables of the marinade tend to become sodden and so are better replaced by fresh vegetables.

THE FLAMING OF FOOD with wine, whisky, brandy or other spirit is another method of introducing a unique flavour to a dish. The wine or spirit is first heated in either a ladle or small saucepan. When hot, it will light easily by drawing to the side of the heat, when the fumes ignite. The flaming liquor is poured over the food where it burns together with any fat or sugar in the dish. Once the alcohol has burned out, one is left with a concentrated essence of delicious flavour. Flaming may be done as a process early in the cooking of some dishes, or as a final flourish in the dining-room.

SAVOURY SAUCES

Sauce-making is a test of culinary skill and a successful sauce contributes greatly to the flavour of the dish which it is to accompany. Indeed, a sauce may be looked upon as a form of liquid seasoning.

While the variety of sauces is considerable, the recipes are usually built from a much smaller number of foundation sauces or " sauces mères ".

FLAVOURED MILK FOR WHITE SAUCES

Sauces in which milk is used are greatly improved if it is first flavoured by infusing a little carrot, onion, celery and a bouquet garni in it. Cook gently together until the milk is well flavoured and reduced a little, then strain.

The flavour of the most elementary white sauce to accompany a vegetable may be improved if only by adding a little of the vegetable water to the sauce before using it.

THE CONSISTENCY OF A SAUCE

A sauce may be used as an accompaniment and handed separately, in which case it should be of a pouring consistency. Sometimes it is necessary to have a sauce which will mask the food and in this case it should be slightly thicker and is called a coating sauce. Again a sauce may be required to bind ingredients together as in the making of croquettes. This is the thickest sauce of all and is known as a panada.

BASIC WHITE SAUCE

Pouring	*Coating*	*Panada*
$^1/_2$ *oz butter*	*1 oz butter*	*1 oz butter*
or margarine	*or margarine*	*or margarine*
$^1/_2$ *oz flour*	*1 oz flour*	*1 oz flour*
$^1/_2$ *pint milk*	$^1/_2$ *pint milk*	$^1/_4$ *pint milk*
seasoning	*seasoning*	*seasoning*

THE POURING and COATING SAUCES: Melt the butter in a small saucepan. Stir in the seasoned flour and cook together over a gentle heat for a few minutes. This forms a white roux. Withdraw the pan from the heat and stir in the milk by degrees. Return to the heat and stir until boiling point is reached. Simmer for 3-4 minutes so that the flour is thoroughly cooked.

THE PANADA is made rather differently:

Make a roux as before and withdraw the pan from the heat. Add the milk all at once and return to the heat. Stir and cook until the mixture is so thick that it leaves the sides of the pan. Cook thoroughly before using.

BÉCHAMEL SAUCE

1 *oz butter or margarine*	$^1/_2$ - $^3/_4$ *pint flavoured milk*
1 *oz flour*	2 *tablespoonfuls cream*
salt and white pepper	

Melt the butter in a small saucepan. Add the flour and mix well with a wooden spoon, then cook for a few minutes over a gentle heat. Draw the saucepan from the heat and add the flavoured milk gradually. Return to the heat and stir constantly until boiling. Simmer for 3-4 minutes. Add the cream and correct the seasoning.

Many sauces are derived from the basic white or béchamel sauce:

ANCHOVY SAUCE

Use a basic white sauce, preferably made with milk flavoured with fish trimmings, a few pieces of vegetables and a bouquet garni. When it is ready, add 2 teaspoonfuls anchovy essence and a drop of pink colouring.

Alternatively, a few pounded anchovies may be used to flavour the sauce.

CAPER SAUCE

If the caper sauce is to accompany boiled mutton, the most satisfactory liquid to use is half milk and half meat liquor. Make as a basic white sauce. When it is ready, add 1 tablespoonful roughly chopped capers and 1 dessertspoonful of caper vinegar to the basic sauce and cook together for a few minutes before serving.

EGG SAUCE

$^1/_2$ *pint white sauce*	1-2 *hard-boiled eggs*
a squeeze of lemon juice	$^1/_2$ *oz butter or margarine*

Prepare the white sauce and when it is ready, add a squeeze of lemon juice and stir in the chopped hard-boiled egg. Remove the saucepan from the heat and stir in the $^1/_2$ oz butter.

Use with boiled fish or chicken.

MORNAY OR CHEESE SAUCE

Use a basic white or béchamel sauce and add $1^1/_2$-2 oz grated cheese when it is cooked. Heat sufficiently to melt the cheese.

This sauce should be well seasoned with salt, a little cayenne and mustard.

MUSHROOM SAUCE

¹/₄ pint white or   *³/₄ oz butter or marga-*
  béchamel sauce   *rine*
3 oz mushrooms   *2 tablespoonfuls cream*

Prepare the sauce and keep hot. Meanwhile, wipe and slice the mushrooms and sauté for 3-4 minutes in the melted butter. Add to the béchamel sauce with the cream. Simmer together for a few minutes before serving.

MUSTARD SAUCE

Prepare a basic white or béchamel sauce adding 1 teaspoonful dry mustard to the flour for the roux. At the last stir in 1 teaspoonful vinegar.

ONION SAUCE

1 onion   *1 tablespoonful flour (or*
¹/₂ pint milk   *cornflour)*
     salt and pepper

Slice or chop the onion and stew in the greater part of the milk until tender. Meanwhile, blend the seasoned flour with the remainder of the milk and use to thicken the onion mixture. Cook well.

PARSLEY SAUCE

Use a basic white or béchamel sauce and add a generous tablespoonful of well-chopped parsley just before serving.

Parsley sauce spoils if it has to be kept hot.

VELOUTÉ SAUCE

Velouté sauce is a white sauce made with stock. It forms the foundation of a number of other sauces such as suprême and Dutch sauce.

1 oz butter or   *¹/₂ pint concentrated*
  margarine   *white stock*
³/₄-1 oz flour   *e.g. chicken or fish*
salt and pepper   *2 tablespoonfuls cream*
     a squeeze of lemon juice

Melt the butter and stir in the seasoned flour. Cook gently until a light straw colour. Draw away from the heat and gradually add the stock. Return to the heat and stir until boiling. Simmer for 5-7 minutes. Lastly add the cream and a squeeze of lemon juice.

SAUCE SUPRÊME

¹/₂ pint velouté sauce   *2 tablespoonfuls cream*
2 egg yolks   *salt and pepper*
     a squeeze of lemon

Heat the velouté sauce in a double pan —the surrounding water being below boiling point. Combine the yolks and the cream and stir carefully into the sauce. Cook slowly until it thickens again. Correct the seasoning and add a squeeze of lemon juice.

Frequently sliced sautéd mushrooms are part of a suprême sauce. They may be added directly, but are probably better if scattered over the food to be coated.

DUTCH SAUCE

1 gill velouté sauce   *1 dessertspoonful vinegar*
¹/₂ gill creamy milk   *or 1 tablespoonful*
     lemon juice
1 egg yolk   *salt, pepper and cayenne*

Heat the velouté sauce, preferably in a double saucepan.

Combine the yolk, milk and seasoning and stir in. Cook gently until thick. The sauce should not boil again. Add the vinegar or lemon juice.

SIMPLE BROWN SAUCE

1 *oz butter or*	1 *oz flour*
margarine	*salt and pepper*
1 *onion*	1 *tomato*
	¹/₂ *pint stock*

Melt the butter and fry the chopped onion. Remove the onion and add the flour and seasoning. Cook gently in the fat until a golden brown roux is formed. Return the onion and add the tomato cut in quarters. Add the stock and stir until boiling. Simmer for 30 minutes. Strain and use.

ESPAGNOLE SAUCE

2 *oz ham or bacon*	1 *pint brown stock*
2 *oz butter or*	6 *mushrooms (or*
margarine	*mushroom stalks)*
1 *onion*	*a bouquet garni*
1 *small carrot*	1 *gill tomato pulp*
2 *oz flour*	1 *tablespoonful sherry*
	salt and pepper

Cut the ham into small pieces and fry in the melted butter. Slice the vegetables and fry them gently. Add the flour and brown all carefully. This takes time and it is important not to burn the ingredients. Add the stock, bouquet garni and quartered mushrooms. Stir until boiling, then simmer 30 minutes. Towards the end of this time, add the tomato pulp and simmer a further 10 minutes. Strain, correct the seasoning and add the sherry.

REFORM SAUCE

The recipe which follows is a simplified one for home use.

¹/₂ *pint Espagnole*	1 *tablespoonful port*
sauce	*wine*
1 *dessertspoonful*	*a few grains of*
red-currant jelly	*cayenne*

Prepare the Espagnole sauce omitting the sherry. Stir in the red-currant jelly, the port and cayenne and simmer for 10 minutes.

HOLLANDAISE SAUCE

the juice of ¹/₂ *lemon*	2 *egg yolks*
1 *teaspoonful water*	4¹/₂ *oz butter*
	salt, cayenne and lemon juice

Put the lemon juice and water into a small bowl and place over a pan of hot water. Add the egg yolks and ¹/₂ oz butter. Whisk well until it begins to show the marks of the whisk. Draw to the side of the heat and add the remaining butter in small pieces, whisking continuously so that each part is worked in before the next is added. Season with salt and cayenne and add more lemon juice as required.

Hollandaise sauce should barely hold its shape when ready and is served luke-warm rather than hot. It is used to accompany boiled salmon and other fish, also asparagus.

BÉARNAISE SAUCE

1 *chopped shallot*	¹/₂ *gill vinegar*
1 *tablespoonful*	2 *yolks*
chopped herbs	4 *oz butter*
—parsley, tarragon	*a little lemon juice*
and chervil	*salt and pepper*

Put the chopped shallot, herbs and vinegar into a small saucepan and reduce to 1 dessertspoonful. Put the yolks and ¹/₂ oz butter into a small bowl and place over a pan of hot water. Beat with a wooden spoon and strain in the vinegar. Mix well. Continue beating and adding the butter in small pats, beating each piece in thoroughly before the next is added. Be careful not to overheat the sauce or it will curdle. Correct the seasoning and add a squeeze of lemon juice.

Béarnaise sauce should be the consistency of mayonnaise. It is used to accompany grilled steaks.

APPLE SAUCE

4-5 *cooking apples*   2-3 *tablespoonfuls sugar*
1 *tablespoonful water*   1 *oz butter or margarine*
a squeeze of lemon juice

Peel, core and slice the apples. Put them in a saucepan with the water and sugar. Simmer together until reduced to a pulp. Add the butter and lemon juice. Apple sauce may either be sieved or left as it is — much depends on the quality of the apples and personal taste.

Apple sauce is used to accompany roast pork, duck and goose.

CRANBERRY SAUCE

$^1/_2$ *lb cranberries*   3-4 *tablespoonfuls sugar*
2 *apples — peeled and*   *a little water*
   sliced (optional)

Combine the ingredients in a small saucepan and cook slowly until the fruit is soft.

Sometimes it is considered better to thicken cranberry sauce with a little blended arrowroot.

Cranberry sauce is used to accompany roast turkey.

GOOSEBERRY SAUCE

$^1/_2$ *lb gooseberries*   *a little water*
3 *tablespoonfuls sugar*   1 *oz butter*

Wash the gooseberries — it is not necessary to top and tail them. Put them in a saucepan with the sugar and a little water. Simmer gently until they are quite soft. Sieve and reheat the pulp with the butter.

Gooseberry sauce is served with fried or boiled mackerel. It is also good with roast duck if apples are not available.

MINT SAUCE

1 *bunch mint*   2 *tablespoonfuls boiling*
2 *tablespoonfuls sugar*   *water*
salt $^1/_2$ *gill vinegar*

Strip the leaves from the mint and wash and dry them. Chop finely with the sugar. Put them into the sauceboat, add salt and the boiling water. Stir in the vinegar.

Mint sauce is very successfully made in the liquidiser of the mixing machine, the combined ingredients being put into the electric blender for chopping.

Mint sauce is served with roast lamb. It should be freshly made and the mint used with generosity.

TOMATO SAUCE

1 *onion*   *a pinch of dried basil*
1 *slice lean bacon*   1 *gill tomato pulp*
1 *oz butter*   1 *gill stock*
salt, pepper and a   1 *teaspoonful cornflour*
   pinch of sugar

Chop the onion and bacon and sauté in the melted butter for 10 minutes. Add the seasoning, basil, tomato pulp and the stock and simmer together until the onion is tender. Sieve and thicken with the blended cornflour.

BREAD SAUCE

2 *cloves*   *salt and pepper*
$^1/_2$ *onion* $^1/_2$ *oz butter or*
$^1/_4$ *bay-leaf*   *margarine*
$^1/_2$ *pint milk*   1 *tablespoonful cream*
2 *oz breadcrumbs*   *(optional)*

Stick the cloves into the onion and put into a saucepan. Add the piece of bay-leaf and the milk. Simmer very gently until the milk is well flavoured. Remove the onion and bay-leaf and add the breadcrumbs, seasoning and butter. Cook together for 4-5 minutes or until a creamy consistency. Do not overcook at this stage otherwise the sauce will become too thick. Stir in the cream.

Bread sauce is served with roast chicken among other things.

CURRY SAUCE

1 oz butter, margarine   1 tablespoonful flour
   or dripping
1/2 onion — chopped   salt
1 apple — chopped   3/4 pint stock
1 tablespoonful curry   a squeeze of lemon juice
   powder

Heat the fat and add the chopped onion and apple. Cook gently until golden brown. Add the curry powder and cook a further 3-4 minutes. Stir in the flour and salt and cook for a minute. Draw the saucepan to the side of the heat and gradually stir in the stock. Bring to the boil stirring all the time, and simmer for 15-20 minutes. Add a squeeze of lemon juice.

If wished, the stock may be flavoured by infusing 1-2 tablespoonfuls cocoanut in it for an hour before using.

This simple curry sauce is suitable for curried eggs, vegetables, prawns and chicken.

HORSE-RADISH SAUCE—HOT

1/2 pint béchamel   a squeeze of lemon
   sauce   juice
1 large tablespoonful   1 tablespoonful cream
   grated horse-radish   (optional)
     1/2 teaspoonful made mustard

Add the freshly-grated horse-radish, mustard and lemon juice to the béchamel sauce and cook gently together for a short time. Stir in the cream.

Horse-radish sauce is served with roast or boiled beef and fish.

HORSE-RADISH SAUCE—COLD

2 tablespoonfuls   2 teaspoonfuls castor
   grated horse-radish   sugar
1/4 teaspoonful made   salt and pepper
   mustard   1 tablespoonful vinegar
     1 gill cream

Mix the horse-radish, mustard, sugar, seasoning and vinegar together. Whip the cream until stiff and stir into the horse-radish mixture gradually.

Refrigerate until required.

Cold horse-radish sauce is served with roast beef. It is also a delicious accompaniment to grilled salmon and trout.

RAISIN AND CIDER SAUCE

1/4 cupful soft brown   1 cup cider
   sugar   1/4 cupful raisins
1 small tablespoonful   8 cloves
   cornflour   2 inch cinnamon stick
salt   1 oz butter or margarine

Put the sugar, cornflour and salt into a saucepan and blend with the cider. Add the raisins and spices. Bring to the boil, stirring all the time, and simmer for 10 minutes. Stir in the butter. Serve with boiled or baked ham.

CUMBERLAND SAUCE

2 heaped tablespoonfuls   2 tablespoonfuls port
   red-currant jelly   1/2 teaspoonful dry
rind of 1 Seville orange   mustard
(or the rind of 1 orange   1/2 teaspoonful salt
   and 1 lemon)

Place the jelly in a bowl over hot water to melt. Peel the zest from the orange and cut into fine shreds. Cook in $^1/_2$ gill water for 5 minutes and strain. Add to the jelly, together with the port and seasonings. Serve cold as an accompaniment to hot or cold meat such as ham, pork, goose or brawn.

VINAIGRETTE SAUCE

2 *shallots*	1 *tomato*
2 *teaspoonfuls capers*	*salt, pepper and a little*
1 *pickled gherkin*	*sugar*
2 *large tablespoonfuls*	$^1/_2$ *gill olive oil*
chopped parsley	1 *dessertspoonful*
	vinegar

Chop the shallots as finely as possible. Chop the capers and gherkins roughly. Combine with the finely-chopped parsley. Skin and seed the tomato and cut into shreds. Add to the parsley mixture together with the seasoning, oil and vinegar. The mixture should be thick and green.

Serve with boiled pig's feet, boiled chicken or fish or use for dressing a cold beef salad.

TARTAR SAUCE

1 *teacupful mayonnaise*	1 *dessertspoonful*
1 *dessertspoonful*	*chopped capers*
chopped gherkins	1 *dessertspoonful*
	chopped parsley

Mix the chopped gherkins, capers and parsley with the mayonnaise. Serve with fried fish.

SWEET SAUCES

CHOCOLATE SAUCE — NO. (1)

2 *oz dark chocolate*	$1^1/_2$ *gills water*
2 *oz sugar*	1 *teaspoonful arrowroot*
a little vanilla flavouring	

Break the chocolate into pieces and combine with the sugar and the greater part of the water. Heat gently until the chocolate is melted. Bring to the boil and boil together for a few minutes. Blend the arrowroot with the remaining water and use to thicken the sauce. Cook thoroughly and add the vanilla flavouring.

CHOCOLATE SAUCE — NO. (2)

$^1/_4$ *lb dessert chocolate*	*a little vanilla*
1 *gill water*	*flavouring*
1 *tablespoonful sugar*	2 *tablespoonfuls cream*
$^1/_2$ *oz butter*	

Dissolve the broken chocolate in the water. Add the sugar and vanilla flavouring. Simmer gently for 20 minutes, then stir in the cream and the butter.

Serve hot with ice-cream.

CUSTARD SAUCE — PLAIN

1 *dessertspoonful*	1 *egg*
cornflour	1 *dessertspoonful sugar*
$^1/_2$ *pint milk*	*flavouring as required*

Blend the cornflour with a little of the milk. Heat the remainder and thicken slightly with the cornflour. Beat the egg and carefully stir in the cornflour mixture. Return to the pan and stir over a gentle heat until the egg is cooked and the custard thickened. Add the sugar and flavouring.

CUSTARD SAUCE — RICH

$^1/_2$ *pint milk*	1 *dessertspoonful sugar*
2 *egg yolks*	*vanilla flavouring*

Heat the milk. Blend the yolks with the sugar and pour over the milk. Strain back into the saucepan and stir over a gentle heat until it thickens sufficiently to coat the back of the spoon. Do not overheat or it will curdle. Add the vanilla flavouring.

FUDGE SAUCE

2 *oz butter or*   4 *oz soft brown sugar*
  margarine   2 *tablespoonfuls creamy*
1 *tablespoonful golden*   *milk*
  syrup

Melt the butter. Add the golden syrup and the sugar and stir over a gentle heat until dissolved. Bring to the boil and simmer gently until a little, when tested in cold water, will form a soft ball. Cool for a minute then beat in the milk.

Serve with steamed coffee pudding.

JAM OR MARMALADE SAUCE

2-3 *tablespoonfuls jam* 1 *dessertspoonful sugar*
  or marmalade   1 *teaspoonful arrowroot*
1 *gill water*   *colouring if necessary*

Put the jam, water and sugar into a saucepan and bring to the boil. Simmer for 5 minutes. Blend the arrowroot with a little extra water and use to thicken the sauce. Cook thoroughly. If necessary strain before serving.

LEMON SAUCE

2 *tablespoonfuls golden* *the rind and juice of*
  syrup   1 *lemon*
1 *gill water*   1 *teaspoonful arrowroot*

Put the golden syrup, water, the rind and juice of the lemon into a saucepan and simmer together for 5 minutes. Blend the arrowroot with a little extra water and use to thicken the sauce. Strain, if wished, and serve with various steamed puddings.

SABAYON SAUCE

2 *egg yolks*   ³/₄ *gill sherry, white*
1 *dessertspoonful castor*   *wine or fruit juice*
  sugar

Put the three ingredients into a bowl and place over a pan of steaming hot water. Whisk until the mixture becomes thick and frothy. Avoid overheating the sauce or it will curdle. Alternatively, if it is under-cooked, it will separate on standing.

Serve with rich steamed puddings.

SWEET WHITE SAUCE OR CORNFLOUR SAUCE

¹/₂ *pint milk*   1 *dessertspoonful castor*
1 *heaped teaspoonful*   *sugar*
  cornflour   *flavouring as required*

Blend the cornflour with a little milk and heat the remainder. Thicken with the cornflour and cook thoroughly. Add the sugar and flavouring.

Sweet white sauce may be flavoured with vanilla, lemon, ginger and nutmeg among other things. It is served with steamed and baked puddings.

SYRUP SAUCE

2 *large tablespoonfuls* 1 *teaspoonful lemon*
  golden syrup   *juice*
1 *tablespoonful water*   *a little grated lemon*
                           rind (optional)

Heat the ingredients together and serve with steamed puddings.

HARD SAUCES

Hard sauces are best represented by the brandy butter served with the Christmas plum pudding. The basic mixture may be given different flavourings. These sauces are more widely used in America than here and are good with steamed puddings.

SPICED HARD SAUCE: 4 oz butter, 4 ¹/₂ oz castor sugar, ¹/₄ teaspoonful ground cinnamon, ¹/₈ teaspoonful ground cloves and a little grated lemon rind.

Cream the butter and sugar until light. Beat in the spices and lemon rind. Serve piled in a little dish, sprinkled with toasted nuts and dusted with icing sugar. Alternatively, spread neatly and thickly on a plate and chill. Cut into cubes and serve piled in a dish.

BROWN SUGAR HARD SAUCE: 4 oz butter, 4 ¹/₂ oz soft brown sugar, 1 tablespoonful cream, vanilla flavouring.

Cream the butter and sugar until very light. Beat the cream in gradually and lastly add the vanilla flavouring. Pile in a small dish and chill. Alternatively, chill and cut into cubes.

Hard sauce may also be flavoured with coffee, rum, whiskey, sherry, lemon or orange. A small quantity of ground almonds is sometimes added to the mixture.

SAVOURY BUTTERS

Savoury butters are used to accompany many dishes such as grilled fish, meat and ham. They are also excellent to spread on bread for sandwiches and for various small savouries.

MAÎTRE D'HÔTEL BUTTER

1 oz butter   *finely-chopped parsley*
a squeeze lemon juice   *salt and pepper*

Work the butter on a plate with a knife and gradually work in the other ingredients. Spread neatly and thickly on the plate and chill. When hard, cut into squares and serve the pats on grilled fish or meat.

ANCHOVY BUTTER

1 oz butter   *a little anchovy essence*
3-4 anchovy fillets   *pepper*

Soften the butter on a plate. Pound the anchovies and add, together with the anchovy essence and pepper. The butter should be a soft pink when ready. Spread neatly and thickly on the plate and chill. When hard, cut into squares and serve the pats with fish.

CHUTNEY BUTTER

1 dessertspoonful   *¹/₂ teaspoonful made*
    chutney   *mustard*
2 oz butter   *a squeeze lemon juice*

Chop the chutney if necessary and gradually work into the creamed butter. Add the mustard and a squeeze of lemon juice.

Chutney butter is useful for sandwiches and small savouries.

DEVILLED BUTTER

1 oz butter   *¹/₂ teaspoonful chutney*
a little curry paste   *a pinch of cayenne*
    a squeeze of lemon juice

Cream the butter and gradually work in the other ingredients. Use with grilled steak, kidneys or cutlets.

SALAD DRESSINGS

FRENCH DRESSING

3 dessertspoonfuls   *salt and pepper*
    olive oil   *¹/₄ teaspoonful made*
1 dessertspoonful   *mustard or a pinch of*
    vinegar   *dry mustard*

Combine the salt, pepper and mustard and gradually stir in the oil. When well blended, add the vinegar and mix until emulsified.

Other ingredients may also be added

as required such as chopped chives, parsley, garlic, onion juice, cayenne, sugar or a crumbled blue-vein cheese.

MAYONNAISE

1 *egg yolk*	*a little pepper*
¹/₄ *teaspoonful made mustard*	*a dust of cayenne*
	¹/₄ *pint olive oil*
¹/₄ *teaspoonful castor sugar*	1-1 ¹/₂ *tablespoonfuls vinegar*
¹/₄ *teaspoonful salt*	*a little lemon juice*

Put the egg yolk in a bowl and mix in the seasonings. Then beat in the oil, adding a few drops at a time especially at the beginning. A wooden spoon or a small sauce whisk are used for this purpose. As the making of the mayonnaise progresses the oil may be added more quickly. Continue beating in the oil until the mixture thickens, then beat in some of the vinegar and lemon juice to correct the consistency. Continue in this way until all the oil is used up. The amount of vinegar and lemon juice may be varied according to the flavour and consistency required in the mayonnaise. The other seasonings may also be varied so that the flavour of the mayonnaise suits the food which it is to accompany. It is sometimes made very thick so that it can be piped for savouries.

Mayonnaise is easily made in the emulsifier of the mixing machine.

SALAD CREAM

1 *heaped teaspoonful flour*	2 *dessertspoonfuls sugar*
	1 *egg yolk*
¹/₂ *teaspoonful dry mustard*	¹/₄ *pint milk*
	1 *oz butter or margarine*
¹/₂ *teaspoonful salt*	2 *tablespoonfuls vinegar*

Blend the dry ingredients with the egg yolk and milk. Bring to the boil

stirring all the time and cook thoroughly. Remove from the heat and stir in the butter and vinegar.

This salad cream stores well. If possible, use combined with a little whipped cream.

RELISHES

SPICED VINEGAR FOR PICKLES

1 *quart vinegar*	¹/₄ *oz whole allspice*
¹/₄ *oz cinnamon stick*	¹/₄ *oz mace*
¹/₄ *oz cloves*	*a few peppercorns*

Tie the spices in muslin and add to the vinegar. Cover with a tight fitting lid and bring to simmering point. Remove from the heat and infuse for 2 hours. Remove the bag of spice and use either hot or cold as required in different pickles.

PICKLED BEETROOT

Wash and boil the beetroot for 1 ¹/₂ hours. Peel and slice or cut into cubes. Pack loosely into pickle jars and cover with cold spiced vinegar. Seal so as to exclude the air.

PICKLED RED CABBAGE

Use fresh crisp red cabbage and remove the outer leaves. Cut into 5 or 6 sections and shred finely. Arrange the shreds in a large basin, sprinkling each layer with salt. Cover and put aside for 24 hours. Drain well and pack loosely into pickle jars. Cover with cold spiced vinegar. Seal so as to exclude the air.

Pickled red cabbage is ready for use after one week. After 2-3 months it loses its crispness.

PICKLED PEARS

4 *lb pears (sound, but*   1 *lb sugar*
   not too large)   1 ¼ *gills vinegar*

It is not necessary for the pears to be ripe. Peel them, keeping them whole and with the stem still attached. Melt the sugar in the vinegar and bring to the boil. Add the pears, cover with a lid and simmer as slowly as possible for 3 hours.

Remove the lid and continue to cook for a further 3 hours. At first the liquid does not nearly cover the fruit, but as the cooking progresses it increases. During the second part of the cooking it becomes amber in colour. Pack into jars with tight-fitting lids. Cover with syrup and seal so as to exclude the air.

PICKLED PEACHES

6 *lb small peaches*   1 *pint vinegar*
1 *pint water*   4 *oz cinnamon stick*
3 *lb sugar*   2 *oz cloves*
        1 *oz root ginger*

Peel the peaches and prepare a syrup with the water and half the sugar. Boil the peaches in this for 5 minutes, then remove from the heat and leave for 2-3 hours. Remove the peaches. Add the vinegar, remainder of the sugar and the spices tied in muslin. Bring to the boil and boil for 10-15 minutes. Return the peaches to the syrup and cook quickly until they are tender and the syrup is thick—about ½ hour. Put aside for some hours or overnight. Remove the bag of spice and pack the peaches into jars. Reheat the syrup and use to cover the fruit. Seal so as to exclude the air.

APPLE AND DATE CHUTNEY

2 *lb cooking apples*   1 *large onion*

1 *lb dates*   1 *oz garlic*
½ *lb crystallised*   2 *oz salt*
   ginger   1 *quart vinegar*
½ *lb soft brown sugar*   4 *chillies*

Peel, core and slice the apples and stew with the sugar until tender. Chop the dates, ginger, onion and garlic. Add to the apples together with the salt, vinegar and chillies tied in muslin. Simmer all together for 2-2 ½ hours or until thick. Bottle in clean warm jars and cover so as to exclude the air.

Chutney improves with keeping.

TOMATO CHUTNEY

2 *lb green tomatoes*   6 *cooking apples*
1 *lb raisins*   1 *lb granulated sugar*
1 *lb sultanas*   4 *oz mustard seed*
2 *oz garlic*   4 *chillies*
2 *oz shallots*   2 *quarts vinegar*

Chop or mince the tomatoes, raisins, sultanas, garlic, shallots and apples. Put in a saucepan and add the sugar, the mustard seed and chillies tied in muslin and the vinegar. Simmer all together for 2-2 ½ hours or until thick. Pot and cover so as to exclude the air.

MINT SAUCE FOR STORING

1 *pint vinegar*   1 *lb brown sugar*
    1 *very large bunch mint*

Bring the vinegar and sugar to the boil. Meanwhile chop the mint finely. Add to the vinegar and bring to the boil again. Bottle and cork. Store for use throughout the winter.

SPICED PRUNES

1 *lb prunes*   ½ *lb sugar*
cold tea   1 *teaspoonful whole*
¾ *pint vinegar*   *cloves*
       1 *stick cinnamon*

Steep the prunes in cold tea for 24 hours. Put the vinegar and sugar in a saucepan and add the spices tied in muslin. Boil together for 15-20 minutes. Meanwhile stew the prunes in the tea until soft. Drain. Measure $1/2$ pint juice and add to the vinegar together with the prunes. Do not use for 2 days.

Spiced prunes make a pleasant accompaniment for a curry dish.

HOME MADE BEVERAGES

CONCENTRATED LEMONADE CORDIAL

3 *lemons*   1 *pint water*
1 *orange*   2 *oz citric acid*
1 *grapefruit*   3 *lb sugar*

Grate the rind and squeeze the juice from the fruit. Add the water, citric acid and sugar. Heat together until the sugar is dissolved. Strain and bottle. Use a little diluted with water.

FRESH LEMONADE

1 *lemon*   2 *oz sugar*
$1/2$ *pint boiling water*

Grate the lemon and squeeze the juice. Add the sugar and pour over the boiling water. Stir until the sugar is dissolved and put aside to cool. Strain before serving.

An orange drink may be made in the same way.

PORRIDGE

A variety of meals may be used to make porridge and include oatmeal — either fine, medium or pin-head; rolled or flaked oats; wheaten meal; maize meal, yellow meal, or Golden Drop. In each case, it is important that the meal is fresh otherwise the flavour of the porridge lacks that nutty quality which is so delicious.

There are also various ways of actually making the porridge:

1. Bring $3/4$ pint water to the boil and sprinkle in 3 tablespoonfuls oatmeal. The water should be kept on the boil and stirred all the time. Add a small teaspoonful salt and cover with a lid., Simmer gently for 15-30 minutes — the time depending on the type of meal used. Should the porridge be too thick the consistency may be adjusted by adding more water.

2. Steep the meal in the water overnight. In the morning, bring to the boil, stirring all the time. Add salt to taste and simmer gently for 15-30 minutes, stirring occasionally to prevent it sticking to the saucepan.

3. Porridge may also be made in a double saucepan. By this method it will require longer cooking time but will need little attention beyond an occasional stir and there is no fear of it burning.

Porridge should be served very hot with milk or cream or sometimes buttermilk. Sugar — white or brown — honey or golden syrup may also be served with it.

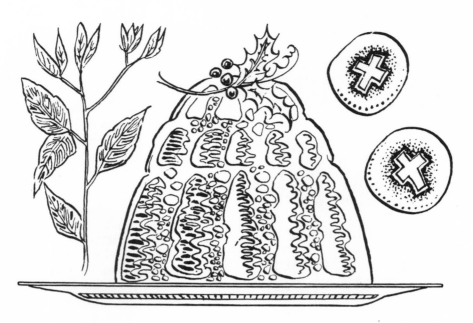

TRADITIONAL FESTIVAL FOOD

CHRISTMAS

Christmas time is celebrated gastronomically with a great wealth of food. It is essentially a family celebration and in every home much the same menu is prepared on Christmas day. A roast turkey is usually the main item followed by plum pudding and mincepies. Other traditional items include roast goose, spiced beef, dressed boar's head and, of course, the iced Christmas cake. These traditional dishes have almost, one might say, a ritual significance, but apart from these there is a lavishness of food of every description.

ROAST TURKEY

Turkeys vary considerably in size but a medium-sized hen bird of 10-14 lb is suitable for the average household. They should be hung for one to two weeks in cold weather or up to four days if the weather is mild. They are hung undrawn. Immediately prior to use, the sinews should be pulled and the bird drawn and singed. The giblets may be made into stock or giblet soup.

STUFFING: A turkey should be stuffed in the breast, but often a second stuffing is used in the body cavity. There is considerable choice and such stuffings as breadcrumbs and herbs, sausage meat, or even whole chestnuts may be used. If chestnuts are used they should be skinned, boiled and used in the body cavity.

TRUSSING: In general the trussing of a turkey is the same as for chicken, the primary aim is to keep it a compact shape and so ensure uniform cooking. The trussing should also improve the appearance and make carving easier.

ROASTING: There are many theories on how to roast a turkey to perfection. Some favour the use of aluminium foil while others cover it with buttered paper or with slices of fat bacon. It should be remembered that the flesh is inclined to be dry and that the cook's task is to see that it remains succulent and tender. The following method of cooking is satisfactory:

Butter the bird all over, season well and lay, breast down, in the roasting tin. Pour sufficient water or giblet stock around to cover the bottom of the pan amply. The steam from this will keep the flesh moist and later form the basis for a good gravy.

The turkey should be cooked slowly in a moderately hot oven.

Suggested oven temperatures — 400° reduced later to 350° or " 4 " reducing to " 3 ".

Turn the bird during the roasting, first on to the other side and finally laying it on its back, so that the whole is evenly browned.

The following table is a useful guide to the actual cooking time:

Stuffed Weight	Time
8-10 lb	2½-3 hours
10-14 lb	3-3½ hours
14-18 lb	3½-4 hours
20 lb	4-4½ hours

THE GRAVY: When the turkey is cooked, lift from the roasting tin, drain free from fat and keep hot. Decant the fat from the top of the liquid in the roasting tin and thicken with blended, seasoned cornflour.

THE ACCOMPANIMENTS: Serve the turkey accompanied by cranberry sauce. Sometimes boiled ham, bacon rolls or roast sausages are also served or bread sauce may be preferred to cranberry sauce.

DRESSED BOAR'S HEAD

The custom of serving a dressed boar's head on Christmas day is a very ancient one and originally it was the most important dish on the table. Today the custom is still observed in some colleges and hotels and it makes an imposing cold dish for a Christmas buffet. It should be noted that it is inexpensive and carves easily to give as many as forty portions.

In ordering the head, ask to have it split open but still hinged down the forehead and snout.

First wash it in plenty of cold water and remove the brains and tongue. Then bone it, being careful not to cut through the skin. Pickle the flesh and the tongue in a brine bath for 2-5 days.

BRINE:

2¼ lb salt	1½ oz saltpetre
¾ lb soft brown sugar	1½ gallons water

Combine the ingredients and bring to the boil. Boil 15-20 minutes, skim and cool before using.

STUFFING: Any good pork forcemeat may be used, but the following will be found most satisfactory:

the pig's tongue	1 finely chopped onion
2-3 pork fillets or	1 tablespoonful chopped
2½ lb pork griskin	parsley
1 lb pig's liver	1 dessertspoonful
1½ lb pork sausage	chopped thyme and
meat	sage
	salt and pepper

Remove the pig's tongue from the pickle, wash and boil until it can be skinned easily. It is then either minced with the other ingredients for the stuffing or cut into dice. Mince the pork and liver using the fine blade of the mincer and combine with the other ingredients.

19

Season well and flavour with freshly-chopped herbs.

The actual stuffing of the head varies somewhat according to the ingenuity of the cook, whose task is to reshape it to its original form. The following is a simple method:

Cut off the ears and set aside. Then lay the pickled flesh from the head skin side down on a damp cloth. Trim the thick parts and place the trimmings over the thin parts to form a fairly level surface. Arrange the forcemeat down the centre, tapering it towards the snout end. Fold in the two outer edges over the stuffing and stitch. Then tie and sew up firmly in the cloth. In doing this keep all shapely, that is to say roughly pear-shaped. Boil the head in stock made from the bones and flavoured with the usual stock vegetables. Simmer gently for 3¹/₂-4 hours. The ears should be added to the liquor one hour before the cooking is complete.

Take the head from the cooking liquor. Cool a little and then remove the cloth. Wash this out and re-tie the head, keeping it firm and a good shape. Leave overnight.

Next day remove the cloth and wipe the head with a cloth wrung out in hot water. Skewer the two ears in position, brush with glaze and decorate.

Another method of stuffing the head involves more work, but the result is very realistic:

Stitch a strip of material along the upper and lower jaw, under the chin of the head and round to the ears. Pack the cavity with the pork forcemeat and stitch across the opening. Steam, preferably for 4-4¹/₂ hours. Remove from the steamer and shape carefully, wiring the ears so that when cold all is a realistic shape.

Next day remove the stitches and material, brush with glaze, and decorate by piping with coloured butters. Simulate eyes from a slice of the white of a hard-boiled egg and a piece of pickled walnut (failing truffle) and contrive tusks from two sticks of celery.

Traditionally, dressed boar's head is served garlanded with bay and rosemary and with a flower or spray of holly stuck behind the ear.

SPICED BEEF

6-10 lb boned brisket

Spiced pickle:

1 *lb cooking salt*	¹/₂ *teaspoonful ground*
1¹/₂ *oz saltpetre*	*allspice*
³/₄ *lb demerara sugar*	¹/₄ *teaspoonful ground*
¹/₂ *cupful treacle*	*peppercorns*
¹/₂ *teaspoonful ground*	¹/₄ *finely chopped onion*
cloves	3 *finely chopped cloves*
¹/₄ *teaspoonful ground*	*of garlic*
mace	¹/₂ *teaspoonful mixed*
¹/₄ *teaspoonful ground*	*herbs*
ginger	

Trim the meat if necessary and place in a roomy vessel. Combine the ingredients for the pickle and rub well into the meat. Cover and put in a cool place. Each day the piece of meat should be turned and the pickle rubbed in. It should remain in the pickle for 14-17 days.

When the meat is sufficiently pickled, remove and wash well. Tie into a firm roll. Put on in cold water, adding a few flavouring vegetables cut in large pieces. Bring slowly to the boil, then simmer gently, allowing ¹/₂ hour to every pound of beef and ¹/₂ hour extra.

When tender remove the meat and press heavily between two boards until the next day.

The joint of spiced beef may be brushed with glaze before serving.

PLUM PUDDING

6 oz crumbs	the rind of 1 lemon and
3 oz flour	a little juice
$^1/_2$ lb demerara sugar	$^1/_2$ grated nutmeg
$^1/_2$ lb prepared suet	4 teaspoonfuls mixed
$^1/_2$ lb raisins	spice
$^1/_2$ lb sultanas	$^1/_4$ teaspoonful baking
2 oz chopped almonds	soda
2 oz quartered glacé	1 tablespoonful milk
cherries	4-5 eggs
1 oz chopped candied	1 glass brandy or
peel	whiskey (optional)

Measure the crumbs, flour, sugar and suet into a roomy basin. Add the prepared fruit, lemon and spices. Mix the baking soda with the milk. Beat the eggs and add to the milk. Use, together with the brandy or whiskey, to mix all to a moist but not sticky consistency. Mix thoroughly and two-thirds fill two greased pudding bowls. Cover with greased paper and steam 6 hours.

When the puddings are cold remove the paper and replace with a fresh covering. Store in a cool place until required, then steam the pudding for a further 2-3 hours.

Traditionally a plum pudding is sent to table dusted with icing sugar, stuck with a piece of holly and flamed with hot brandy. It is served accompanied by brandy or rum butter, a plain hard sauce, brandy sauce or custard.

A plum pudding improves with keeping and so it is usual to make several at a time. They are generally made in the late autumn, but may be made to mature for a year before eating.

LEFT-OVER PLUM PUDDING

Cold plum pudding may be sliced and fried in butter and served sprinkled with castor sugar and brandy or hard sauce.

In parts of England the left-over pudding is crumbled up, mixed with a little extra brandy and used as a filling for a pastry tart. Traditionally this is made after the style of a large Eccles cake.

In other parts the cold plum pudding is cut into thick sticks or blocks. These are arranged criss-cross in a pie-dish and a custard mixture poured round. The pudding is then baked gently as one would a baked custard.

CUMBERLAND RUM BUTTER

$^1/_2$ lb Barbados sugar	$^1/_2$ glass rum
grated nutmeg	$^1/_4$ lb fresh butter
a little icing sugar	

Grate a little nutmeg over the sugar and add the rum. Melt the butter and beat it into the sugar mixture. Continue beating until the mixture begins to set. Pile in a dish and serve sprinkled with icing sugar.

BRANDY BUTTER OR SENIOR WRANGLER SAUCE

3 oz fresh butter	2-3 tablespoonfuls
3 oz castor sugar	brandy

Cream the butter and sugar until light. Then gradually beat in the brandy. The mixture is apt to curdle if the process is hurried. Pile in a glass dish and put aside to firm before serving.

Alternatively the mixture may be spread about half-an-inch thick and put in a cool place to harden. It is then served in small blocks piled in a glass dish.

BRANDY SAUCE

1 *oz butter*	1 *oz sugar*
¹/₂ *oz flour*	1 ¹/₂ *gills water*

¹/₂-1 *glass brandy*

Melt the butter in a small saucepan. Add the flour and mix to a smooth roux. Draw the pan from the heat and gradually stir in the water. Bring to the boil and cook throughly. Stir in the brandy and sugar and bring to the boil again.

MINCEMEAT

1 *lb beef suet*	1 *teaspoonful ground*
³/₄ *lb soft brown sugar*	*ginger*
6 *large apples*	1 *teaspoonful ground*
1 ¹/₄ *lb currants*	*cloves*
1 *lb raisins*	1 *teaspoonful ground*
³/₄ *lb chopped candied*	*allspice*
peel	1 *grated nutmeg*
¹/₄ *lb chopped almonds*	*the rind of 1 lemon and*
1 *teaspoonful salt*	*the juice of 2*
	brandy or rum to
	moisten (optional)

Chop the suet finely using the sugar to keep it from sticking to the knife. Chop the apples. Combine with the fruit, spices, lemon rind and lemon juice. Add sufficient brandy or rum to moisten and stir all well together. Leave aside for an hour or two, stir again then press into jars and cover.

This mincemeat stores well.

MINCEPIES

Mincepies may be made using either a rich short crust pastry or one of the puff pastries. The former is probably best if they are to be handed at informal parties, while the latter can be enjoyed if the mincepies are to be served as a course at a meal.

Roll out the pastry and cut into rounds to suit the patty tins being used. Re-roll the trimmings and cut these into rounds for lining the patty tins. Fill generously with mincemeat. Damp the edges and cover with the first rounds of pastry. Press the edges well together and decorate. Make a slit in the cover of each pie and bake for approximately 20 minutes. The oven temperature will vary according to the type of pastry used. Serve hot, dusted with icing sugar.

CHRISTMAS CAKE (1)

¹/₂ *lb butter*	1 *teaspoonful ground*
¹/₂ *lb barbados sugar*	*ginger*
4-5 *eggs*	¹/₂ *teaspoonful ground*
¹/₂ *lb flour*	*allspice*
1 *lb currants*	¹/₂ *teaspoonful ground*
¹/₂ *lb sultanas*	*cinnamon*
¹/₄ *lb raisins*	¹/₂ *teaspoonful ground*
¹/₄ *lb candied peel*	*cloves*
¹/₄ *lb glacé cherries*	¹/₂ *teaspoonful ground*
2 *oz ground almonds*	*coriander seed*

¹/₂ *gill brandy, whiskey*
or rum (optional)

On the day prior to baking the cake wash and dry the fruit, halve or quarter the cherries, chop the peel and line an eight-inch cake tin.

Next day mix cake as follows:

Cream the butter and sugar and gradually beat in the eggs alternately with the flour and spices. Lastly, add the prepared fruit and turn the mixture into a lined tin. Bake in a moderate oven for approximately 3 hours.

Suggested oven temperature 325º-300º or " 3-2 ".

When the cake is cooked it may be basted with the spirits while it is still hot.

When cold wrap it in greaseproof paper and store in an air-tight tin for icing later.

Christmas cake is iced with almond paste or almond paste and, royal or mountain icing and then decorated.

CHRISTMAS CAKE (2)

1/2 lb sultanas	1/4 lb chopped glacé
3 tablespoonfuls	pineapple
brandy	2 oz chopped preserved
1/2 lb butter	ginger
1/2 lb castor sugar	2 oz chopped candied
4 eggs	citron peel
1/2 lb flour	3 oz chopped angelica
1/2 lb chopped glacé	2 oz chopped walnuts
cherries	

the grated rind and juice of 1 lemon

Steep the sultanas in the brandy overnight.

Cream the butter and sugar. Then gradually beat in the eggs, adding these alternately with the flour. Lastly, add the prepared fruit and the lemon rind and juice. Turn the mixture into a prepared 8 inch cake tin and bake in a moderate oven for approximately $2^1/_2$-3 hours.

Suggested oven temperature — 325° 300° or " 3-2 ".

CHRISTMAS YULE LOG OR BÛCHE DE NOËL

The cake eaten in France at Christmas time.

2 eggs	1/2 teaspoonful baking
3 oz castor sugar	powder
2 oz flour	a little vanilla flavouring
1/2 oz cocoa	2 tablespoonfuls milk

Chocolate butter icing:

4 oz butter	2 oz melted chocolate
6 oz icing sugar	a little vanilla flavouring

Prepare the sponge cake in the usual way, folding in the cocoa, milk and vanilla flavouring at the same time as the flour.

Spread in a lined and greased swiss-roll tin and bake in a hot oven for approximately 8-10 minutes.

Suggested oven temperature — 475° or " 7 ".

Turn out on to a piece of lightly floured paper and roll up without filling. Leave for a few minutes then carefully unroll.

Prepare the chocolate butter icing in the usual way. Spread some over the slab of cake and roll up. Dust off any surplus flour. Then cover the cake with the remainder of the icing — roughing it up into peaks to simulate bark. Trim the ends. If wished, a diagonal wedge may be cut from one end of the cake before it is iced. This piece can be placed at the side of the roll to give an even more realistic appearance.

CHESTNUT YULE LOG

1/2 lb chestnuts	8 oz dark chocolate
1/4 lb butter	(melted)
4 oz castor sugar	1 1/2 teaspoonfuls vanilla
	flavouring

Make a slit in each chestnut and put in a pan with water. Bring to the boil and boil 30 minutes. Take from the water one at a time and remove both outer and inner skins. Sieve or pass through a food mill.

Cream the butter and sugar and gradually work in the sieved chestnuts, melted chocolate and vanilla flavouring. Put aside to firm, then form into a log shape. Mark with a fork to represent the bark and rings of a tree and decorate with a spray of artificial holly. Dust lightly with icing sugar.

NEW YEAR

In Scotland Hogmanay is celebrated rather than Christmas and so it follows that the dishes particularly associated with the New Year come to us from Scotland.

SCOTS CURRANT BUN

6 oz flour	cold water
3¹⁄₂ oz butter	1 teaspoonful
a pinch of salt	castor sugar

1¹⁄₂ lb currants	¹⁄₄ oz ground ginger
¹⁄₄ lb raisins	¹⁄₄ oz ground cinnamon
¹⁄₄ lb chopped candied peel	¹⁄₄ teaspoonful pepper
¹⁄₄ lb chopped almonds	¹⁄₂ teaspoonful baking soda
¹⁄₄ lb sugar	¹⁄₂ teaspoonful cream of tartar
6 oz flour	
¹⁄₄ oz ground allspice	1 gill milk

Make the pastry as for short crust pastry and divide the dough into three pieces. These are for covering the sides, bottom and top of the bun respectively. Begin by greasing an 8 inch cake tin and roll one piece of the pastry into a long thin strip for the sides. Press into position, keeping the join as neat as possible. Next roll out the two remaining pieces of pastry thinly and cut two circles for the top and bottom. Damp the bottom edge of the pastry already lining the sides of the tin and press the bottom circle into position.

Now prepare the filling:

Put the fruit, nuts, peel, flour and other dry ingredients into a large basin. Add the milk and mix all thoroughly together. The mixture when ready should be moist but not sticky. Press into the lined tin, making the surface flat and smooth.

Turn in a ¹⁄₄ inch of the pastry lining the sides, damp and place the circle of pastry for the top in position. Make all secure and neat. Prick well and brush with beaten egg. Bake in a very moderately heated oven for approximately 3¹⁄₂ hours.

Suggested oven temperature — 325°—300° or " 3-7 ".

SCOTS SHORTBREAD

7 oz flour	2 oz castor sugar
1 oz ground rice	4 oz butter

Measure the flour, ground rice and sugar on to a working surface. Put the butter in the centre and knead with the hands, gradually drawing in the dry ingredients. After the flour is worked in, knead the whole for a little then shape into a cake. Pinch the edges with the fingers and prick. Transfer to a baking sheet and fasten a band of greaseproof paper around. Bake in a slow oven for about ³⁄₄ hour. The actual temperature required for baking shortbread will vary according to the thickness of the cake.

The suggested oven temperature —325° or " 2 ".

Dust with castor sugar while still warm.

SHROVE TUESDAY

In bygone days Shrove Tuesday was a time of feasting, being the last day, before the austerities of Lent began.

To-day the only tradition remaining is that of making and eating pancakes.

PANCAKES

4 oz flour	1 egg
a pinch of salt	1/2 pint milk
sugar and lemon for serving	

Measure the flour and salt into a bowl and make a bay in the centre. Drop in the egg and sufficient milk to make a creamy batter. Beat thoroughly, then add the remainder of the milk and set aside for at least one hour before using.

TO FRY THE PANCAKES: Choose a small, strong frying pan and heat thoroughly then heat a little lard, butter or oil in it. When the fat is hot pour in a little of the batter. There should be just enough to cover the bottom of the pan. When brown shake the pancake loose, toss it over and brown on the other side. Turn on to sugared paper, sprinkle with more sugar and a little lemon juice. Roll up and serve hot with extra sugar and wedges of lemon.

EASTER

Good Friday and Easter are associated in the culinary world with hot cross buns, Easter biscuits and Simnel cake. The latter more strictly belongs to Mothering Sunday which was originally a day to honour the Mother Church at Jerusalem. It is believed that the marzipan balls which are traditionally used in the decoration represent the apostles who founded the original church. Nowadays, however the tendency is to think of a Simnel cake as a cake for Easter.

HOT CROSS BUNS

1/2 lb flour	1 oz castor sugar
1/2 teaspoonful salt	1/2 oz yeast
1 teaspoonful mixed spice	3/4-1 gill warm milk
	1 egg
1 oz margarine	2 oz sultanas

Put the flour, salt and spice into a warm bowl and rub in the margarine. Add the sugar. Blend the yeast with the warm milk and add the beaten egg. Use to mix the flour into a soft dough. Knead thoroughly. Cover with a damp cloth and put in a warm place to rise until double its size. Add the fruit and knead again. Divide into 8-10 pieces and knead each into a ball. Place on a greased tray and put to rise for approximately 10 minutes. Brush with egg and mark with a cross. This may be done with a knife or using scraps of pastry. Bake the buns in a hot oven for approximately 15 minutes.

Suggested oven temperature — 475° or "9".

EASTER BISCUITS

5 oz butter or margarine	2 egg yolks
4 oz castor sugar	1/2 lb flour
the grated rind of 1 lemon	a pinch of salt
	2 oz currants
egg white and castor sugar for finishing	

Cream the butter, sugar and lemon rind together. Beat in the yolks and lastly work in the flour, salt and currants. The mixture should be stiff, but if necessary leave in a cool place to firm.

Turn the dough on to a board sprinkled with rice flour and roll out fairly thinly. Cut into large biscuits using a 3 1/2 inch fluted cutter. Brush with lightly-beaten egg white and sprinkle with sugar. Bake in a moderate oven until a light golden colour.

Suggested oven temperature — 375⁰ or " 4 ".

SIMNEL CAKE

6 *oz butter or margarine*	2 *teaspoonfuls mixed spice*
6 *oz castor sugar*	¹/₂ *lb sultanas*
4 *eggs*	¹/₂ *lb raisins*
6 *oz flour*	2 *oz chopped candied peel*

Almond paste for the centre of the cake:
6 *oz ground almonds*   3 *oz icing sugar*
3 *oz castor sugar*   1 *egg*
   a little almond and vanilla flavouring

Begin by preparing the almond paste in the usual way and roll into a 8 inch circle.

Now prepare the cake mixture:

Cream the butter and sugar. Beat in the eggs alternately with the flour. Lastly, stir in the spice and fruit. Spread half this mixture in the bottom of a prepared 8 inch cake tin. Lay the circle of almond paste on top and cover with the remainder of the cake mixture. Bake in a moderately-heated oven for approximately 2 ¹/₂-3 hours.

Suggested oven temperature — 325⁰ or " 3-2 ".

Finish the cake with another layer of almond paste made using 8 oz ground almonds and decorate with the traditional balls or rope of marzipan and glacé fruits or Easter novelties.

HALLOWE'EN

All Hallows' Eve is a holiday in Ireland celebrated by parties and fireworks. The traditional fare includes roast goose, apple cake or dumpling, nuts and toffee apples. Charms such as a ring or three-penny piece are wrapped in paper, perhaps accompanied by a suitable " motto " and buried in the apple cake or dumpling. In some parts of the country when the potatoes are being lifted, the very large ones, too big for storing, are grated and made into boxty.

ROAST GOOSE

An average goose will weigh from 10-12 lb and should serve approximately 8-10 persons.

It should be well hung before cooking, the time varying with the weather, but allowing anything from five to ten days.

A goose should be stuffed in the body cavity, trussed and placed on a greased roasting tin. The actual roasting should be done slowly, particularly if the bird is fat. Allow approximately 2 ¹/₂-3 hours for cooking, starting with a temperature of 400⁰ or " 6 " and reducing the heat to 350⁰ or " 3 " after the first 20 minutes.

Serve accompanied by brown gravy, made using giblet stock and apple or cranberry sauce.

A suitable stuffing is one made with sage and onion. The liver is often diced or mixed through it.

APPLE CAKE

8-12 *oz short crust or rich short crust pastry*
4-5 *cooking apples*
4-6 *tablespoonfuls granulated sugar*
a few cloves

Cut the piece of pastry in two and use half to line a suitable plate. Damp the edge and run a narrow strip of pastry round. Fill the centre with finely-sliced apples, layered with sugar and a few cloves. Cover with the remainder of the pastry and flake and scallop the edges or pinch with the fingers. Bake in a fairly hot oven for 40-45 minutes, the exact oven temperature depending on the choice of pastry.

Serve hot, dusted with castor sugar.

APPLE DUMPLING

6 oz suet pastry
approximately 4-5 cooking apples
4-5 tablespoonfuls granulated sugar
a few cloves

Butter a pudding bowl generously and sprinkle with demerara sugar.

Cut the suet pastry into two pieces of approximately two-thirds and one-third each. Use the larger piece to line the bowl, working it up the sides with the fingers. Fill with layers of finely-sliced apple, sugar and a few cloves. Damp the edges and cover with a lid rolled from the smaller piece of pastry. Cover with greased paper and steam for 2-2 ½ hours.

Serve accompanied by a jug of cream though sometimes slices of firm butter and a sprinkling of sugar are preferred.

Apple dumpling is sometimes made using potato cake instead of suet pastry.

BOXTY PANCAKES

4 large potatoes
2 tablespoonfuls flour
1 teaspoonful baking powder
½ teaspoonful salt
milk to mix
½-1 teaspoonful caraway seeds (optional)

Peel and grate the potatoes and squeeze as dry as possible in a strong cloth. Keep the liquid and put aside for 4-5 hours, when a starchy sediment will form. Meanwhile keep the grated potato tightly screwed up in the cloth. A little discolouration will take place, but will do no harm.

When the pancakes are to be made put the grated potato into a bowl, add the flour, baking powder and salt. Pour off the liquid in the other bowl and add the sediment to the mixture. Mix to a fairly soft batter with milk, the consistency being such that it is necessary to help it to spread in the frying pan. Fry the pancakes in butter in a small pan, cooking until well browned on both sides.

Serve hot with fried bacon or with butter and sugar.

If caraways are appreciated they may be stirred into the batter before frying.

TOFFEE APPLES

6-8 small red eating apples
Caramel:
8 oz granulated sugar
a little water
a pinch of cream of tartar

Impale the apples on wooden poultry skewers.

Put the sugar in a small saucepan and add sufficient water to moisten it. Dissolve over a gentle heat and stir in the cream of tartar. Remove the spoon and bring to the boil. Boil gently until a golden brown. Remove from the heat, allow the bubbles to subside and quickly dip the apples in the caramel.

Cool on a greased surface.

WEDDINGS AND CHRISTENINGS

It is traditional at a wedding to have a rich fruit cake appropriately iced and decorated for the occasion. It is a cake which is cut with ceremony by the bride assisted by the groom, all the guests sampling it. Indeed, it is considered lucky to do so and, in consequence, absent friends are sent small fingers of the cake so that they too may share in the good fortune of the newly-married couple.

The wedding cake is often tiered and the top cake may be kept for use later as a christening cake for the first child. The middle cake may also be kept and cut on the occasion of the twenty-fifth anniversary of the wedding.

WEDDING CAKE

The actual recipe for the wedding cake is similar to that used for a Christmas cake and it is advisable to use one which is familiar and liked. The quantities required will vary from wedding cake to wedding cake, depending on the number of tiers and the size of the cakes. They can be calculated, however, as follows:

If the recipe to be used is familiar it follows that the size of the cake tin will be known exactly and, using water, it is easy to find the volume of the cake. From this, it is a simple matter to find the volume of the tins to be used for the wedding cake, and so to calculate the quantities of cake mixture necessary.

A wedding cake may consist of one, two or three tiers and if it is to have good proportions, it is important that the dimensions of each should be carefully chosen. Suitable sizes are a 12 inch cake for the base, an 8-8 $1/2$ inch one for the centre and a 6 inch cake for the top.

To bake these cakes in a domestic size oven requires care and it is advisable to line the tins with 3-4 thicknesses of paper and in addition to tie several folds of newspaper round the outside of the large tin. The cakes may be prepared in one mixing and baked separately if that is necessary.

Suggested oven temperature — 300° or "2".

A 12 inch cake will require approxim-

ately 4 $1/2$ hours, an 8 inch cake 3-3 $1/2$ hours and a 6 inch cake 2-2 $1/2$ hours. When baked, remove from the oven and baste with brandy or other spirits. Allow to cool in the tin and next day wrap in generous layers of greaseproof paper for storing.

A wedding cake is improved if it is given time to mature before it is required. As the wedding approaches, it should be covered with a layer of almond icing and this given a little time to dry before being coated with royal icing. The cake is usually given two layers of icing and is then decorated by piping appropriately.

A FRENCH CHRISTENING CAKE

As an alternative to the usual rich fruit cake, iced and decorated with royal icing, the following French christening cake is good.

For it, prepare an 8 egg Genoese sponge and bake it in two Charlotte moulds or cake tins, one slightly wider than the other.

Prepare a crème au beurre and flavour it with Kirsch. Cut each cake into 3 layers and sandwich together again with the filling. As the work progresses, soak each layer of sponge with more Kirsch. Superimpose the smaller cake on the larger using the filling to stick them together. Spread the surface of the cake with a little apricot jam glaze and ice all with a white fondant or water icing. Decorate with pink or blue sugared almonds, the colour depending on the sex of the child. Five or six almonds should be arranged to form a flower on the top of the cake and the remainder scattered here and there over the sides. Silver balls should also be scattered attractively between the almonds.

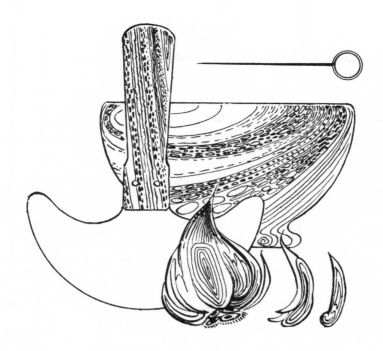

FOREIGN FOOD

THE recipes in this chapter are just a miscellany. They are given as an indication of the wealth of ideas on the cooking of food that awaits exploration.

JOINTS AND POULTRY

The French, in particular, can teach us much about the cooking of a joint, all their efforts being directed towards flavour and simplicity. It is particularly interesting to note that in spite of their fame for cooking, many homes were at one time without a suitable oven for roasting. Out of this seeming disadvantage has grown a method of cooking known as " à la boulangère " which is very adaptable to our own kitchens. The joint, surrounded by sliced potatoes and vegetables moistened with stock was given to the baker, who put it into his oven after the bread was baked. There it cooked slowly until collected at dinner time. The variety of vegetables can be varied to suit circumstances, probably the simplest being sliced potatoes and onions, perhaps flavoured with a little garlic. A joint of lamb cooked in this way has been described as a French Irish stew.

ÉPAULE D'AGNEAU À LA BOULANGÈRE

1 *shoulder of lamb*	*a bouquet garni or spray*
— boned and rolled	*of rosemary*
slivers of garlic	*approximately* 6-8
salt and pepper	*potatoes*
2 *onions*	
a little stock	

Trim away excessive fat from the shoulder of lamb and insert the slivers

29

of garlic here and there. Sprinkle the outside with salt and pepper. Put the bouquet garni or spray of rosemary into the roasting tin and place the meat on top. Peel and slice the potatoes and onions finely. Add a little finely-chopped garlic, sprinkle with seasoning and arrange around the joint. Moisten with a little stock and cover with well buttered paper. Bake in a moderate oven allowing 15-20 minutes to the pound and 15-20 minutes over. Stir the vegetables occasionally to ensure even cooking.

Serve the joint on a hot dish accompanied by the savoury mixture of potatoes and onion. No gravy is necessary as the vegetables are moist with the juices from the meat.

Leg or loin of lamb may also be cooked by this method and sliced carrots or mushrooms make good additions to the vegetable mixture.

GIGOT D'AGNEAU
À LA GRAND'MÈRE

approximately 3-4 lb	*4 oz streaky bacon*
leg of lamb	*1-2 onions*
slivers of garlic	*6-8 potatoes (or as*
salt and pepper	*required)*
a bouquet garni or	*a little butter to flake*
spray of rosemary	*finely-chopped parsley*

Trim the leg of lamb as necessary and insert the slivers of garlic into the fat and near the bone. Sprinkle with salt and pepper. Put the bouquet garni or spray of rosemary into the roasting tin and place the joint of meat on top. Rind the bacon and cut into match-stick pieces. Arrange around the meat. Put into a moderate oven for 20-25 minutes until the cooking starts and a little of the fat has run into the roasting tin. Meanwhile, chop the onion finely

and cut the potatoes into $1/2$ inch cubes. Combine and sprinkle with seasoning. Arrange around the meat stirring through the bacon. If the mixture is dry flake with a little butter. Continue the cooking in the oven allowing 15-20 minutes to the pound and 15-20 minutes over. Stir the vegetables occasionally so that they cook and brown evenly.

Serve the joint of meat on a hot dish. Sprinkle the vegetables with finely-chopped parsley and use as a garnish and an accompaniment.

Other joints of lamb may be cooked in the same way and, if wished, sliced mushrooms may be incorporated with the potato and onion towards the end of the cooking.

A well buttered, stuffed chicken is also good cooked in this way. It should be kept turned so that it browns evenly.

CHICKEN ROAST
IN THE FRENCH STYLE

In France, it is not usual to stuff a chicken. Instead, the inside of the bird is sprinkled with seasoning and herbs. The favourite for this purpose is fresh tarragon, but if this is not available, chopped thyme may be used, while in Italy the leaves of rosemary are favoured. These give the chicken a flavour slightly reminiscent of game. A little finely-chopped garlic may also be mixed with the herbs and will be appreciated by those who like its flavour. Lastly, put a knob of butter into the body cavity and truss in the usual way. Brush the chicken with olive oil and sprinkle with salt. Place in a roasting tin breast side down and cook in a moderately hot oven for $3/4$-1 hour according to the size of the chicken. During the cooking the bird should be turned, first onto the other side of the breast and later on to its back. This, together with the brushing with olive oil, should ensure a beautifully-browned bird.

When the chicken is tender, lift it on-to a hot dish and garnish with cress. The juices in the roasting tin are all that are necessary by way of gravy, but if too greasy, a little should be decanted off. Sometimes a tablespoonful of dry white wine is bubbled up with the chicken juices to make a slightly more elaborate gravy.

Serve the roast chicken accompanied by a tossed green salad and fried potatoes. Alternatively, a savoury rice mixture may be served instead. This latter suggestion is not, of course, of French origin.

STEWS AND OTHER SAVOURY MEAT DISHES

Every country has its own national stew and a study of these is rewarding. They are always practical as well as interesting and tasty.

RAGOÛT DE BOEUF BOURGUIGNONNE

This is a classic French stew and should be made, if possible, with burgundy, though a cheap red wine will serve.

The recipe which follows is a simplified one for home use.

1-1 ½ lb round steak	a pinch of sugar
1 oz dripping	3-4 oz mushrooms
1 onion	1 dessertspoonful flour
2-3 rashers of streaky bacon	1 glass burgundy or rough red wine
1 clove of garlic	stock or water
salt and pepper	a bouquet garni

Cut the meat into pieces as for a stew. Melt the dripping and when hot put in

the meat and brown quickly. Meanwhile, chop the onion, cut the rinded bacon into match length strips and chop the clove of garlic finely. Remove the meat from the pan and put in the onion, bacon and garlic. Add the seasoning and sugar and cook slowly until the onions are brown. Slice the mushrooms and add. Continue the cooking for a further 4-5 minutes until they are softened. Strain off any excess fat and sprinkle in the flour. Cook for a few minutes. Return the pieces of meat, add the wine and sufficient stock to cover all nicely. Add the bouquet garni. Bring to simmering point and cook slowly until the meat is tender — approximately 1 ½-2 hours.

Remove the bouquet garni and serve the stew in a hot dish. Suitable garnishes include fried croûtons, whole mushrooms or whole small onions stewed with the meat for a short period towards the end of the cooking time.

Alternatively, the ragoût may be cooked in a casserole in the oven.

This stew, like many other dishes of this type, improves in flavour on being kept overnight.

CARBONADE DE BOEUF

Carbonade de Boeuf is a Flemish stew made using Belgium beer.

1-1 ½ lb round steak	salt and pepper
1 onion	a little grated nutmeg
1 clove garlic	a pinch of sugar
1 oz dripping	1 tablespoonful flour
a bouquet garni	1 tin brown ale

To finish: *slices of French bread spread with butter and a little French mustard*

Cut up the meat as for a brown stew and chop the onion and garlic. Melt the dripping in a saucepan and fry the onion and garlic gently until brown. Add the meat, bouquet garni and

31

seasonings. Cover with a lid and turn up the heat until the cooking starts. Then cook gently for 30 minutes. Blend the flour with the ale and add. Bring to the boil, stirring all the time and transfer to a casserole. Continue the cooking in a moderate oven for 1-1 $^1/_2$ hours or until nearly tender.

Remove the lid and cover the top of the stew with the slices of prepared bread. Press into the gravy (it is necessary to have plenty) and return the casserole to the oven to toast the bread.

If a French roll is not available, slices of buttered bread smeared with mustard and cut into cubes serve instead. The bread is not an essential feature of a carbonade, but it makes good eating and is an interesting departure from customary methods.

GOULASH

Goulash is a Hungarian stew generally made with beef, though veal may also be used. The gravy is rich with tomatoes and seasoned with paprika pepper.

1-1$^1/_2$ *lb round steak*	*a bouquet garni*
1 *large onion*	1 *dessertspoonful*
1 *oz dripping*	*paprika pepper*
1 *dessertspoonful flour*	*salt and a little sugar*
	stock or water

1 *tablespoonful tomato purée*
6-8 *ripe tomatoes*

Cut up the meat as for a brown stew and slice the onions. Melt the dripping and when it is hot, add the onion and fry gently until a light golden colour. Remove and add the meat. Fry quickly but without allowing it to become very brown. Add the flour and return the onions. Add the bouquet garni, paprika pepper and other seasonings. Barely cover with stock or water and add the

tomato purée. Bring to simmering point and cook gently for half-an-hour. Skin the tomatoes and remove the seeds. Chop roughly and add to the stew. Continue cooking until the meat is tender — approximately 1$^1/_2$-2 hours. Remove the bouquet garni and serve in a hot dish accompanied by boiled potatoes.

Alternatively, the goulash may be cooked in a casserole in the oven.

MOUSSAKA

Moussaka is a savoury dish served in eastern Mediterranean countries and, as with many such dishes, it does not have a rigid recipe, each cook interpreting it in a slightly different way. Often it is made with aubergines. The following version, made with minced steak, potatoes, tomatoes and cheese is probably more useful.

Moussaka may be made in a buttered Charlotte mould and turned out, or, alternatively, use a deep earthenware dish. In the restaurants in Greece, it is generally baked in a large rectangular mould for cutting into individual square portions.

1 *medium onion*	1 *tablespoonful chopped*
1-2 *cloves of garlic*	*thyme and parsley*
2 *oz butter or*	*salt and pepper*
margarine	$^3/_4$ *lb tomatoes*
$^3/_4$ *lb minced steak*	1 $^1/_2$ *lb potatoes*
3 *oz grated cheese*	

Chop the onion and garlic and cook gently in the melted butter. When soft and transparent, add the minced steak and stir until each particle is separate. Add the chopped herbs and seasoning. Skin and slice the tomatoes or, better still, remove the seeds and chop roughly.

Add to the meat and cook together for a few minutes.

Meanwhile, peel and slice the potatoes thinly and sprinkle with seasoning. Put a layer in the bottom of a well-buttered baking dish, then a layer of meat and tomatoes and a sprinkling of cheese. Repeat the layers finishing with a covering of sliced potatoes and a good layer of grated cheese. Bake in a moderate oven for 2 - 2$^1/_2$ hours according to the depth of the mixture.

Moussaka is also frequently made using cooked minced mutton.

KEBABS

Schish Kebabs are typical of Turkish cookery, but are also served in other eastern Mediterranean countries and in India. They consist of small portions of meat, generally mutton, but sometimes veal or pork threaded on metal or wooden skewers. Kebabs are cooked over glowing embers, but may also be fried lightly and the cooking completed in a curry sauce. The word "schish" refers to the skewer; a "Kebab" means grill.

Cut up a piece of tender lamb into inch cubes. Season with salt, pepper, lemon juice and chopped marjoram. Cut some tomatoes in two and thread a portion onto each skewer. Then thread on squares of meat alternating with small pieces of bacon, mushroom caps, bay-leaves and wedges of parboiled onion or parboiled whole little onions. Brush with oil or melted butter and cook slowly under the grill. While it is not authentic, many cooks may prefer to bake the kebabs in the oven.

Kebabs may be served without further embellishment, except for a garnish of parsley or cress. Otherwise serve them with a rice pilaff.

Kebabs cooked in a curry sauce are accompanied by the usual curry accompaniments.

WIENER SCHNITZEL

Wiener Schnitzel is a favourite Viennese dish.

thin escalopes of veal	1 *dessertspoonful olive*
seasoned flour	*oil*
beaten egg	*breadcrumbs*
	a little lemon juice

Garnish: *Slices of lemon, stoned olives, fillets of anchovy and chopped parsley*

Flatten the escalopes and dip in seasoned flour.

Add the olive oil to the beaten egg. Dip the pieces of meat in this mixture and then in the breadcrumbs. Melt a little butter in a frying pan and fry the escalopes gently. Serve on a hot dish garnished with slices of lemon and stoned olives surrounded by an anchovy fillet. Add a squeeze of lemon juice to the butter still in the frying pan and strain over the meat. Dust with chopped parsley.

Veal cutlets may be cooked and served in the same way.

SWISS FONDUE

The name "fondue" is used in connection with a number of dishes, but the one made in Switzerland is probably the best known in this country.

1 *clove of garlic*	$^1/_2$ *pint white wine*
1 *lb grated cheese —*	3 *teaspoonfuls cornflour*
preferably Gruyère	*salt and pepper*

Rub the inside of a saucepan or earthenware casserole with the garlic.

Put in the grated cheese, wine, cornflour and seasoning and stir over a gentle heat until the cheese melts and the mixture is hot.

The Swiss fondue is sent to table in the pan or casserole in which it is cooked and the cooking continued at table over a spirit lamp. In fact, there are special fondue sets for the purpose, complete with long dipping forks. Crusty bread, cut into convenient pieces, accompanies the fondue. These are pierced with a fork and dipped into the cheese mixture — all eating from the same dish. Fondue should also be accompanied by a glass of wine and, according to ritual, the one who loses his bread in the cheese must pay for the bottle of wine.

CURRIES

Curries are universally known, but have their origin in countries with a hot climate, notably India and Africa. The actual curry powder is made from a combination of spices ground together, and that sold in grocers' shops is generally a mixture of some fifteen to twenty. Those who really appreciate curry, however, use special combinations of spices for different dishes. While many curries are hot and peppery, indeed very hot, others are quite mild.

CURRY ACCOMPANIMENTS

A dish of curry may be accompanied by one or two or many and varied accompaniments. Plainly boiled rice is always handed first and, after a generous helping is received, the curry itself is served and is spooned on top of the rice. After this comes a variety of accompaniments served in small dishes. Indeed a curry is sometimes described as a " one boy curry " or a " ten boy curry " each " boy " representing a different dish.

A choice of accompaniments may be made from the following suggestions:

Sliced hard-boiled egg — served on top of the curry
Sliced tomatoes — raw and fried
Sliced cucumber — raw and fried
Sliced bananas in dressing or fried
Onion — plain and fried
Peanuts — plain and fried
Coco-nut — plain and fried

Also chutney, spiced prunes, poppadums and Bombay duck. The poppadums are very thin, savoury wafer biscuits which are attractive when fried. They are usually broken over the curry by the diners. Curry is often eaten with a spoon and fork, depending on the consistency, while it is useful to know that it improves in flavour if made the day before it is required.

CURRIED CHICKEN

2 oz coco-nut	1 chicken — jointed
water	salt and a little sugar
4-5 potatoes	a pinch of saffron
2 tablespoonfuls olive	2 teaspoonfuls curry
oil or 2 oz butter	powder
1 medium onion	1 chilli pod
2 cloves of garlic	a piece of cinnamon stick
2 tomatoes — skinned, seeded and chopped	

Garnish: *rings of fried onion*

Steep the coco-nut in water.

Peel the potatoes and cut in two or into quarters. Heat the olive oil and fry the potatoes in this until brown all over. Remove and fry the sliced onion and chopped garlic. Remove. Fry the joints of chicken until brown. Return the potatoes and onion to the pan and add the other ingredients. Strain the water from the coco-nut and add. Bring to the boil and simmer gently until the chicken is tender — approximately 30-35 minutes.

Remove the chilli pod and arrange

the pieces of chicken on a hot dish. Place the potatoes at either end and pour the sauce over all. Scatter rings of fried onion over the top of the curry.

For a " one boy " curry, serve with the following version of pellao.

PELLAO: *1 onion, 4 tablespoonfuls olive oil or butter, 1 cupful rice, 2¹/₂ cupfuls water, 1 teaspoonful salt, ¹/₂ teaspoonful sugar, 12 cloves, 2 bay-leaves, a pinch saffron and 2 oz sultanas — soaked in hot water.*

Chop the onion finely and fry in the hot oil. Remove when a light golden colour. Add the rice to the oil and fry lightly.

Return the onions to the pan and add the water and other flavourings. Bring to the boil. Cover with a lid and cook gently for approximately 20 minutes or until the rice is tender and the liquid absorbed. Lastly stir in the sultanas using a carving fork.

MEAT AND POTATO CURRY

1 *lb lean beef or mutton*	1 *dessertspoonful tomato purée*
1 *onion*	*salt*
1 *clove of garlic*	¹/₂ *pint water*
2 *oz butter or margarine*	*a squeeze of lemon juice*
1 *tablespoonful curry powder*	1 *lb small potatoes — cut in quarters*

Cut the meat into convenient pieces. Chop the onion and garlic finely and fry in the melted butter. When brown, add the curry powder and continue cooking slowly for 2-3 minutes. Stir in the tomato purée and salt. Add the meat, water and lemon juice. Bring to the boil, cover with a lid and simmer gently for ³/₄ hour. Then add the potatoes and continue cooking until the meat is tender.

Serve with plainly-boiled rice and other accompaniments, as required.

BOBOTIE

A mild South African curry.

1 *lb minced steak*	2 *oz sultanas*
1 *thick slice of bread*	1 *tablespoonful flaked almonds*
1 *onion*	
2 *tablespoonfuls olive oil or butter*	1 *tablespoonful apricot jam*
1 *tablespoonful curry powder*	*salt*
	the juice of ¹/₂ *lemon*
¹/₄ *pint stock or water*	

Custard:

2 *eggs*	¹/₂ *pint milk*
	salt and pepper

Soak the slice of bread in water. Chop the onion finely and fry in the hot oil. Squeeze the bread dry and mash smoothly. Add to the onion. Add the curry powder, sultanas, almonds, jam and meat. Stir all together until the meat particles separate and brown. Add the salt, lemon juice and stock and simmer together for 5 minutes. Turn the mixture into a deep oven dish.

Next prepare the custard:

Beat the eggs and add the milk. Season and pour gently over the meat. Bake in a slow oven for approximately 40-45 minutes.

Suggested oven temperature — 350° or " 3 ".

FRENCH AND ITALIAN SAVOURY TARTS

The savoury tarts of France and Italy are well known. They are generally regional dishes often taking their name from the district in which they were originally made. The French tarts in particular are rich and delicious with cream and we in this country have to adjust ourselves to using this expensive item in this type of dish. The recipes, however, may be modified if economy is vital. While suitable as lunch or supper dishes they are served in France as a hot hors-d'oeuvre.

QUICHE LORRAINE NO. (1)

The word " quiche " indicates an open tart and there are many recipes for this type of dish. They are mostly connected with the regions of Lorraine and Alsace. Originally, quiches were made with a bread dough rolled out very thinly, but nowadays a short crust or flaky pastry are usually preferred.

6 oz rich short crust pastry

Filling:

slices of Gruyère cheese   *2 eggs*
(or sliced processed   *¹/₂ pint cream (or use*
   cheese)   *¹/₂ cream and ¹/₂*
4-6 oz streaky bacon   *milk)*
         salt and pepper

Use the pastry to line a deep dish pie-plate. Prick, then cover the pastry with thin slices of cheese. Rind the bacon and cut into 1 inch pieces. Fry lightly and scatter over the cheese. Beat the eggs. Add the cream and seasoning. Pour over the bacon. If the dish is not sufficiently full, top up with a little more milk. Bake in a moderate oven for 40-50 minutes.

Suggested oven temperature — 400° or " 6 ".

QUICHE LORRAINE NO. (2)

6 oz short crust pastry

Filling:

4-6 oz streaky bacon   *1 ¹/₂ gills of milk*
2 eggs   *1 dessertspoonful flour*
         salt and pepper

Use the pastry to line a deep dish pie-plate and prick. Rind the bacon and cut into 1 inch pieces. Fry lightly, then scatter over the pastry. Beat the eggs. Blend the flour with the milk and add to the eggs. Add a little of the bacon fat and seasoning. Pour over the bacon and, if necessary, top up with more milk. Bake in a moderate oven for approximately 45 minutes.

Suggested oven temperature — 400° or " 6 "

QUICHE AUX POMMES DE TERRE

4 large potatoes   *4 rashers of streaky*
2 oz flour   *bacon*
2 oz butter or   *2 eggs*
   margarine   *1 gill cream and a*
salt   *little milk*
       1 clove garlic
       1 oz grated cheese

Boil the potatoes and sieve while still hot. Add the flour, butter and mix all together. Turn into a well-greased deep dish pie-plate and spread thickly over the inside of the dish. Decorate the edges using floured fingers. Rind the bacon, cut into 1 inch pieces and fry lightly. Scatter over the potato mixture.

Beat the eggs, add the cream, the finely-chopped garlic and seasoning. Pour over the bacon and, if necessary, top up with a little milk to fill the dish. Sprinkle generously with grated cheese and bake in a moderate oven for approximately 30-40 minutes.

Suggested oven temperature — 400° or " 6 ".

TARTE À L'OIGNON

Onion tart is connected with Alsace and Lorraine and particularly with the town of Strasbourg.

36

6 oz short crust pastry

Filling:

2-3 onions	2 eggs
2 oz butter or margarine	2 oz grated cheese salt and pepper
	a little milk

Begin by preparing the filling:

Slice the onions finely and melt the butter. Add the onions and cook very gently in a covered pan for approximately 30 minutes. When ready, they should be soft, yellow with butter and transparent. This preliminary cooking should be done with care as it is important for the success of the tart. Beat the eggs and add to the onions, together with the grated cheese and seasoning.

Use the pastry to line a deep dish pie-plate and prick. Fill with the onion mixture, topping up with a little milk, if necessary. Bake in a moderate oven for approximately 40-45 minutes.

Suggested oven temperature — 400° or " 6 "

PIZZA ALLA NAPOLETANA

A pizza is an Italian dish, the word denoting a pie or tart. There is a whole range of recipes, the most famous being the version made in and around Naples. It has as its base a thin round of yeast dough covered with tomatoes flavoured with herbs and topped with cheese and anchovy fillets. In private houses, the pizza is usually made with a plain pastry. The savoury mixture may be varied too and might include mussels, salame, ham, mushrooms, onions or olives.

Individual pizza are called pizzette, while sweet pizza are also made, though they are not so usual.

Yeast mixture:

4 oz flour	a little warm milk
1/2 teaspoonful salt	1 egg

1/4 oz yeast	1 oz butter or margarine

For the top:

4-5 ripe tomatoes	6-8 anchovy fillets
1 dessertspoonful chopped basil or marjoram	3 oz cheese — Bel Paese if possible
	a little olive oil

Measure the flour and salt into a bowl. Cream the yeast with the warm milk. Add the beaten egg and use to mix all to a light dough. Beat thoroughly. Have the butter soft and beat into the yeast mixture. Cover with a damp cloth and put aside in a warm place to rise until twice the size — approximately 45 minutes.

Turn the dough onto a floured surface, knead and roll out in a circle approximately 8 inch in diameter and 1/4 inch thick.

Peel the tomatoes and remove the seeds. Chop roughly and use to cover the round of dough. Sprinkle with seasoning and the chopped herbs. Scatter the diced or coarsely-shredded cheese on top and decorate with the anchovy fillets. Sprinkle with a little olive oil. Put in a warm place for 10 minutes to prove and bake in a fairly hot oven for 20-30 minutes.

Suggested oven temperature — 450°. or " 7 "

FRITTO MISTO

In Italy the quality of the fried food is excellent, undoubtedly due to the use of Italian olive oil as a cooking medium. In particular, their Fritto Misto (mixed fried), in all its various forms, is famous and quite delightful to eat. It may take various forms such as mixed fried fish, a variety of offal, various vegetables and fruit. The pieces of food are also coated in a variety of ways, some with batter, others with egg and crumbs or even seasoned flour. Some items will be fried in deep fat and others cooked in shallow, so that there is plenty of variety.

FRITTO MISTO MARE

The wealth of Mediterranean fish is used to best advantage in this dish of mixed fried fish and while the authentic items are not always available here, an excellent Fritto Misto Mare may be made using a carefully chosen variety of the local fish. Some of these should be left in fairly large pieces. In this instance, dabs dipped in flour and fried in shallow fat are very suitable. Larger plaice or sole may be left on the bone, but chopped into 3 or 4 pieces. Dip in seasoned flour and fry in shallow fat. Alternatively, fillets of plaice or sole may be cut gudgeon style and coated with egg and crumbs for frying.

Other items may include:
1. Scampi or prawns dipped in batter and fried in deep fat.
2. Scallops — poached and coated with egg and crumbs for frying. If wished, they may first be cut into quarters.
3. Fish roes such as cod or herring roe coated with egg and crumbs and fried.
4. Anchovy fillets dipped in batter and fried.

Serve the fried fish piled in a hot dish accompanied by wedges of lemon and fresh brown bread and butter or rolls. A sharp sauce may also be served, though this is not usual in Italy where the excellence of the fish and the standard of frying make a sauce unnecessary.

FRITTO MISTO OF BRAINS, SWEETBREAD AND OTHER MEAT

A mixture of fried meat and vegetables is used in another version of Fritto Misto. Ingredients suitable to include are:

1. Thin escalopes of veal.
2. Brains — poached and cut into suitable pieces. These should be dipped in egg and breadcrumbs for frying.
3. Sweetbreads — poached, pressed and suitable pieces dipped in egg and breadcrumbs.
4. Lamb's liver sliced and fried.
5. Sometimes even pieces of sliced Bel Paese cheese are included. They are dipped in batter and fried quickly in deep fat.

Suggested vegetables include mushroom caps and sprigs of parboiled cauliflower dipped in batter and fried.

The various fried items should be piled in a hot dish, garnished with lemon and accompanied by a sharp sauce.

FRITTO MISTO DI VERDURE

Mixed fried vegetables, including some herb fritters, can make an excellent dish. Choose a selection from the following suggestions:

Mushrooms — dip the caps of medium-sized mushrooms into batter and fry in deep fat.

Onion — cut into thin slices, toss in seasoned flour and fry immediately in deep fat.

Chestnuts — use parboiled nuts and dip in egg and crumbs for frying. Alternatively, make small chestnut croquettes.

Cauliflower — sprigs of parboiled cauliflower, dipped in batter and fried.

Potatoes — make into small croquettes and fry. Grated cheese is often added and a delicious result can be obtained if flaked almonds are used in the coating instead of breadcrumbs. Again potatoes may be sliced thinly and the pieces dipped in batter and fried.

Parsnips — make into a croquette mixture, form into little balls, press between two pieces of walnut and dip in egg and breadcrumbs. Fry in deep fat.

Herbs, such as chopped parsley, chives and thyme may be added generously to the following batter and fried in small spoonfuls:

2 tablespoonfuls flour, $^1/_2$ teaspoonful baking powder, salt and beaten egg to give a fairly stiff consistency.

Serve the mixture of fried vegetables piled in a hot dish.

SAVOURY RICE DISHES

While many tend to think of rice in terms of a milk pudding or perhaps plainly boiled to accompany a curry, there are a great many other uses for this staple food. Its bland flavour makes it a suitable medium to combine with more highly flavoured foods and there are a great number of savoury rice dishes which are world famous:

The risottos of Italy, paella from Spain, the pilaffs of the eastern Mediterranean and their equivalent — the pillau — of India. Rice is, of course, a great feature of Chinese cooking.

In preparing such dishes the quality of the rice is of great importance. It should be a hard grained variety which will cook without breaking up.

PLAIN BOILED RICE

There are two recognised methods of cooking plain boiled rice suitable to serve with a curry.

The first method requires care and an attention to detail:

Wash the rice in running water. Then add it to a large saucepan of fast-boiling salted water. If wished, add a squeeze of lemon juice. Boil rapidly for 12-15 minutes or until a grain, when tested between the thumb and finger is soft without being mushy. It is most important to avoid overcooking. Drain and wash under running cold water. Return to a saucepan lined with buttered paper. Cover with a lid and steam for half-an-hour until dry and hot.

The second method has now largely superseded the first. It is much simpler, but a specially-prepared rice is necessary:

To every cup of rice allow 2 $^1/_2$ cupfuls of water. Add a teaspoonful salt and cover the pan with a close-fitting lid. Cook over a gentle heat until the water is absorbed and the rice tender. The time required is approximately 25 minutes.

This quantity will give 4-6 portions.

Correctly-boiled rice should be snowy white with each grain separate, never sticky or gummy. If stirring is necessary, a carving fork should always be used, not a spoon.

FRIED RICE

Cook a cupful of rice as just described. Chop a quarter of an onion finely and to it add a finely-chopped clove of garlic. Cook together in a knob of melted butter. When soft and transparent, add the boiled rice. Season well and stir with a carving fork until it begins to colour. If very dry, it may be necessary to add more butter. Add a tablespoonful of finely-chopped herbs or colour and flavour with paprika pepper. Serve piled in a hot dish.

RISOTTO ALLA MILANESE

Northern Italy is the home of the risotto and there are many versions. The different recipes are often connected with a town or district and probably the best known is that made in Milan. Risotto is served as a first course at a lunch, or may make a meal in itself. It is always served accompanied by finely-grated cheese. In this country, we often take the liberty of using it as an accompaniment to a roast chicken or a grilled steak instead of the more usual potatoes.

2 ½ oz butter	6 oz Italian rice
¼ onion	a good pinch of saffron
1 clove of garlic	salt and pepper
	1 pint chicken stock

2 oz grated cheese — Parmesan if possible

Melt half the butter in a saucepan and add the finely-chopped onion and garlic. Fry gently until golden in colour. Add the rice — it should not be washed for a risotto. Stir with the onion in the hot fat for 4-5 minutes. Add the saffron, seasoning and stock. Bring to the boil. Cover with a lid and cook gently until the rice has absorbed the liquid — approximately 25-30 minutes. Lastly, using a carving fork, stir in the remaining butter and grated cheese.

CHICKEN PILAFF

A pilaff is a type of dish common in the eastern Mediterranean particularly Greece, Turkey and Egypt. It consists of a savoury rice mixture with chicken, meat — particularly mutton — and fish added to it. Other additions may include nuts and dried fruit.

A similar type of dish is also made in India and is known by quite a few variations of the word such as pilau, pillau, pilaw or pellao.

1 chicken	seasoning
a few flavouring vegetables	olive oil

Rice mixture:

1 onion	3 oz raisins
1 oz butter	6-8 oz rice
2 oz almonds or pine kernels	salt and pepper
	1-1¼ pints chicken stock

Joint the chicken and cut the flesh into nice pieces free of bone. Put the carcase, bones, giblets and flavouring vegetables into a saucepan. Add cold water to cover and simmer gently to give a concentrated chicken stock.

When the chicken stock is ready, prepare the rice mixture:

Slice the onion finely and put aside the better rings for a garnish later. Melt the butter and fry the remainder of the onion until golden. Add half the blanched split almonds and half the raisins. Add the rice, seasoning and chicken stock. Bring to the boil. Cover and cook gently until the rice is tender and has absorbed the liquid.

Meanwhile, season the pieces of chicken and fry in a little olive oil — the time required will be approximately 15-20 minutes according to the size of the pieces. Remove from the pan and keep hot. Fry the remainder of the onion, adding the rest of the almonds and raisins when it is nearly brown and crisp.

Serve the rice mixture in the centre of a hot dish. Arrange the fried chicken at either end and garnish with a scattering of fried onion, almonds and raisins over the whole.

PASTA

Pasta is the collective name for a large group of farinaceous foods with their origins in Italy. In this country the best known are macaroni, spaghetti and vermicelli, but there are countless others. They are made from wheat flour.

THE COOKING OF PASTA

It is essential to cook pasta in a large pan of boiling, salted water and it should not be overcooked. The long lengths are gradually lowered and curled into the water and are cooked at simmering point until a little, when tested between the finger and thumb, is still very slightly resistant or " al dente ". The average time required is 20 minutes. Stir gently once or twice during the cooking to prevent the pasta sticking to the bottom of the saucepan. Drain in a colander. Serve with a knob of butter.

The boiled pasta is accompanied by a sauce from which the dish will take its name. This sauce may either be mixed through the pasta or served separately. Plenty of grated Parmesan cheese is always served separately.

SPAGHETTI ALLA BOLOGNESE

$1/_2$ lb spaghetti	a knob of butter

Bolognese sauce:

1 onion	1 dessertspoonful flour
1 clove of garlic	salt and pepper
1 tablespoonful olive oil or 1 oz butter	1 $1/_2$ gills stock
	a bouquet garni
$1/_4$ lb minced steak	1 dessertspoonful tomato purée

Accompaniment: *grated cheese — Parmesan if possible*

Begin by preparing the Bolognese sauce:

Chop the onion and garlic finely and fry in the hot oil until golden. Add the minced steak and stir until each particle is separate and the meat brown. Add the flour and seasoning and mix well.

Stir in the stock and add the bouquet garni and tomato purée. Bring to the boil and simmer gently for 30 minutes.

While the sauce is cooking, boil the spaghetti. Drain and toss a knob of butter through it.

Pile the spaghetti in a hot dish and pour the Bolognese sauce over it. Sprinkle with grated cheese and serve more grated cheese separately.

SPAGHETTI ALLA NAPOLETANA

6 oz spaghetti	a knob of butter

Tomato sauce:

1 lb tomatoes	1 small carrot — finely shredded
1 medium onion — finely chopped	1 dessertspoonful chopped herbs — basil, thyme and parsley
1 clove of garlic — finely chopped	

salt, pepper and a pinch of sugar

Accompaniment: *grated cheese — Parmesan if possible*

Begin by preparing the sauce:

Skin the tomatoes and remove the seeds. Chop roughly and put in a saucepan with the onion, garlic, finely-shredded carrot, chopped herbs and seasoning. Stew together until a fairly thick purée is formed.

If preferred, the tomatoes need not be skinned and seeded. The sauce should then be sieved before use.

Meanwhile, boil the spaghetti. Drain in a colander and return to the saucepan. Add the knob of butter and the tomato sauce, tossing one through the other. When throughly hot, pile in a heated dish. Sprinkle with grated cheese and serve accompanied by more grated cheese.

SWEET DISHES

On the Continent fruit is generally served instead of a pudding and on this account, there is not a wealth of recipes for this type of dish. There are a few, however, which have won an international reputation.

ZABAIONE OR ZABAGLIONE

This is an Italian sweet of great fame. It is generally served while still warm and is an excellent dish to give to invalids.

The following recipe is sufficient for two, or perhaps three, portions.

4 *egg yolks* 1 *tablespoonful castor sugar*
2 *glasses Marsala*

Put the three ingredients into a bowl and whisk over hot water until thick. Pour into heated individual glasses and serve at once, accompanied by sponge fingers or other dainty biscuits.

An alternative method is as follows:

Whisk the yolks and the sugar together until light. Stir in the wine and transfer all to a strong saucepan. Stir over a gentle heat until the mixture thickens.

APPLE STRUDEL

Apple Strudel is a dish associated with Austria, Hungary and Germany and to be completely successful, depends greatly on the fine quality of the flour used. The flour from the central plains of Europe has the necessary character to produce the paper-thin strudel paste. A good strudel should be delicately crisp when baked.

Strudel paste:

$^1/_2$ *lb flour* 1 *egg*
a pinch of salt *approximately* $^1/_4$ *pint tepid water*

Filling:

1 $^1/_2$ *lb apples* 6 *oz brown sugar*
2 *oz currants* $^1/_2$ *teaspoonful ground cinnamon*
2 *oz sultanas*
$^1/_2$ *teaspoonful mixed spice*

melted butter to brush
4 *tablespoonfuls buttered crumbs*

Measure the flour and salt into a bowl and mix to a soft dough using the beaten egg and tepid water. Beat well until thoroughly elastic. Cover and put in a warm place for 15 minutes.

Spread a cloth over a small table and dust with flour. Turn the pastry onto this and roll out into a square shape. Brush with olive oil and leave for a further 10 minutes. Now pull it out carefully, using the hands lightly under the paste. Pull on all sides until it is paper thin.

Trim away any thickness at the edges — scissors being the best tool to use. Leave in a warm place to dry.

Meanwhile, prepare the filling:

Chop the apples finely and combine with the dried fruit, sugar and spices.

When the strudel paste has dried, dab it generously with melted butter and scatter with the buttered crumbs. Spread it with the apple mixture. Turn in the edges of the paste and roll up. The cloth is useful at this stage. It should be held by two corners and, by tilting it gently, it is possible to roll the strudel over and over quite easily. Finally tilt onto a greased tray. If the strudel is too long for the tray, it may be curved gently. Brush with more melted butter and bake in a fairly hot oven for approximately 45 minutes.

Suggested oven temperature — 400° or "6".

Dust thickly with icing sugar and serve while freshly baked.

PETITS POTS DE CHOCOLAT

A French chocolate mousse.

4 *oz dessert chocolate* *a knob of butter*
4 *eggs* *flavouring*

Break the chocolate into pieces and put into a bowl placed over a pan of hot water. Separate the yolks from the egg whites and stir the yolks into the melted chocolate, adding them one at a time. Add the butter and flavouring and stir in. Fold in the stiffly-beaten egg whites. Pour into small glasses and put aside in a cool place for at least 12 hours. The mousse improves on standing.

Suitable flavourings include:
— 2 tablespoonfuls rum, brandy or other liqueur.
— the rind and juice of 1 Seville orange.
— 1 tablespoonful coffee essence.

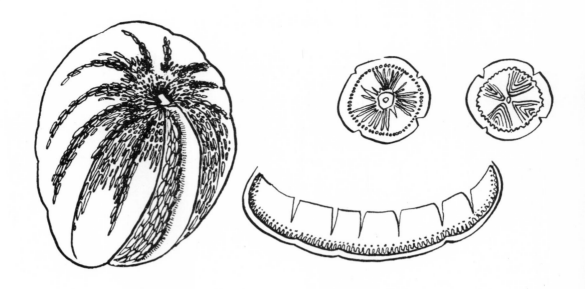

HORS-D'OEUVRE OR APPETISER

THE term hors-d'oeuvre is applied to the light appetising little dishes which are intended to stimulate the appetite at the beginning of a lunch or dinner. A wide range of foods may be included, always provided they are piquant and attractive both to the palate and the eye. While hors-d'oeuvres are generally cold, they are not necessarily so and broadly speaking they can be sub-divided as follows:

THE MIXED HORS-D'OEUVRES or hors-d'oeuvres variés where a choice of four, five, six or more different kinds is presented, usually in a special hors-d'oeuvre dish. The choice offered should be varied and include tasty meats, fish, dressed eggs, vegetable salads and sometimes fruit. The dressings used should also be varied and include both vinaigrette dressing and mayonnaise.

THE ONE DISH HORS-D'OEUVRE which is increasingly popular. Of this type of hors-d'oeuvres the aristocrats are caviare, oysters and smoked salmon. All are served with the greatest simplicity.

CAVIARE: True caviare is the roe of the sturgeon, but on the market at present there are many substitutes generally labelled " caviare type ".

It should be served in its original container or in a dish surrounded by crushed ice and accompanied by wedges of lemon and brown bread and butter.

The correct spoon for serving it is one of bone or ivory; never a metal one. OYSTERS are generally eaten uncooked. They should not be opened until required, when they are loosened and served in the deep half of their shells and surrounded by crushed ice. They should be accompanied by wedges of lemon, freshly-ground pepper or cayenne and brown bread and butter.

Oysters are in season from September to May.

SMOKED SALMON is served in paper-thin slices on individual plates accompanied

44

by wedges of lemon and brown bread and butter.

SMOKED EEL is also good. It should be cut into fillets and served with lemon and brown bread and butter.

LIVER PÂTE

$^1/_2$ *pint béchamel*   4 *oz fat bacon*
   sauce   4 *anchovy fillets*
$^3/_4$ *lb liver* (*preferably* *a pinch of ground cloves*
   chicken)   *a pinch of allspice*
      3-4 *bacon rashers*

Prepare the béchamel sauce in the usual way. Cut up the liver, bacon and anchovies and pass through the mincer using the small blade. Either mince a second time or feed slowly into the liquidiser of the electric mixing machine. It is necessary to have the mixture very smooth and free from fibre. Combine with the sauce, ground cloves and allspice. Line the bottom of a small casserole with the bacon rashers and pour in the liver mixture. Cover and set in a larger dish of hot water. Bake in a very slow oven for 1 $^1/_4$ hours.

Suggested oven temperature — 300° or " 1 ".

Press until the next day.

Liver Pâte may be served as an hors-d'oeuvre in one of two ways:

(1) It may be pressed firmly, turned out and cut into fairly thick slices.

(2) It may be pressed lightly so that the texture is creamy and then scooped out with two spoons to give an egg shape. Garnish across the top with an anchovy fillet.

In either case, serve accompanied by freshly-made toast and butter.

HAM AND PINEAPPLE SALAD

4 *slices of cooked ham*   2 *rings of pineapple*

Dressing:
4 *pickled walnuts*   1 *tablespoonful tomato*
1 *pickled gherkin*   *ketchup*
$^1/_2$ *gill whipped cream* *a little lemon juice*
            cayenne

Cut the ham and pineapple into shreds.

Chop the pickled walnuts and slice the gherkin. Add to the whipped cream, together with the tomato ketchup, lemon juice and seasoning. Toss through the combined ham and pineapple.

Arrange one or two lettuce leaves on individual plates and spoon a portion of the salad mixture to one side.

EGG MAYONNAISE

3 *hard-boiled eggs*   *mayonnaise*
salt and pepper   6 *anchovy fillets*
         a little cress

Cut the hard-boiled eggs in two by the length. Season with salt and pepper arrange on a cake wire placed over and a plate. Mask with the mayonnaise and decorate each half egg with a looped anchovy fillet.

Serve garnished with cress.

DEVILLED EGGS

3 *hard-boiled eggs*   *mayonnaise*
salt and pepper   *a little cress*

Cut the hard-boiled eggs in two and remove the yolk. Season the egg white. Sieve the yolk and beat in a little mayonnaise and seasoning. Transfer this mixture to a forcing bag fitted with a large star pipe, and pipe in swirls into the little cases made by the egg whites. Serve garnished with cress.

Additional flavourings can be added to the yolk mixture, such as curry powder, anchovy essence, chopped herbs or grated cheese.

EGG MOUSSE

3 *hard-boiled eggs*	2 *tablespoonfuls water*
¹/₂ *gill mayonnaise*	¹/₂ *gill lightly-whipped*
a few anchovy fillets	*cream*
¹/₂ *level dessertspoonful*	*cayenne*
gelatine	*salt*

Salad:

2 *sticks of celery*	*a few black or green*
1 *oz walnuts*	*grapes*
	French dressing

Chop the hard-boiled eggs roughly and mix with the mayonnaise. Chop four or five of the anchovy fillets very fine, and add. Dissolve the gelatine in the water and add. Season. Fold in the cream and pour into dariole moulds when beginning to thicken.

When set, pass through hot water and turn out. Garnish each with a looped anchovy fillet and serve accompanied by a salad made from the shredded celery, chopped walnuts and pitted grapes tossed in French dressing.

MUSHROOMS À LA GRECQUE

6-8 *oz mushrooms*	¹/₂ *gill vinegar*
¹/₂ *gill olive oil*	¹/₂ *gill water*
	salt and pepper

If the mushrooms are small they are usually left whole, but if large they should be sliced. Heat the oil a little, add the prepared mushrooms, cover and sweat together for 5 minutes. Add the vinegar and water and cook together for a further 15 minutes. Season. Serve cold.

Mushrooms à la Grecque are suitable to serve in a mixed hors-d'oeuvre.

AVOCADO PEAR

Avocado pear is a tropical fruit which is pear-shaped and of a greenish purplish colour. In the centre is a kernel about the size of a walnut. If the avocado pear is ripe and of choice quality, it requires few, if any additions, the flesh having a nutty flavour and a buttery consistency. Otherwise the fruit is cut in two, the kernel removed and the hollow filled with a French dressing. Serve chilled, accompanied by brown bread and butter.

Alternatively, the flesh may be scooped out, crushed, mixed with a dressing and returned to the casing.

It is usual to allow half a pear per person.

TOMATO, CUCUMBER AND ONION SALAD

3-4 *tomatoes*	*French dressing*
¹/₄ *cucumber*	*a few lettuce leaves*
	or cress
a few thinly-sliced rings of onion	

Skin the tomatoes and slice. Slice the cucumber. Dress with the French dressing and chill. Arrange one or two lettuce leaves on individual plates and on this arrange the tomato and cucumber. Garnish with thinly-sliced rings of onion and serve accompanied by brown bread and butter.

GRAPEFRUIT

Choose large heavy grapefruit and allow half per person. Cut in two and remove the seeds and centre pith. Then, using a special grapefruit knife, loosen the flesh completely from the skin and cut into neat sections. Be careful to avoid losing the juice and for this reason, it is best to work on a plate and even to have an extra half grapefruit to top up those halves which are to go to table. Sprinkle each portion with sugar and leave in a cool place until required. If correctly prepared, the grapefruit should be easy to eat, juicy and have an unhandled look.

Serve in grapefruit glasses or on small plates, garnished with cherry, a sprig of mint or rosemary.

GRAPEFRUIT SALAD

2 *grapefruit*	4-6 *oz pitted green*
1-2 *oranges*	*grapes*
	sugar

Cut the grapefruit and the oranges in two and remove the seeds and centre pith. Then, using the special grapefruit knife, remove the flesh and cut into sections. Combine with the pitted grapes and sweeten with sugar. Pile back into the half grapefruit skins. Serve garnished with cherry, a sprig of mint or rosemary.

MELON

Ripe melon makes an admirable appetiser. Generally, it is simply served in generous wedges accompanied by sugar or a mixture of sugar and a little ground ginger. The melon should be chilled.

If preferred, the wedge of melon may receive a little more attention in order to make it look more attractive and easier to eat:

With a long cut, remove the flesh from the skin of the melon. Cut it into neat pieces and rearrange on the skin alternately to either side to give a zig-zag effect. Garnish with cherry and serve very cold with the usual accompaniments.

TOMATO JUICE

1 *pint tomato juice*	1 *teaspoonful vinegar*
the pared rind and	1 *teaspoonful Worcester*
juice of 1 *lemon*	*sauce*
	a scrape of onion juice

seasoning to include a little sugar and a grating of nutmeg

Combine the ingredients and put aside in a cool place to infuse for an hour. Just before serving, remove the lemon rind. Serve very cold in small glasses.

SOUPS

STOCK

While stock will always have a place where good cooking is respected, nevertheless, few private homes now boast a stock-pot, or make stock regularly. When a small quantity is required it is often more practical to use the bouillon cubes available in the shops. Alternatively, first class stock becomes available during some cooking processes as, for example, when boiling a fowl or piece of mutton or pork. Meat boilings such as these have a full flavour, especially if a bouquet garni and a few vegetables have been added during the cooking.

Apart from these and particularly if fairly large quantities are required, there are occasions when a supply of stock is necessary for the success of a dish. From the great variety of stocks which can be made, the most generally useful and practical is:

HOUSEHOLD OR GENERAL STOCK: This stock is made from miscellaneous ingredients as available including bones (without marrow which would make it greasy), chicken carcases, bacon rinds and vegetables such as carrot, onion, leek and celery.

Mushroom trimmings, if available, may also be added. The bones may either be those from cooked meat or fresh bones.

Place the bones in a strong saucepan, cover with water and bring slowly up to simmering point. Skim. Add the vegetables, cut in large pieces and a bouquet garni, and simmer gently for 4-5 hours. Strain and use as required.

A richer stock can be made by the

addition of meat such as a piece of shin of beef.

As deep freezing becomes more generally available, it will be well to remember that stock may be successfully preserved by this means for use as required.

Stock can also be made using a pressure cooker.

BROTCHAN ROY

"Brotchan" is an old word meaning broth and " Brotchan Roy " indicates a broth made with leeks. This recipe has its origins in a very old Irish one.

2 oz butter or	1/2 pint milk
margarine	1 pint finely-shredded
2 oz flaked oatmeal	leek
1 1/2 pints stock or	salt, pepper and a little
water	ground mace
chopped parsley	

Melt the butter, sprinkle in the flaked oatmeal and toast gently together. Stir in the stock and milk and bring to the boil. Add the leeks and seasoning and bring to the boil again. Simmer gently for 3/4-1 hour. Just before serving add plenty of chopped parsley.

VEGETABLE BROTH

2 lb vegetables — potatoes, carrot, celery, onion and leek as available

2 oz butter or	3 pints stock or water
margarine	1 oz fine sago
salt and pepper	1/2 pint milk
chopped parsley	

Cut the vegetables into fine dice. Melt the butter, add the vegetables and sweat together for approximately 20 minutes. Add the seasoning and stock and bring to boiling point. Simmer gently for 1 1/2-2 hours. Sprinkle in the sago and continue cooking for a

further 20 minutes or until the sago is clear. Add the milk and bring to the boil again. Just before serving add plenty of chopped parsley.

COTTAGE SOUP

1/2 lb potatoes	1 oz butter or margarine
1/2 lb carrots	salt and pepper
1 onion or leek	1 1/2 pints stock or water
2 sticks celery	1 oz flour
1/2 pint milk	
2 oz grated cheese	

Cut the vegetables into fine dice and sweat in the melted butter for 10-15 minutes. Add the seasoning and stock or water and bring to the boil. Simmer gently for 1 1/2-2 hours. Blend the flour with the milk and use to thicken the soup. Sprinkle in the grated cheese.

SCOTCH MUTTON BROTH

1 1/2 lb neck or	2 quarts water
shoulder of mutton	1 carrot — diced
1 tablespoonful barley	1 piece turnip
(steeped overnight)	1/4 small cabbage
2 tablespoonfuls dried	2 leeks or 1 onion
peas (steeped	salt and pepper
overnight)	1 carrot — grated
chopped parsley	

Put the meat, barley and peas in a roomy saucepan. Add the water and bring slowly to the boil. Skim and then simmer gently for 1 hour. Prepare the vegetables, dicing the carrot and turnip and shredding the cabbage and leeks. Add the vegetables to the broth and continue cooking for a further 2 hours. Twenty minutes before serving, add the second carrot grated and just before serving, add plenty of chopped parsley. Season to taste and serve the meat separately with a little of the broth poured round it.

CHICKEN BROTH

3 pints concentrated   3 oz each of carrot,
   chicken stock   turnip and leek
1 1/2 oz rice   2 oz each of onion and
                          celery
           salt and pepper
           chopped parsley

Put the chicken stock and the rice in a saucepan and bring to the boil. Meanwhile, cut the vegetables into very fine dice and add together with the seasoning. Simmer all gently for 1 1/2 hours.

Just before serving, add the chopped parsley.

MINESTRONE

2 large tomatoes   1 oz butter or
   (peeled)   margarine
1 carrot   1/4 cabbage
1 potato   1 clove of garlic
1 leek   salt and pepper
1 onion   1 quart water
3 sticks celery   2 oz vermicelli or
2 oz green peas   spaghetti
       grated Parmesan cheese

Dice or shred the vegetables. Melt the butter, add all the vegetables except the cabbage and sweat together for 10-15 minutes. Add the finely-chopped clove of garlic, the seasoning and the water. Bring to the boil and simmer together for 1 hour. Break the pasta into short lengths and add, together with the shredded cabbage. Simmer for a further 30 minutes.

Serve with the grated cheese handed separately.

LENTIL OR SPLIT PEA SOUP

4-6 oz lentils   1 oz butter or
1 onion   margarine
a piece each of carrot   salt and pepper
   and turnip   1 ham bone
2 large potatoes   2 pints water

Wash the lentils and steep overnight. Drain. Chop the onion and dice the carrot, turnip and potatoes. Melt the butter. Add the lentils and the other vegetables and sweat together for 20 minutes. Add the seasoning, the ham bone and the water and bring to the boil. Simmer gently for 2 hours. Remove the ham bone and serve.

POTATO SOUP

1 large onion   salt and pepper
1-2 leeks   2 pints stock or water
1 oz butter or   1 tablespoonful
   margarine   sago
2 lb potatoes   1/2 pint milk
       chopped parsley

Chop the onion and shred the leeks. Melt the butter, add the vegetables and sweat together for 10-15 minutes. Meanwhile, slice the potatoes thinly and add, together with the seasoning and stock. Bring to the boil and simmer gently for 1 1/2 hours. Sprinkle in the sago and continue cooking for a further 20 minutes or until the sago is clear. Add the milk and break down any large pieces with a wooden spoon. Just before serving, stir in the chopped parsley.

FRENCH ONION SOUP

1-2 Spanish onions   1 1/2 pints stock or
1 1/2 oz butter or   water
   margarine   salt and pepper
1/4 oz flour   1 bay-leaf
       slices of French bread
        grated cheese

Cut the onion in thin slices. Melt the butter. Add the onions and cook slowly together until the vegetable is brown. Dust in the flour. Pour on the boiling stock and the seasoning and bay-leaf and simmer together for 1/2 hour. Remove the bay-leaf.

To serve: put a few slices of oven toasted French bread in the bottom of a casserole, pour the hot soup over, sprinkle with the grated cheese and brown in a hot oven.

Alternatively, if French bread is not available, butter a slice of fresh toast, cut into cubes, toss in grated cheese and brown in a hot oven. Float these croûtons on the top of the soup.

ARTICHOKE SOUP

1 onion	1¹/₂ lb artichokes
2 sticks celery	(weighed after
1 oz butter or	peeling)
margarine	salt and pepper

1 tablespoonful rice flour
1¹/₄ pints stock or water
¹/₂ pint milk

Chop the onion and celery and sweat in the melted butter for 10-15 minutes. Peel and slice the artichokes and add, together with the seasoning and stock. Simmer gently for 1 hour. Sieve. Blend the rice flour with the milk and use to thicken the soup.

BRUSSELS SPROUTS PURÉE

¹/₂ lb Brussels sprouts	1 oz butter or
1 onion	margarine
1 oz ham (or a ham	salt and pepper
bone)	2 pints stock or water

2 oz flour
1 gill milk

Chop the sprouts, onion and ham and sweat in the melted butter. Add the seasoning and stock and simmer for 1 hour. Sieve. Blend the flour with the milk and use to thicken the soup.

CAULIFLOWER SOUP

1 cauliflower	salt and pepper
2 small onions	1 ¹/₂ pints water
1 oz ham (or ham	2 oz butter or margarine
bone)	2 oz flour

¹/₂ pint milk

Put the cauliflower, chopped onions, ham, seasoning and water into a saucepan. Simmer together until the cauliflower is just cooked, then remove some nice sprigs for serving in the soup later. Continue cooking the soup for 1 hour in all. Sieve. Melt the butter, stir in the flour and add the milk gradually. Add the sieved soup and bring to the boil, stirring all the time. Lastly, add the cauliflower sprigs and reheat.

CELERY SOUP

1 head celery	1 bay-leaf
1 onion	1 piece mace
2 oz butter or	1 quart stock or water
margarine	2 oz flour
salt and pepper	¹/₂ pint milk

Chop the celery and onion. Melt the butter. Add the vegetables and sweat together for 20 minutes. Add the seasoning, bay-leaf, mace and stock and bring to the boil. Simmer gently for 1-1 ¹/₂ hours. Sieve. Return the soup to the saucepan and reheat. Blend the flour with the milk and add to the soup gradually, stirring all the time. Bring to the boil and simmer for a few minutes before serving.

The addition of a little cream is an improvement to this soup.

CREAM OF CHICKEN SOUP

1 pint concentrated	¹/₄ pint milk
chicken stock	salt and pepper
1 dessertspoonful	2 egg yolks
ground rice	¹/₂ gill cream

cooked chicken to garnish

Put the strained chicken stock into a saucepan and bring to the boil. Blend the ground rice with the milk and thicken the stock with this. Season and simmer together for 30 minutes. Combine the yolks with the cream. Draw the soup from the heat and add the yolk mixture gradually, stirring all the time. Cook for 2-3 minutes, but without letting the soup boil again. Lastly, add a little cooked chicken, cut in Julienne strips, and heat through before serving.

LENTIL PURÉE

¹/₄ *lb lentils*	*salt and pepper*
1 ¹/₂ *pints water*	1 *small piece of mace*
¹/₂ *onion*	*liaison:* ³/₄ *oz butter or*
1 *stick celery*	*margarine*
1 *spray parsley*	³/₄ *oz flour*
	¹/₂ *pint milk*

Wash the lentils and steep overnight. Drain. Then put them on to boil with the water. When boiling point is reached, skim. Then add the chopped onion, celery, parsley, seasoning and mace and simmer slowly for 1 ¹/₂ hours. Sieve. Return the soup to a clean pan and reheat.

Make the liaison: Melt the butter and stir in the flour to form a roux. Gradually stir in the milk. Use to thicken the soup and stir until boiling. Simmer for a few minutes longer.

Add a little cream, if available, before serving.

MUSHROOM SOUP

¹/₄ *lb mushrooms*	2 *pints stock or water*
¹/₄ *lb onion*	*liaison:* 2 *oz butter or*
1 *oz butter or*	*margarine*
margarine	2 *oz flour*
salt and pepper	¹/₂ *pint milk*
1 *bouquet garni*	*a little cream or evapor-*
	ated milk

Chop the mushrooms and onion, making sure that the latter is cut very fine. Melt the butter, add the vegetables and

sweat together for 10 minutes. Add the seasoning, the bouquet garni and stock. Simmer together for ³/₄-1 hour. Remove the bouquet garni.

To thicken: melt the butter and stir in the flour. Gradually stir in the milk and add carefully to the soup. Stir until boiling, then cook for a few minutes longer. Just before serving stir in a little cream or evaporated milk.

POTATO PURÉE

1 ¹/₂ *lb potatoes*	1 *oz butter or margarine*
1 *onion*	*salt and pepper*
1 *stick celery*	1 ¹/₂ *pints stock or water*
¹/₂ *pint milk (or milk and cream)*	

Slice the potatoes and chop the onion and celery. Melt the butter. Add the vegetables and sweat together for 10-15 minutes. Add the seasoning and the stock and simmer together for 1 hour. Sieve. Return the soup to a clean pan, add the milk and bring to the boil again.

If wished, chopped parsley may be added just before serving.

TOMATO SOUP

1 *small onion*	*seasoning to include a*
¹/₂ *carrot*	*little sugar*
1 *stick celery*	1 *bouquet garni*
1 *oz ham (or a ham*	1 *pint tomato pulp or*
bone or bacon rinds)	1 *lb fresh tomatoes*
1 *oz butter or*	1 *pint stock or water*
margarine	1 ¹/₂ *oz flour*
	¹/₂ *pint milk*

Chop the onion, carrot, celery and ham and sweat together in the melted butter for 15 minutes. Add the seasoning, bouquet garni, tomato pulp and stock. Simmer together for 1-1¹/₂ hours. Sieve. Reheat and thicken with the blended flour and milk.

The addition of a little cream is an improvement to this soup.

TURKISH SOUP

1 *onion*	1/2 *lb lentils (steeped*
1 *carrot*	*overnight)*
1 *stick celery*	1 *pint tomato pulp*
1 *oz ham (or ham*	3 *pints water*
bone or bacon rinds)	*liaison:* 1 *oz butter or*
1 *oz butter or*	*margarine*
margarine	
seasoning to include a	1 *oz flour*
little sugar	1/2 *pint milk*

Chop the onion, carrot, celery and ham and sweat together in the melted butter. Add the seasoning, lentils, tomato pulp and water. Bring to the boil and skim. Simmer gently for 1-1 1/2 hours. Sieve. Return to the saucepan and reheat.

Melt the second quantity of butter, stir in the flour and gradually add the milk. Add to the sieved soup and bring to the boil, stirring all the time. Cook for a few minutes more before serving.

This soup is improved by the addition of a little cream.

KIDNEY SOUP

1/2 *ox kidney*	*a piece of turnip*
1 *oz butter*	*a bouquet garni*
1 *onion*	2 *cloves*
1 *carrot*	*salt and pepper*
1 *stick celery*	2 *pints brown stock*
	1 1/2 *oz cornflour*

Skin and core the kidney and cut into dice. Fry quickly in the butter. Remove and fry the onions until well browned. Slice the carrot and turnip. Tie the vegetables, the bouquet garni and cloves loosely in a piece of muslin. Put in a saucepan with the kidney, seasoning and stock. Simmer gently for 2 hours, skimming as necessary. Remove the vegetables and thicken with the blended cornflour.

OXTAIL SOUP

1 *ox-tail*	2 *sticks celery*
2 *oz flour*	24 *black peppercorns*
2 *oz dripping*	*a few parsley stalks*
2 *quarts stock or water*	*a sprig of thyme*
1 *carrot*	1 *tablespoonful ketchup*
1 *onion*	*a squeeze of lemon juice*
a piece of turnip	*salt*

Cut the tail into joints and blanch as follows:

Put the pieces into cold water; bring gently to the boil; simmer 10 minutes, then discard this water and dry the pieces before proceeding. Sometimes the pieces of tail are steeped overnight before blanching.

Now proceed with the making of the soup:

Put half the flour on a plate, add seasoning and coat the pieces of tail with the mixture. Melt the dripping and when hot fry the meat until brown on all sides.

Remove and fry the chopped onion until a rich brown. Return the pieces of tail to the pan. Add the stock and bring to the boil. Skim if necessary. Leave to simmer while the vegetables are prepared. These should be cut in rough pieces and added together with the herbs and seasoning. Continue to simmer gently for 4 hours or until the pieces of tail are tender and the meat is easily eased from the bone. Strain into a basin and, if possible, leave until the next day when the layer of fat will have hardened and so be easy to remove.

Next day proceed as follows:

Put 2/3 of the soup into a saucepan and bring to the boil. Blend the remainder of the flour and use to thicken the soup. Add the ketchup, lemon juice and check for seasoning. Cut the meat neatly from the smaller joints of ox-tail and add. Sometimes a little dry sherry is also added to oxtail soup just before serving.

The remainder of the soup can now be thickened and used as a gravy to serve with the best joints of the tail.

Alternatively, serve the large joints, country fashion, in deep plates with the soup poured around and boiled potatoes broken through it.

BROWN MEAT STOCK FOR A CONSOMMÉ

To make a successful consommé it is essential to have a good brown meat stock or bouillon as a foundation.

1¹/₂ *lb shin of beef*	*or 2 lb shin of beef*
1 *chicken carcase*	
a bouquet garni	1 *teaspoonful salt*
¹/₂ *onion*	6 *peppercorns*
¹/₂ *carrot*	2 *cloves*
1 *stick celery*	4 *pints water*

Wipe the meat and remove any marrow from the bone. Cut the meat into blocks. Cut up the carcase and slice the vegetables thickly.

Heat a strong pan and fry the meat, bones and onion until well browned. It may be necessary to use a little extra fat at this stage if the meat is very lean. When brown add the carrot, celery, bouquet garni, seasonings and water. Bring slowly to the simmer and cook gently until reduced by approximately half—in all about 3-4 hours. Strain and put aside until the next day.

The meat left after the straining may be used again with fresh vegetables to give a second stock.

CONSOMMÉ

2 *pints brown meat stock*	1 *egg white and the egg shell*
8 *oz shin of beef*	1 *lump of sugar*
	sherry — optional

Remove any trace of fat from the top of the stock and put in a clean pan. Remove all fat from the beef and either shred, as in the making of beef tea, or mince.

Add to the stock, together with the egg white and the washed crushed egg shell. Whisk over the heat until the soup just approaches boiling point. Then remove the whisk and let it come up to the top of the pan. Draw aside where it will keep hot, but not simmer, and leave to infuse for 1 hour.

Meanwhile place a close textured cloth in an upturned sieve and scald. Gently strain the soup through this, repeating the process as necessary. In repeating add a lump of sugar which will help the soup to sparkle.

The consommé should now be clear. In reheating it, avoid letting it boil again. Now add a little sherry, if wished, and the chosen garnish.

The consommé receives its name from the garnish which is added, for example: CONSOMMÉ JULIENNE has a garnish of cooked carrot, turnip, onion, leek and celery cut in fine match-stick pieces. CONSOMMÉ BRUNOISE has a garnish of similar vegetables cut into tiny dice and cooked. CONSOMMÉ A L'ITALIENNE has a garnish of cooked pasta such as vermicelli or spaghetti. CONSOMMÉ with PROFITEROLES — has a garnish of tiny profiteroles.

CLAM SOUP

A Portaferry recipe:

1 *oz butter or margarine*	6 *clams or scallops*
	salt and pepper
¹/₂ *onion — finely chopped*	1 *pint water*
1 *small carrot — diced*	1 *tablespoonful cornflour*
	¹/₄ *pint cream*

Melt the butter and add the onion and carrot. Sweat together for 10-15 minutes. Meanwhile, cut the clams into 4-6 pieces. Add to the onion and carrot. Season with salt and pepper and add the water. Bring to the boil and simmer gently for ³/₄-1 hour. Blend the cornflour with a little extra water or milk and use to thicken the soup. Stir in the cream.

QUICK SOUPS

Soup out of tins and packets need not be disdained, and can often be used as the base for a quick soup:

WHITE FOAM SOUP: *1 tin celery soup, 1 tin milk, 1 egg, 2 oz grated cheese and a little finely-chopped parsley.*
Dilute the soup with the milk. Combine the egg yolk with the cheese adding sufficient soup to make it a pouring consistency. Heat the soup. Stir in the yolk and cheese and cook for a few minutes without boiling. Whisk the egg white until stiff and put in the bottom of the soup tureen. Pour the hot soup over and serve sprinkled with chopped parsley.

TOMATO SHRIMP BISQUE: *1 tin tomato soup, 2 teaspoonfuls finely-chopped onion, 1 teaspoonful chopped basil (or a pinch of dried basil), 1 small tin shrimps and 2-3 tablespoonfuls whipped cream.*
Dilute the soup if condensed, using equal quantities of milk and water. Add the onion and basil and bring to the boil. Cook gently for 5 minutes. Lastly add the shrimps and heat these through. Put the cream into the bottom of the soup tureen and pour the hot soup over.

OXTAIL SOUP with ONION RINGS: *1 tin oxtail, soup, 1 tin water, 1 onion and butter for frying.*

Dilute and heat the soup in the usual way. Slice the onion into rings and fry gently in the butter. Fry until golden. To serve: float a few rings in each portion of soup.

CELERY SOUP with SAUSAGEMEAT BALLS: *1 tin celery soup, 1 tin water and milk, 2 pork sausages and some grated cheese.*
Dilute and heat the soup in the usual way. Meanwhile, skin the sausages and form into tiny balls. Roast or fry until brown. Add to the soup. Serve with grated cheese handed separately.

Another interesting way to serve cream of celery soup is to garnish it at the last moment with small, firm pats of parsley butter. Stir these lightly into the soup.

QUICK MUSHROOM SOUP: *1 tin mushroom soup, 1 tin milk, 4-8 oz mushrooms and a little cream if possible.*
Dilute the mushroom soup with the milk and heat. Chop the mushrooms and add. Simmer together for 5 minutes. Add a little cream before serving.

ACCOMPANIMENTS FOR SOUP

TOASTED CROÛTONS: Remove the crusts from freshly-toasted bread and cut into dice. Serve with purées and cream soups.

FRIED CROÛTONS: Remove the crusts from sliced bread and cut into cubes. Fry a golden brown in deep fat. Serve with purées and cream soups.

FAIRY TOAST: Cut bread, paper thin and dry out and toast in a very moderately-heated oven.

MELBA TOAST: Toast slices of bread of moderate thickness. Split and dry and crisp in a moderately-heated oven.

EGG AND CHEESE DISHES

BOILED EGGS

An egg for boiling should be very fresh and there are a number of different methods of carrying out this seemingly simple job. In each case importance is attached to gentle cooking, so that the yolk and white set without toughening.

Three simple and successful methods are:

1. Place the eggs in a pan of boiling water, cover with a lid and draw aside from the heat. Cook, without boiling, for 7-9 minutes according to the size and temperature of the eggs.
2. Place the eggs in cold water and bring to the boil. Simmer gently for 2 1/2-3 minutes according to size and temperature.
3. If an electric cooker with a solid plate is used, the following method of steaming the egg is recommended:

Place the egg in a pan with a tight-fitting lid and add 3-4 tablespoonfuls of cold water. Cover with the lid and place on the solid plate. Switch to " high " until the water reaches boiling point. Then switch to " off ". Leave on the plate for 4 minutes for a lightly-cooked egg; one or two minutes longer

for a medium-cooked egg and 10 minutes for a hard-boiled egg.

With radiant plates, the method requires adjusting and, instead of switching to " off " it should be turned to " low ". The timing remains the same.

The time required for boiling eggs may be varied according to personal taste and it should be noted that they are better not taken direct from the refrigerator. The sharp contrast in temperature might cause them to crack and besides it affects the exact timing of the cooking.

HARD - BOILED EGGS: Put the eggs in cold water and bring slowly to the boil, simmer gently for 10-12 minutes. Immediately they are cooked, they should be plunged in cold water. This helps to prevent the yolk discolouring and also makes the eggs easier to shell.

If a large number of eggs are to be boiled, it is convenient to place them in a frying basket.

SCRAMBLED EGG

To each egg allow:

1/4-1/2 oz butter salt and pepper
1 tablespoonful milk hot buttered toast

Melt the butter in a small, strong

56

saucepan. Add the milk and seasoning. Beat the egg slightly and add. Stir gently over a moderate heat until the egg begins to set and the mixture is of a creamy consistency. An extra piece of butter stirred in at this stage is an improvement. Remove from the heat immediately and pile the mixture onto the toast. Garnish with parsley and serve at once.

Variations of scrambled egg include the following:

SCRAMBLED EGG with CHEESE: Prepare the scrambled egg in the usual way adding 1 tablespoonful grated cheese and a little mustard to each egg.

SCRAMBLED EGG with TOMATOES: Allow half a tomato to each egg. Skin, chop and stew in the melted butter and milk. Add the slightly-beaten egg and continue scrambling the mixture in the usual way.

SCRAMBLED EGG with HERBS: Chopped parsley or chives may be added to the basic mixture.

POACHED EGG

Half fill a shallow saucepan with water or, alternatively, use a frying-pan. Add salt and vinegar in roughly the proportion of 1 tablespoonful vinegar to each quart. Bring to the boil, then stir rapidly. Meanwhile, have the egg broken into a cup and slip it gently into the whirling liquid. Poach gently for 3 minutes or until the egg is nicely set. Lift out with a perforated spoon or egg slice and serve immediately on hot buttered toast.

FRIED EGG

Eggs may be fried in bacon fat, butter or oil. Heat a little fat in the pan. It should be barely smoking. Break in the egg, season and baste first with a little of the egg white to veil the yolk and give the egg a good shape. Now baste with hot fat and fry gently until set. Sometimes the egg is turned and browned on the other side.

SAVOURY OMELET

3 eggs
seasoning
1 tablespoonful water

a little finely-chopped parsley, thyme, marjoram or other herbs

approximately ¹/₂ oz butter

Break the eggs into a bowl and stir, rather than beat, with a fork until the yolks are mixed with the whites. Stir in the seasoning, water and chopped herbs, while sometimes a few pieces of butter the size of a pea are also added. Meanwhile, heat the omelet pan (one 7 inch across will suit an omelet made with 3-4 eggs). Add the butter and, when hot and on the point of turning colour, pour in the eggs. Tip the pan towards the person and, with a fork, draw the mixture from the far side to the centre. Again tilt the pan so that the liquid eggs run to replace those from the space made. Continue in this fashion until the omelet shows signs of setting. Finally tilt the pan away from the person and fold the omelet over into the lip of the pan to give a half-moon shape. Cook a second longer, then quickly turn onto a heated dish. Serve immediately.

BACON OMELET

Allow approximately 2 rashers of bacon to a 3 egg omelet. Remove the rind and fry until crisp. Break into small pieces, add to the omelet mixture and cook all together in the usual way.

CHEESE OMELET

A cheese omelet may be made in various ways and the result depends greatly on the quality of the cheese used.

Failing Gruyère, a processed cheese which will melt easily is best. It should be cut in dice and sprinkled over the omelet once it is set. Cook a second longer, before folding the omelet in two.

Alternatively, 1 tablespoonful grated cheese may be incorporated into the egg mixture and more grated cheese sprinkled over the omelet before it is folded in two.

MUSHROOM OMELET

3-4 *oz mushrooms*	*salt and pepper*
1 *shallot*	$^1/_2$ *oz butter*
1 *teaspoonful chopped parsley*	1 *savoury omelet*

Chop the mushrooms and shallot finely. Add the parsley and seasoning and sauté in the melted butter for 5 minutes. Make the omelet in the usual way and spread half with the mushroom mixture before folding it over.

SCOTCH EGGS

To each hard-boiled egg allow:

1 *pork sausage*
egg and bread crumbs

Remove the shell from the hard-boiled egg and roll lightly in flour. Skin the sausage and flatten into a round cake. Work round the egg enveloping it completely.

Flatten slightly at either end and pass through beaten egg and bread-crumbs. Fry slowly in deep fat. Drain well and cut in two. Serve either hot with a sauce such as tomato sauce, or cold with salad.

EGG CUTLETS

2-3 *hard-boiled eggs*	1 *oz flour*
1 *oz cooked ham or fried bacon*	1 *gill milk*
3-4 *mushrooms (cooked)*	*salt, pepper and cayenne*
1 *oz butter or margarine*	*a little grated nutmeg*
	1 *egg yolk*
	egg and breadcrumbs

Chop the hard-boiled eggs, the ham or bacon and the mushrooms. Make a panada with the butter, flour and milk. Remove from the heat and add the chopped ingredients, together with the seasoning, nutmeg and egg yolk. Spread the mixture on a plate and put aside until cold. Cut into eight wedges and form these into cutlet shapes. Pass through egg and crumbs and fry.

CURRIED EGGS (HOT)

4-6 *hard-boiled eggs*	*a little lemon juice*
$^1/_2$ *pint curry sauce*	3 *oz boiled rice*

Cut the hard-boiled eggs in two. Place in the curry sauce and heat through. Arrange the eggs on a hot serving dish. Add a little lemon juice to the sauce and use to coat the eggs. Garnish with a border of boiled rice.

CURRIED EGGS (COLD)

6 *hard-boiled eggs*	1 *dessertspoonful vinegar*
1 *teaspoonful curry powder*	1 *tablespoonful mayonnaise*

Sauce:

2 *oz butter or margarine*	1 *teaspoonful flour*
1 *dessert apple*	2 *oz sultanas*
4 *shallots*	$^1/_2$ *gill milk*
1 *teaspoonful coriander seeds*	*mayonnaise*
1 *tablespoonful curry powder*	*a squeeze of lemon juice*
	salt and pepper
	a pinch of sugar

Cut the hard-boiled eggs in two by the length. Remove the yolks and sieve. Add the curry powder, vinegar, mayonnaise and seasoning as necessary. Beat the mixture well and use to stuff the eggs. Put the two halves together again and lay in a serving dish.

Meanwhile prepare the sauce:

Melt the butter and add the diced apple and finely-chopped shallots. Sweat together for 10-15 minutes. Crush the coriander seeds a little and add together with curry powder, flour and sultanas. Gradually stir in the milk. Bring to the boil and cook gently for a few minutes. Cool. Stir in an equal quantity of mayonnaise. Add the lemon juice, seasoning and sugar. Spoon over the eggs and serve suitably garnished with perhaps some spiced prunes and shredded pimento.

Good accompaniments include spiced prunes, banana and rice salads.

EGGS MORNAY

4-6 *hard-boiled eggs* 2 *oz grated cheese*
$^1/_2$ *pint béchamel or* *a little butter or mar-*
white sauce *garine*

Cut the hard-boiled eggs in two and arrange on a heat-proof dish. Season the béchamel sauce highly including a little mustard with the salt and pepper. Stir in half the cheese and pour this sauce over the eggs. Sprinkle with the remainder of the cheese, flake with pieces of butter and brown in a hot oven.

Suggested oven temperature 450° or "7".

CUMBERLAND PIE

Potato pastry:

6 *oz butter or* 10 *oz cooked*
margarine *riced potato*

6 *oz flour* 1 *teaspoonful salt*
Filling:
6-8 *oz streaky bacon* 3-4 *eggs*
seasoning

Begin by preparing the potato pastry:

Cream the butter and gradually work in the flour, riced potato and salt. Knead well and cut in two pieces, one being rather bigger than the other. Use the larger piece to line a pie-dish.

Rind the bacon and make into little rolls. Arrange lightly in the pie-dish. Beat the eggs, season sparingly and pour over the bacon rolls. Cover with the remainder of the pastry. Brush with egg and bake in a moderate oven for approximately 50-60 minutes.

Suggested oven temperature — 400° or "5".

BACON AND EGG PIE

6-8 *oz short crust* 4 *eggs*
pastry 6 *oz streaky bacon*
salt and pepper

Cut the short crust pastry in two and use half to line a sandwich tin or heat-proof plate. Rind the bacon and cut into $^1/_2$ inch pieces. Arrange on the pastry making four nests in the bacon for the eggs. Crack the eggs into these hollows and sprinkle each with salt and pepper. Cover with the remainder of the pastry and neaten the edges attractively. Brush with egg and bake in a fairly hot oven for approximately 45 minutes.

Suggested oven temperature—450°-400° or "7-6".

This pie may be served hot or cold. It will look particularly attractive if, when cut, the cross-section shows bacon, egg white and egg yolk.

WELSH RAREBIT OR RABBIT

1/4 *lb cheese*
1-2 *tablespoonfuls milk (traditionally beer is used)*

1 *oz butter*
seasoning including a little cayenne
2 *slices hot buttered toast*

Grate the cheese and put in a saucepan with the milk, butter and seasoning. Stir and cook over a gentle heat until the cheese has melted and the mixture is quite smooth. Avoid overheating. Pour over the toast and serve immediately.

Alternatively, the Welsh rarebit may be browned under the grill in which case the bread is only toasted on the under side.

MACARONI CHEESE

2 *oz macaroni*
3-4 *oz cheese*
1/2 *pint white sauce*
salt and pepper

1/2 *teaspoonful made mustard*
1 *tablespoonful breadcrumbs*
a knob of butter

Fill a roomy pan with water, add salt and bring to the boil. Add the macaroni and simmer until tender — about 20-30 minutes. Drain and chop roughly. Grate the cheese and add the greater part of it to the white sauce. Season highly including the made mustard. Stir in the macaroni and pour into a greased pie-dish. Sprinkle with the remainder of the cheese and the breadcrumbs mixed together. Flake with butter and brown in a hot oven.

Suggested oven temperature — 475º or " 9 ".

CHEESE AND MACARONI CUTLETS

2 *oz macaroni*
2-3 *oz cheese*
1 *oz butter or margarine*
1 *oz flour*

1 *gill milk*
1 *egg yolk*
seasoning including a little made mustard
egg and crumbs

Boil the macaroni and drain. Chop finely. Grate the cheese. Make a panada with the butter, flour and milk. Add the macaroni, cheese, egg yolk and season the mixture highly. Spread on a plate and put aside until cold. Cut into 6-8 wedges and form each into a cutlet shape. Pass through egg and breadcrumbs and fry in hot fat. Drain and stick a piece of macaroni into each cutlet to imitate a bone.

FRIED CHEESE SANDWICHES

Make sandwiches with well-buttered bread and slices of processed cheese or a cheese filling — the bread should be rather thicker than for normal sandwiches. Trim off the crusts and fry in melted butter until golden and crisp on both sides. Serve very hot.

BREAD AND CHEESE FRITTERS

6 *slices of bread cut from a sandwich pan*
  butter for spreading
  a little made mustard
4 *slices of processed cheese*
  egg and breadcrumbs

Butter the slices of bread generously and spread with a little made mustard. Make into decker sandwiches using three slices of bread and two slices of cheese to each. Remove the crusts and cut each round into three oblong sandwiches. Pass through beaten egg and bread-crumbs and fry in deep fat until golden and crisp.

CHEESE PUDDING (1)

1/2 *pint milk*
1 *oz butter or margarine*

2 *oz breadcrumbs*
2-3 *oz grated cheese*
1-3 *eggs*
salt and pepper
1/4 *teaspoonful made mustard*

Heat the milk and butter together and pour over the breadcrumbs and cheese. Leave to soak for a short time. Stir in the lightly-whisked eggs and season highly with salt, pepper and mustard. Pour into a greased pie-dish and bake in a moderate oven for approximately 30 minutes.

Suggested oven temperature — 400° or " 6 ".

CHEESE PUDDING (2)

approximately 4 oz thinly-sliced bread and butter
a little made mustard   3 oz grated cheese
salt and pepper   ¹/₂ pint milk
1 egg

Smear the bread with a little made mustard and cut into dice. Season the cheese and combine with the bread in a greased pie-dish. Heat the milk and pour over the beaten egg. Pour the mixture over the contents of the pie-dish and put aside to soak for a short time. Bake in a moderately-heated oven for approximately 30-40 minutes.

Suggested oven temperature — 400° or " 6 ".

CHEESE PIE

4 oz short crust pastry

Filling :
¹/₂ *lb grated cheese*   *3 well-beaten eggs*
1 tablespoonful flour   *salt and pepper*
1 cupful milk   *a little made mustard*

Use the pastry to line a flan ring or a deep pie-plate. Grate the cheese into a bowl and stir the flour through evenly. Add the milk, well-beaten eggs and seasoning. Pour the mixture into the pastry case and bake for 15 minutes in a fairly hot oven, then continue at a reduced heat for approximately 30 minutes.

Suggested oven temperature — 400° reduced to 350° or " 6 " reduced to " 3 ".

CHEESE, LEEK AND POTATO PIE

6-8 potatoes   *3-4 leeks*
6 rashers of bacon   6 oz grated cheese
salt and pepper

Boil the potatoes. Rind, chop and cook the bacon sufficiently to draw the fat. Shred the white part of the leek, add this to the bacon and sweat together until soft.

Slice the boiled potatoes and arrange half of these in the bottom of a pie-dish. Add the bacon and leeks and sprinkle with half the grated cheese. Cover with the remainder of the sliced potatoes and finally sprinkle all with cheese. Season each layer carefully. Brown in a hot oven for approximately 30 minutes.

Suggested oven temperature — 450° or " 7 ".

CHEESE SOUFFLÉ

1 oz butter or   *salt, pepper and a pinch*
margarine   *of cayenne*
1 oz flour   *4 oz grated cheese*
¹/₄ pint milk   *2 eggs*
1 extra egg white

Make a panada with the butter, flour and milk. Cook thoroughly. Remove from the heat and cool a little. Add the seasoning, grated cheese and the yolks of the two eggs. Beat until smooth and creamy. Whisk the egg whites until stiff. Fold into the cheese mixture and bake in a 5¹/₂ inch soufflé dish for approximately 30 minutes.

Suggested oven temperature — 425° or " 6 ".

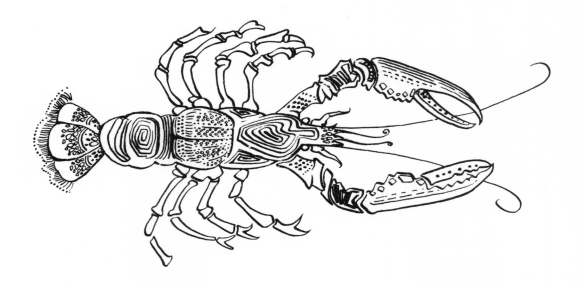

FISH

THE heritage that exists in Northern Ireland in the matter of fish and fish cookery is not insignificant if simple, and sometimes begotten, as is much of our cookery, out of hard times.

The Bann silver eel fisheries are probably the largest of their kind in western Europe, while there are also eel fisheries on the River Erne. The eels are mostly exported live to the London markets, though attempts have been made to smoke them on Lough Erne. Otherwise it is sad to think they are only esteemed by the folk who catch them. In passing, it is interesting to note that at one time the elvers too, were caught, cooked in milk and pressed into a kind of eel-cheese.

In Lough Neagh pollan are caught. These may be described as fresh water herring and are peculiar to some Irish and Scottish lakes. They make good eating if dipped in seasoned flour and fried in butter.

Excellent trout abound, particularly in the spring and early summer, while salmon is plentiful, but expensive. Indeed it is so plentiful in the River Bann that at one time a bargain was often made between master and servant to limit the number of times it might be served in the week.

Around the coast sea fish abound. Apart from the usual cod, haddock, whiting and flat fish, herrings are probably the most important catch. They are sold fresh, salted and as red herring — that is a herring which has been salted and then smoked. At Ardglass, Portavogie and Annalong large prawns are caught, and their fat tails find their way to the deep freeze and the London markets under the name of scampi. Scallops, also spoken of as clams along some parts of the coast, are in good supply in the spring, and in the Portaferry district they are used in several interesting ways. Sometimes they are made into a clam soup or again they may be baked:

The scallops or clams are first heated on top of the range or in the oven till the shell opens. They are then washed and trimmed so that only the white flesh and orange roe are left. Each fish is cut in four, laid in the deep half of the shell, sprinkled with lemon juice, seasoning, covered with crumbs, generously flaked with butter and baked in a moderate oven for approximately 30-35 minutes.

In the past and occasionally today, blocking and lythe were dried by the fisher folk. This was done, of course, by hanging the filletted fish in the open and exposing it to the elements. Later this dried fish was steeped and then gently cooked, laid skin side down on the coals of a turf fire. Served with plenty of butter, this was tastier fare than one might suppose.

FRIED FISH

Any small whole fish, piece of fish or fillet is suitable for frying. All must, however, have a coating and the usual are:

> milk and seasoned flour
> batter
> egg and breadcrumbs, after a
> preliminary coating of flour

Fish coated with milk and flour is usually fried in shallow fat, while fish coated with egg and breadcrumbs may be fried in shallow or deep fat. Of the two, the second is easier and the result generally more satisfactory. On the other hand fish coated in batter should be dropped immediately into hot deep fat, no frying basket being necessary.

FRIED HERRING

There are a variety of ways to fry herring, and the most usual method is as follows:

Remove the scales, fins and head and gut the herring. Wash and dry, then toss in seasoned flour or fine oatmeal. Fry gently in a little butter or dripping until the skin is brown and crisp on both sides. Serve with a wedge of lemon and mustard sauce if wished.

Alternatively, the herring may be split, boned and opened out before frying as already described.

Yet another method is to heat a frying pan, sprinkle it well with salt and, when hot, fry the prepared herring dry, except for its own fat. It is not necessary to coat it with flour or oatmeal in this instance.

FRIED MACKEREL

Mackerel must be perfectly fresh if it is to be enjoyed, and then it is very good. The usual way to cook it is to fillet it and to dip the pieces in seasoned flour or fine oatmeal before frying in butter.

Mackerel may also be poached whole and, in either case, is excellent accompanied by gooseberry sauce.

FRIED EEL

Eel must be kept alive until just prior to cooking, when it should be stunned by a blow on the head. The further preparation for cooking is to skin it. This may be done in various ways depending on circumstances:

Perhaps the most usual method is to cut off the head, then turn back the skin at the neck and draw it downwards with the aid of two forks — as one would draw off a stocking.

Alternatively, it may be hung up on a hook by a string tied at the neck.

Cut through the skin below this point, loosen so that it can be gripped in a cloth and pulled down and off in one movement.

Another way is to cut the eel into short lengths, place these under a grill for a short time, turning the pieces frequently. The heat causes the skin to blister so that it can be removed easily.

If the eel to be fried is small, no further preparation is necessary beyond cutting into short lengths and the usual tossing in seasoned flour. Fry gently in butter and serve accompanied by a little fried bacon.

If the eel is large, it is better to parboil it before frying. Alternatively, it may be preferable to bone it and cut into fillets for cooking.

PLAICE OR SOLE MEUNIÈRE

This is a classic method of cooking fish and one which may be used for many types other than plaice or sole.

fillets of plaice or sole   *extra butter for*
  (skinned)   *serving*
seasoned flour   *chopped herbs including*
clarified butter for   *parsley (optional)*
  frying

a squeeze of lemon juice

Dip the fillets of fish in the seasoned flour. Clarify the butter and heat in a frying-pan. When foaming lay the fillets in it, placing them presentation side down. Cook gently until nicely browned, then turn and cook on the other side. Transfer to a hot serving dish. Wipe the pan and in it melt the second quantity of butter. Heat until just turning colour, then add the herbs and lemon juice and quickly pour over the fish.

Serve with wedges of lemon.

RIBBON FILLETS OF PLAICE OR SOLE

The fillets of fish should be skinned, then cut each in two by the length. Dip the strips in seasoned flour and tie loosely in a knot. Pass through beaten egg and toss in breadcrumbs. Fry in deep fat. Serve accompanied by wedges of lemon and a suitable sauce.

PLAICE/SOLE — GUDGEON STYLE

The gudgeon or goujon is a small fresh water fish found in shoals in the lakes and rivers of Europe. It is usually fried. When plaice or sole is served gudgeon style the fillets are cut diagonally across in strips in imitation of this little fish. The pieces are dipped in milk and seasoned flour and fried in deep fat.

Alternatively, the pieces of fish may be passed through egg and crumbs before frying.

Serve piled in a hot dish garnished with wedges of lemon and parsley and accompanied by a suitable sauce.

FRIED SCALLOPS

Poach the flesh and roe of the scallops in a little court-bouillon or milk flavoured with onion, thyme and bay-leaf. Do not overcook as they quickly become tough. Drain and dip in batter or egg and crumbs and fry in hot deep fat. Serve garnished with parsley and lemon and accompanied by a suitable sauce.

Allow 2-3 scallops per person.

SOLE COLBERT

Skin and trim the sole, then slit the fish down one side. Raise the two fillets and roll back neatly. Using scissors, cut the centre bone in two or three places so that it can easily be removed later.

Dip the fish in seasoned flour, then in egg and crumbs. Fry in hot deep fat. After draining remove the back bone carefully and fill the cavity with maître d'hôtel butter.

One large sole may be used or allow one smaller one for each person.

POACHED FISH

Poaching seems a better and more accurate term for this method of cooking fish than boiling, since in fact, fish should never be boiled. It should rather be cooked slowly at a temperature just below boiling point.

Large whole fish, large pieces or fillets are all suitable for cooking by this method, and the cooking may either be done using top heat or in the oven.

The liquid for poaching is called a "court-bouillon". At its simplest, it may take the form of water to which is added salt, peppercorns, a bouquet garni, a little vinegar, carrot, onion and celery. More elaborately, it may be made with the addition of a cheap white wine or cider. The ingredients are boiled together for $1/2$-$3/4$ hour and cooled before use.

Whole fish are put into a cool court-bouillon and pieces of fish into boiling liquor in order to seal the juices in immediately. For large fish, the cooking time is 8-10 minutes to every pound. For convenience a fish kettle is ideal to use for the cooking, but few households now possess this piece of kitchen equipment. As an alternative, the fish may be tied in a piece of muslin in order to make it easy to lift out without breaking.

Large fish, or large pieces such as cod, halibut, turbot, salmon trout or salmon cooked in this way may be served quite plainly, with a suitable sauce and boiled potatoes.

Poached fish intended to be eaten cold should be cooled in the court-bouillon.

SOLE MORNAY

1 sole of approximately 1-1 $1/2$ *lb*

a piece of onion	*6 peppercorns*
a piece of carrot	*salt*
a bouquet garni	*approximately* $3/4$ *pint water*

Mornay sauce:

1 oz butter or margarine	*salt, pepper and a little made mustard*
1 oz flour	$1/2$ *pint milk*
2 oz grated cheese	

Skin and fillet the sole and make a stock with the bones, fish trimmings, vegetables, bouquet garni, seasonings and water. Simmer together for 30 minutes. Strain and cool.

Lay the fillets on a board with the skinned side uppermost. Season and sprinkle with a little lemon juice. Either fold in two or fold under the tips of the fillets. Lay in a buttered dish and pour over sufficient stock to just cover. Lay a piece of buttered paper on top and poach in a moderately-heated oven for 15-20 minutes.

Meanwhile prepare the sauce:

Make a roux with the butter and flour. Add the seasoning and gradually stir in the milk. Stir until boiling. Simmer for a few minutes and lastly stir in the greater part of the cheese.

Arrange the fillets on a hot dish. Coat with the sauce, sprinkle the remainder of the cheese on top and brown in the oven or under the grill.

Sautéed mushrooms make a pleasant garnish for this dish, which is also a useful method of serving fillets of haddock and plaice.

SOLE VÈRONIQUE

1 *sole of approximately* 1-1 ½ *lb*
a piece of onion   *salt*
a piece of carrot   *approximately* ¾ *pint*
a bouquet garni   *water or preferably*
6 *peppercorns*   *water and white wine*
                              or cider

Sauce:
1 *oz butter*   1 ½ *gills milk*
1 *oz flour*   ½ *gill of the liquor*
salt and pepper   *from the fish*
Garnish: 4-6 *oz green grapes*

Skin and fillet the fish and make a
stock with the bones, fish trimmings,
vegetables, bouquet garni, seasonings and
water. Simmer together for 30 minutes.
Strain and cool.

Season the fillets and sprinkle with a
little lemon juice. Fold the two ends
under and lay in a buttered dish. Pour
over barely sufficient stock to cover and
lay buttered paper on top. Poach in a
moderately-heated oven for 15-20
minutes.

Meanwhile prepare the sauce in the
usual way from a roux foundation.
Correct the consistency with the strained
liquor from round the fish.

Skin and pip the grapes and heat. If
possible they should be heated in a little
white wine.

Arrange the fillets on a hot dish, coat
with the sauce and garnish with the
grapes.

BAKED STUFFED FISH

Herrings, cod steak and small whole
haddock lend themselves to stuffing and
baking and a suitable stuffing is as
follows:
3 *oz breadcrumbs*   *a scraping from a juicy*
1 ½ *oz butter or*   *onion*
   margarine

chopped parsley   *salt and pepper*
chopped thyme   1 *egg*
                         milk

Rub the butter into the breadcrumbs
and add the chopped herbs, the onion
juice and seasoning. Bind with the
beaten egg and a little milk.

Use to stuff the fish. Lay on a greased
baking dish, flake with butter and cover
with buttered paper. Bake in a moderate
oven.

Suggested oven temperature — 375° or
" 4 ".

Serve hot with a suitable sauce.

Herrings may also be stuffed with an
oatmeal stuffing as follows:
4 *boned herrings*   *a little finely-chopped*
2 *tablespoonfuls fine*   *onion*
   oatmeal   *salt and pepper*
chopped parsley   2 *oz dripping*

Lay two of the open herrings on a
greased baking tray with the skin side
down. Combine the ingredients for the
stuffing and lay on top. Cover with
the remaining two herrings placed skin
side uppermost. Flake with butter and
bake in a moderate oven for approximately 30 minutes.

BAKED SALMON TROUT

Instead of poaching a salmon trout,
it may be baked — wrapped in aluminium foil. This is particularly
convenient if no fish kettle is available.

Have a piece of foil rather larger than
the fish so that it can be enveloped
securely, and either butter it generously
or brush with olive oil. The latter is
better if the fish is to be eaten cold.
Place the prepared fish in the centre
and parcel it firmly, twisting the two
ends tightly so that no juice can escape.
Lay on a baking tray and bake in a
very moderately-heated oven.

Suggested oven temperature — 300° or "1".

The foil should not be opened until the fish is cooked, and the time depends on the weight and thickness of the fish. The cooking is very gentle, however, and $^3/_4$-1 hour is not too long for a 2 lb trout.

When ready, slide the fish and its juices onto a hot dish. The simplest and perhaps best accompaniment for hot salmon trout is a little melted butter served separately.

If it is to be served cold, remove the skin gently while it is still warm and serve within a few hours. Serve with mayonnaise, cucumber and other salads.

Salmon or a piece of salmon may also be baked as just described.

FISH IN PASTRY

6 oz flaky or rough puff pastry

Filling:

$^1/_2$ *lb filleted haddock*	1 *chopped gherkin*
(*or 6 oz cooked fish*)	1 *teaspoonful chopped*
1 *hard-boiled egg*	*capers*
1 *gill anchovy sauce*	*a squeeze of lemon juice*
	salt and pepper

Cut the fish in 1 inch pieces (or flake the cooked fish). Chop the hard-boiled egg and combine the fish and egg with the sauce. Add the chopped gherkin, capers, lemon juice and seasoning.

Roll the pastry to a 12 inch square and trim the edges. Spread the fish mixture in the centre of the pastry. Brush the edges of the pastry with water and fold the four corners to the centre, overlapping the edges a little. Brush with egg and decorate with pastry leaves. Brush these with egg also, and bake in a hot oven until the pastry is set.

Suggested oven temperatures — 475° or "9".

Reduce the heat and complete the cooking. The time required will vary from approximately 30 to 45 minutes depending on whether the fish is cooked or not.

If preferred, the fish in pastry may be shaped like a large sausage roll.

SAVOURY HADDOCK

1 *lb smoked filleted*	1 $^1/_2$ *oz flour*
haddock	*salt and pepper*
1 *onion*	4-5 *tomatoes*
$^3/_4$ *pint milk*	2 *tablespoonfuls grated*
1 $^1/_2$ *oz butter or*	*cheese*
margarine	

Cut the fish into convenient pieces and slice the onion. Place both in a saucepan and add the milk. Poach gently until cooked. Remove the fish and break into flakes. Strain the milk and make it into a creamy sauce with the butter and flour. Stir in the fish and season as required. Pour into a greased pie-dish. Cover with sliced tomatoes and sprinkle with seasoning and grated cheese. Place in a fairly hot oven for 20-30 minutes to heat thoroughly and toast the cheese.

SCALLOPED FISH

$^1/_2$ *lb cooked fish* $^1/_2$ *pint white sauce*

buttered crumbs

Butter 4 or 5 deep scallop shells and in them lay some pieces or flakes of cooked fish. Pile these rather high in the centre. Spoon over some well-flavoured white sauce and sprinkle the whole generously with buttered crumbs. Bake in a hot oven for 10-15 minutes.

The scallops should be browned on top. Serve with a wedge of lemon and a sprig of parsley on top of each portion. A little grated cheese may be added either to the sauce or the crumbs.

Alternatively, the flaked fish may be combined with the sauce, poured into a pie-dish and the surface covered generously with buttered crumbs. Place in a fairly hot oven for 20-30 minutes to heat through and brown.

FISH PIE

¹/₂ lb cooked fish	*approximately 1 lb*
1-2 hard-boiled eggs	*potatoes*
(optional)	*1 ¹/₂ oz butter or*
chopped parsley	*margarine*
¹/₂ pint béchamel or	*a little hot milk*
white sauce	*seasoning*

Fish pie may be made by various methods:

Generally the flaked fish, chopped hard-boiled eggs and parsley are combined with a well-flavoured sauce. Pour this mixture into a buttered pie-dish and top with creamy mashed potatoes. Flake with butter and brown in a hot oven.

Alternatively, the sauce may be omitted and the flaked fish added to the riced potatoes, the whole being beaten to a creamy consistency with melted butter and hot milk. Season well, including a little grated nutmeg, and add plenty of chopped parsley.

Pile in a greased pie-dish, flake with butter and brown in a hot oven.

Fish pie is particularly tasty if grated cheese is added to the creamed potatoes.

FISH CAKES — No. (1)

¹/₂ lb cooked fish	*chopped parsley*
¹/₂ lb potatoes (boiled)	*1 oz melted butter or*
salt and pepper	*margarine*
1 egg (optional)	
egg and breadcrumbs	

Flake the fish and sieve or rice the potatoes. Combine and add the seasoning, chopped parsley and melted butter.

Whisk the egg and beat into the mixture. Spread on a plate and put aside in a cool place to firm. Form the mixture into small cakes. Brush with egg and toss in crumbs. Fry, either in shallow or deep fat.

FISH CAKES — No. (2)

¹/₂ lb cooked fish	*1 oz flour*
1 oz butter or	*1 gill milk*
margarine	*salt and pepper*
chopped parsley	
egg and breadcrumbs	

Flake the fish. Make a panada with the butter, flour and milk. Add the fish, seasoning and chopped parsley. Spread the mixture on a plate and put aside in a cool place to firm.

Form into small cakes or croquettes. Dip in beaten egg and then in breadcrumbs and fry in hot deep fat.

A richer and more creamy fish cake may be made using milk flavoured with bay-leaf and a little onion and beating an egg into the mixture. If they are to be made like this they should be prepared well in advance so that they have an opportunity to firm in the refrigerator before shaping.

FISH FRITTERS

³/₄ lb fish (cooked)	*salt and pepper*
3 oz flour	*chopped parsley*
³/₄ teaspoonful baking	*1 egg and a little*
powder	*milk*

Flake the cooked fish and to it add the flour, baking powder, seasoning and chopped parsley. Mix to a stiff batter with the beaten egg and milk. Drop the mixture from a dessertspoon into deep fat which is just faintly smoking. Fry gently, turning when golden brown on the underside. Serve piled in a hot dish garnished with lemon and parsley.

Alternatively, uncooked fish may be used in which case it should be prepared by scraping or mincing.

KEDGEREE

¹/₂ *lb smoked filleted*	*4 oz Patna rice*
haddock (cooked)	*(boiled)*
2-3 oz butter or	*salt and pepper*
margarine	*1 egg*
1-2 hard-boiled eggs	

Flake the fish. Melt the butter. Add the fish and the greater part of the rice, stirring preferably with a carving fork. Season as required and stir in the beaten egg. Continue stirring over the heat until thoroughly hot. Serve piled on a hot dish, garnished with the remainder of the rice and quarters of hard-boiled egg.

If wished, the egg may be omitted and more butter used in the mixture, the amount depending on how well the rice has been dried. Sometimes 1-2 tablespoonfuls thick cream is also added.

Other fish may be used for making Kedgeree such as any white fish, or tinned or fresh salmon.

BAKED FISH SOUFFLÉ

¹/₂ *gill milk*	*a scant 1 ¹/₂ gills milk*
1 oz breadcrumbs	*flavoured with the*
¹/₂ *lb cooked fish*	*fish, bay-leaf and a*
1 oz butter or	*little onion*
margarine	*salt and pepper*
1 oz flour	*chopped parsley*
3 egg yolks	
3-4 egg whites	

Bring the milk to the boil and pour over the breadcrumbs. Put aside to soak. Flake the fish very finely.

Make a thick béchamel sauce with the butter, flour and flavoured milk.

Stir in the fish, breadcrumbs, seasoning and chopped parsley. Beat in the egg yolks. Lastly fold in the stiffly beaten egg whites and turn the mixture into a buttered soufflé case. Set in a bain-marie of hot water and bake in a moderate oven for approximately ¹/₂ hour.

Suggested oven temperature — 350° or " 3 ".

Serve immediately.

STEAMED FISH SOUFFLÉ

4 oz fish, e.g. any white fish, lobster or salmon	
³/₄ *oz butter or*	*a little anchovy essence*
margarine	¹/₂ *teaspoonful vinegar*
³/₄ *oz flour*	*seasoning*
1 gill milk	*2 eggs*
¹/₂ *pint anchovy sauce*	

Sieve or scrape the fish. Make a panada with the butter, flour and milk. Add the fish, flavouring and seasoning. Beat in the egg yolks and fold in the stiffly beaten egg whites. Turn the mixture into a prepared soufflé tin. Steam gently for 25-30 minutes. Turn out onto a hot dish and coat with the anchovy sauce. Garnish with lemon and parsley and serve immediately.

POTTED OR SOUSED HERRING

Remove the heads, fins and scales of the herring and arrange heads to tails in a pie-dish.

Place a bay-leaf in the centre, add a few slices of onion and sprinkle in some peppercorns, cloves and salt. Cover with a mixture of vinegar and water using these in roughly the proportion of ²/₃ vinegar to ¹/₃ water. Cover closely with well-buttered paper and bake in a cool oven for 3-4 hours. Long slow cooking is essential and does much to dissolve the small bones and give the herrings a good flavour.

Alternatively, the herring may be boned and rolled for potting, but they are not so good to eat as when cooked whole.

Potted herring keep well for a day or two and are, therefore, usually cooked in fairly large numbers. Serve cold with fresh bread and butter and salad if wished.

Mackerel may also be potted.

FISH SALAD

3/4 *lb cold cooked fish* 1 *dessertspoonful*
2-3 *tablespoonfuls* *chopped capers*
 shrimps (optional) 1 *dessertspoonful*
1 *dessertspoonful* *chopped parsley*
 chopped gherkins *a little scraped onion*
   salt and pepper
  mayonnaise (or salad cream)
Garnish: *lettuce, watercress, cucumber and tomato*

Flake the fish. Add the shrimps, gherkins, capers, parsley, onion and seasoning. Toss lightly together and mix with a little mayonnaise. Arrange in a dish, piling the mixture lightly. Cover with mayonnaise and garnish with salad material. Serve very cold with an accompanying salad.

SALMON MAYONNAISE

approximately 3/4 *lb* *lettuce, cucumber,*
 salmon   *radishes and cress*
1/2 *gill mayonnaise* *a little extra aspic*
1/2 *gill aspic jelly* *jelly (for glazing)*

Poach the salmon carefully in a court-bouillon and leave to cool in the cooking liquor. Remove the skin and bone and divide into 4 portions. Arrange on a cooling wire placed over a plate. Combine the mayonnaise with the just liquid aspic and stir until it begins to show signs of setting. When thick enough to coat the back of a spoon, use it to coat the pieces of salmon. When set decorate with neatly-cut pieces of cucumber and radish, and glaze with a final coating of aspic jelly.

When set, arrange on a dish and garnish with lettuce, crimped cucumber, radish and cress.

If preferred, the piece of salmon may be left whole.

The aspic jelly may also be omitted and mayonnaise alone used to coat the fish. The appearance will not be so good, however.

CRAB AND LOBSTER

Crab and lobster may be purchased cooked, but are best if bought alive as they should be used as soon as possible after cooking. Choose heavy fish of medium size, and give preference to those with large claws.

The crab or lobster should first be prepared for boiling in as humane a manner as possible:

Either they may be killed by running a skewer between the eyes or by plunging into rapidly-boiling water, which kills them immediately. Others prefer to put them in cold water to which has been added a little vinegar and to bring slowly to the boil. In this way, they are believed to lose their sense of feeling gradually, but from a culinary point of view the flesh is not so good to eat.

Crab and lobster may be boiled in salted water, sea-water, or a simple court-bouillon. Allow 10-15 minutes for every pound and preferably let them cool in the cooking liquid.

Lobsters are in season all the year round, but are at their cheapest and best from June to September. Crabs are best from April to October.

DRESSED CRAB

Rinse a cooked crab and place on its back. Break off the large claws, crack the shells and remove the white meat. Twist off the smaller claws and set aside for a garnish.

Next separate the body from the shell. This can be conveniently done if the crab is placed on the table with the flap next the person, and, using the thumbs push under the tail until it breaks away. Discard the gills or " dead men's fingers ", the stomach — recognisable as a small sac lying near the head — and with it a little twist of intestine. The remainder of the shell contains edible meat, but of a darker colour than found in the claws. Generally the two meats are kept separate and more of the white flesh can be picked out with a skewer from the body. Chop the white meat finely and mash or sieve the dark meat. To it add two tablespoonfuls crumbs, seasoning and a little cream or salad dressing. Moisten the white flesh with a little salad dressing also.

Now prepare the shell of the crab for dishing:

A natural line will be found marked on the under-side and the shell should be gently cracked and removed at this point all round. Wash well and rub with a little salad oil.

Arrange the dark flesh across the centre of the shell and the white flesh on either side. Finally decorate with hard-boiled egg and chopped parsley.

Place on a dish and steady and garnish further with the small claws and salad material as convenient.

LOBSTER MAYONNAISE

Lobster mayonnaise may be prepared in a variety of ways, and many prefer to relish it if it is served with simplicity, split in two, the claws cracked and accompanied by mayonnaise and a green salad.

A little more elaborately, it may be prepared as follows:

Remove the claws from a freshly-boiled lobster, then place it on a chopping board with the tail extended. Using a large cook's knife, cut it in two by the length. Remove the bag in the head and the dark line running to the tail which is the intestine. Carefully lift out the flesh from the tail shells, and, if wished, cut in slanting slices and return to the opposite shell so that the red side is now uppermost. Moisten the flesh in the head shells with a little mayonnaise.

Arrange the two halves on a dish garnished with the cracked claws and salad material. Serve accompanied by mayonnaise and perhaps a potato salad.

Another method of presenting lobster mayonnaise is as follows:

In the bottom of a glass dish arrange a layer of shredded lettuce, and over it arrange neat pieces of meat from the lobster's claws and any miscellaneous meat from the head. The pieces should not be too small and should be slightly domed. Next cover with slices cut from the tail meat. Season with salt and mask with mayonnaise. A recognised decoration consists of a lattice of anchovy fillets. Caper or slices of stuffed olive may be placed in the squares or diamonds thus formed. Complete the dish with a border of quartered hard-boiled eggs and the small leaves from the heart of the lettuce.

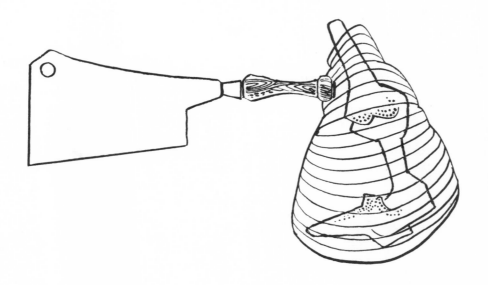

MEAT

BEEF

Prime beef should be well hung; the lean a bright red and marbled with fat which, in turn, should be creamy white with the suet firm and dry.

PRINCIPAL JOINTS for ROASTING: Sirloin, fillet or under-cut and ribs. Occasionally, a piece of top-side may also be cooked by roasting, but since it is lean, it tends to be dry, and requires slow cooking to make it tender.

PRINCIPAL JOINTS for BOILING: Brisket, silverside — either fresh or salted — and pickled ox tongue.

PRINCIPAL CUTS for GRILLING and FRYING: rump steaks, sirloin steaks, rib steaks and fillet of beef sliced.

PRINCIPAL CUTS for STEWING: Round or buttock steak, shoulder steak, brisket, flank, shin, ox-tail, liver, kidney and tripe.

BOILED BEEF — UNSALTED

For this purpose select a piece of boned and rolled brisket or cut of silverside weighing 3-6 lb. Put it into a roomy saucepan in which there is sufficient boiling water to cover it. Bring to the boil again and boil for 5 minutes. Skim and add salt and flavourings such as a bunch of herbs, some black peppercorns and a few cloves. Simmer gently allowing from 20-30 to the pound and 20-30 minutes over, according to the kind and shape of the piece of meat. Boiled meat should always be well cooked. About 45 minutes before the cooking is complete, add a mixture of carrot, turnip and onion cut into medium-sized pieces and continue to cook slowly until the meat is tender and the vegetables soft.

TO SERVE HOT: Lift the meat onto a hot dish and arrange the vegetables in a separate dish. Sometimes they may be served at either end of the meat dish, providing there is sufficient room for carving. Serve some of the broth in a sauceboat, as gravy. Alternatively, the boiled beef may be accompanied by an onion or horse-radish sauce.

TO SERVE COLD: Press the meat between two boards or dishes, with a weight on top. When cold, brush with a meat glaze if wished.

BOILED CORNED BEEF WITH DUMPLINGS

Select a compact piece of salted brisket or silverside weighing between 3 and 6 lb. Wash it, and if it is thought to be too salty, soak overnight or for a few hours in cold water. Put into a saucepan with cold water to cover. Bring fairly quickly to the boil, reduce the heat and simmer slowly until it is quite tender, allowing 20-30 minutes to the pound and 20-30 minutes over, according to the size and shape of the meat. Skim as necessary.

About 45 minutes before the cooking is complete, add a mixture of carrot, turnip and onion cut in fairly large pieces. Small suet dumplings may also be cooked with the meat and make a favourite accompaniment.

DUMPLINGS: 6 *oz flour*, $^1/_2$ *teaspoonful salt*, $^1/_2$ *teaspoonful baking powder*, 2 *oz prepared suet and water for mixing.*

Combine the dry ingredients and mix to a light dough with water. Make up into small balls and cook for 20 minutes along with the meat and vegetables. The water must be kept simmering at this stage, otherwise the dumplings will be heavy.

Serve the boiled salt meat on a hot dish, garnished with the dumplings and some of the vegetables. Serve extra vegetables separately. A little of the broth should accompany the boiled meat as a gravy.

ROAST SIRLOIN OR RIB OF BEEF

There are two methods of roasting meat:

The first and more usual method is to cook the joint fairly quickly at a temperature of 425° or " 6 " reducing the heat, if necessary after the first $^1/_2$ hour to 400° or " 5 ".

The second method is spoken of as " low temperature roasting " and, while not so usual, has the advantage that there is much less shrinkage of the joint and therefore more portions. The meat is put into a cold oven and the heat control turned to 350° or " 3 ". This method takes rather longer cooking time.

The favourite joints of beef for roasting are sirloin and rib. The meat may either be left on the bone or the joint boned and rolled. If it is left on the bone, it is necessary to have the rib bones sawn through at the streaky end so that the short lengths can be removed and the meat doubled under and secured with string or a carefully placed skewer. The chine bone may also be sawn through for removal after cooking to make carving easier. Sprinkle the joint with seasoning, including mustard if wished. Slivers of garlic may also be inserted here and there if the flavour is enjoyed. Place in a roasting tin and, if the meat is lean, spread with a little dripping.

Roast, or more correctly, bake in a fairly hot oven, allowing 15 minutes to the pound and 15 minutes over. Baste occasionally. Roast beef should be served rather underdone so that the flesh is still pink when carved.

When cooked, lift the joint onto a hot dish, remove any string or skewers and keep hot while the gravy is being made.

GRAVY: Pour the fat gently from the roasting tin, leaving any meat juices and sediment behind. To these add seasoning and stock or water as required. Bring to the boil and boil for a few minutes to dissolve the glaze from round the sides of the pan. The gravy may be left thin or slightly thickened with a little blended flour. Strain, if necessary, and serve.

THE ACCOMPANIMENTS to hot roast beef include Yorkshire pudding, gravy and and horse-radish sauce. The garnish is slivers of freshly shredded horse-radish. Roast potatoes generally accompany a roast joint. They may be served round the meat providing there is sufficient room left for carving.

YORKSHIRE PUDDING

4 oz flour   *1 egg*
a pinch of salt   *¹/₂ pint milk*

Measure the flour and salt into a bowl and make a bay in the centre. Drop in the egg and add sufficient milk to make a creamy batter. Beat thoroughly, then add the remainder of the milk and set aside for at least one hour before using.

Meanwhile put a little beef dripping into a Yorkshire pudding tin or large patty tins. Heat thoroughly in the oven with the joint. When very hot, remove and pour in the batter. Bake quickly until well risen and set. The Yorkshire pudding which is cooked in a sheet should be cut into square portions for serving.

A POT ROAST

Small joints of meat may be roasted in a heavy pan and this is often a more convenient and economical method than oven roasting.

Melt a little dripping in the pan and when it is hot, put in the prepared meat. Baste and cover with the lid. Continue the cooking at a steady even heat. The meat should be turned during the process so that it is evenly browned. Potatoes may also be cooked round the pot roast, but care is necessary so that they brown evenly.

Serve in the same way as an oven roasted joint.

"POT-OVENS" form part of the kitchen equipment of the Irish cottage and were ideal for cooking a pot roast or chicken. The live "coals" or turf were arranged on the lid as well as underneath, so that this native method of cooking is somewhat similar to the French method of braising.

BRAISED BEEF

Braising is a combination of roasting and stewing in a closely-covered pan. The meat cooked in this way is tender and well-flavoured with the vegetables cooked under it.

It is a suitable method of cooking joints of meat not sufficiently tender to roast. Preferably, however, the meat should have a proportion of fat, otherwise it becomes dry. If lean, it requires larding with strips of bacon fat. Suitable pieces are top-side or rump steak or other inexpensive stewing meats.

3 lb braising beef   *a little dripping*
approximately ¹/₂   *trimmings of bacon or*
cupful each of: *ham*
carrot   *seasoned flour*
turnip   *1 pint stock or water*
onion   *a bouquet garni*
celery   *salt and pepper*
2-3 cloves

Tie the meat into a compact shape and cut the vegetables into pieces of moderate size. Melt the dripping in a roomy pan. Add the bacon trimmings and cook a little together. Put in the piece of meat and brown on all sides. Remove and add the vegetables and brown lightly. Place the piece of meat on top. Add the stock, bouquet garni, seasoning and cloves. Cover with a close-fitting lid and cook slowly until the meat is tender. The cooking may be done on the top of the stove or in the oven. Alternatively, it may be cooked $1/2$ hour on top and the remainder of the time in the oven. Baste occasionally with the stock and, if it reduces too much, a little more should be added. The time for cooking will depend on the kind and the size of the piece of meat.

When ready, lift the meat on to a hot dish, remove the string and keep hot while the gravy is being made.

Strain the liquid from the braising pan into a smaller saucepan. Boil for a few minutes, remove any grease from the top, pour some round the joint and serve the remainder in a sauceboat. The vegetables cooked with the braise may also be served with it — bourgeois style — or, more elaborately, freshly-cooked vegetables may be served with the piece of braised beef.

It should be noted that the word " braise " is frequently used incorrectly to describe various dishes on a menu. For example, braised steak is often nothing more than a brown stew and similarly braised celery is all too frequently merely tinned celery hearts dressed with melted butter.

A " daube " is another French culinary term referring to a method of cooking similar to braising.

BROWN STEW

1 *lb stewing steak*	1 *carrot*
1 *onion*	*a piece of turnip* } *optional*
1 *oz dripping*	*water*
seasoning	1 *tablespoonful flour*

Cut the meat into small pieces and slice the onion. Melt the dripping. When hot, add the onion and fry gently until brown. Add the meat and seasoning and stir round. Cover with a lid and leave to cook slowly for $3/4$ hour. Stir occasionally.

Add the sliced carrot and turnip and sufficient water to cover all. Continue the cooking for a further hour or until the meat is quite tender. Thicken the gravy with the blended flour.

Dish the meat and vegetables and pour the gravy over. Garnish with freshly-boiled carrots tossed in melted butter and sprinkle with chopped parsley.

An alternative method of making a brown stew is as follows.

Cut the meat into square pieces and toss them in seasoned flour. Slice the onion. Melt the dripping. When hot, fry both the meat and onion until well browned. Add the carrot, turnip and sufficient water to cover all. Bring to the boil and simmer gently for 2 hours or until the meat is tender.

STEWED SHIN OF BEEF

1 $1/2$ *lb shin of beef*	4 *cloves*
1 $1/2$ *oz flour*	1 *Oxo cube or gravy*
salt and pepper	*browning*
1 *onion*	$3/4$ *pint stock or water*

Remove the meat from the bone and cut into cubes. Scoop out the marrow — it should not be included in the stew as it would make the gravy greasy. Toss the meat in seasoned flour and arrange in a casserole. Quarter the onion and stick a clove into each piece.

Arrange through the meat. Dissolve the Oxo cube in the stock and pour over all. Cover with a lid and cook in a moderate oven for 2-2 ¹/₂ hours or until the meat is tender. Stir occasionally.

Suggested oven temperature — 350⁰ or " 3 ". Reduce the temperature once the cooking has started.

EXETER STEW

1 *lb stewing beef*	1 *oz dripping*
1 *oz flour*	1 *pint stock or water*
salt and pepper	1 *tablespoonful vinegar*
1 *onion*	1 *bay-leaf*

Dumplings:

3 *oz flour*	¹/₄ *onion (finely*
1 *oz prepared suet*	*chopped)*
¹/₂ *teaspoonful baking*	¹/₂ *teaspoonful chopped*
powder	*parsley*
a pinch of dried herbs	*salt and pepper*
	water

Cut the meat into squares and toss in the seasoned flour. Slice the onion. Melt the dripping in a saucepan. When smoking hot, put in the prepared meat and fry until brown on all sides. Remove the meat, add the onion and brown also. Stir in any remaining flour and add the stock, vinegar and bay-leaf. Stir until boiling. Return the meat and simmer slowly until the meat is tender — approximately 1 ¹/₂-2 hours. Three-quarters of an hour before the stew is ready, prepare the dumplings:

Measure the ingredients into a bowl and mix to a light dough with the water. Divide into 8 and shape into little balls. Drop into' the stew and complete the cooking.

Remove the bay-leaf. Serve the meat and gravy in the centre of a hot dish with the dumplings arranged around.

VICTORIA STEAK

1-1 ¹/₂ *lb round steak*	1 *tablespoonful*
(*cut thin and in one*	*seasoned flour*
piece)	*a bouquet garni*
	stock or water

Stuffing:

2-3 *oz breadcrumbs*	*a little grated lemon*
1 *tablespoonful*	*rind*
prepared suet	*salt and pepper*
1 *dessertspoonful*	1-2 *oz chopped ham*
chopped parsley	(*or* ¹/₂ *onion*)
1 *teaspoonful dried*	*egg to bind*
herbs	

Lay the meat on a board and beat a little with a rolling-pin. Season with salt and pepper and, if necessary, trim and lay the trimmings in the centre or over the thinner parts. Prepare the stuffing.

Combine the ingredients, flavouring and seasoning. Bind with the beaten egg. Arrange on the steak, roll up and fasten with string. Toss in the seasoned flour. Melt the dripping in a saucepan. When smoking hot put in the meat and brown on all sides. Add the bouquet garni and sufficient stock to half cover the meat. Cover the pan and simmer gently until the meat is tender — approximately 2 hours.

Remove the roll, cutting away the string, and place on a hot dish. Remove the bouquet garni and thicken the gravy with blended flour. Pour over the meat. Garnish with freshly-cooked carrots or peas tossed in melted butter or small baked tomatoes.

BEEF OLIVES

1-1¹/₂ *lb round steak*	*a little carrot, turnip*
(*cut thin and in a*	*and onion*
neat piece)	*salt and pepper*
1 *oz dripping*	³/₄ *pint stock or water*
	1 *tablespoonful flour*
	3-4 *creamed potatoes*

Stuffing:

2-3 *oz breadcrumbs*	*a little grated lemon*
1 *oz prepared suet*	*rind*
1 *dessertspoonful*	*salt and pepper*
chopped parsley	1 *egg*
1 *teaspoonful dried*	*a little milk if*
herbs	*necessary*

Cut the meat into small oblong pieces suitable for rolling up. Beat a little with a rolling pin. Any nice pieces of meat too small or ragged to make into rolls may be laid on the top of the other pieces. Prepare the stuffing.

Combine the ingredients, flavouring and seasoning well. Bind with beaten egg and milk if necessary. Divide around the pieces of meat, roll up and tie with a strong thread. Melt the dripping in a saucepan and, when smoking hot, fry the rolls of meat turning them so that they brown all over. Lift on to a plate, drain away any surplus fat, add the flavouring vegetables, seasoning and the stock. Bring to the boil. Return the rolls of meat, cover with a lid and simmer gently until the meat is tender — approximately 1-1½ hours.

Arrange a border of creamed potatoes on a hot dish. Remove the thread from the beef olives and place on top of the potatoes. Thicken the gravy and strain over.

If preferred, the potato border may be omitted.

An alternative method of preparing beef olives is as follows:

Stuff the oblongs of steak as before and roll up firmly. It is not necessary to tie them with thread. Arrange in a casserole so that they are firmly packed and with the end of each roll underneath. Place a bouquet garni in the centre.

Slice the onion and fry in hot dripping until brown. Add the stock and bring to the boil. Simmer for a short time and thicken with blended seasoned flour. Pour over the meat rolls. Cover with a lid and bake in a moderate oven for 1½-2 hours or until the meat is tender. Stir occasionally. Serve from the casserole.

Suggested oven temperature — 350° or "3". It may be necessary to reduce the heat once the cooking has started.

STEWED MINCE OR MINCE COLLOPS

1 *onion*	1 *lb minced steak*
2-3 *cloves of garlic*	2 *teaspoonfuls flour*
1 *oz dripping*	*salt and pepper*
¼ *pint stock or water*	

Garnish: *sippets of toast*

Chop the onion and garlic finely. Melt the dripping and, when hot, put in the onion, garlic and minced steak. Stir until each particle is separate and nicely browned. Blend the flour and seasoning with the stock and add. Bring to the boil and simmer gently for ½ hour.

Serve on a hot dish garnished with sippets of toast.

STEWED MINCE WITH LENTILS

1 *onion*	¼ *lb lentils (steeped*
2-3 *cloves of garlic*	*overnight and*
1 *oz dripping*	*strained)*
1 *lb minced steak*	*salt and pepper*
½ *pint water*	
1 *Oxo cube*	
1 *small tablespoonful flour*	

Garnish: *sippets of toast*

Chop the onion and garlic finely. Melt the dripping and, when hot, add the onion and fry until brown. Add the minced steak, lentils and seasoning. Stir until each particle is separate. Add the water and the crumbled Oxo cube. Bring to the boil and simmer gently for ¾ hour. Thicken with the blended flour.

Serve in a hot dish garnished with sippets of toast.

STEWED OX-TAIL

1 *ox-tail*
1 *onion*
1-2 *oz dripping*
a piece of carrot and turnip
a bouquet garni
1 *pint stock or water*
a little lemon juice
2 *oz flour*

Divide the tail into joints and trim away any unnecessary fat. Put the pieces into a saucepan of cold water, add a little salt and bring to the boil. Boil for 10 minutes, then strain and rinse the pieces of tail. Chop the onion. Melt the dripping, and, when smoking hot, fry the ox-tail until brown on all sides. Remove and fry the onion. Add the sliced carrot, cubed turnip, bouquet garni, stock and lemon juice. Bring to the boil. Return the pieces of tail, cover with a lid and simmer gently until tender — approximately 3 hours.

Arrange the pieces of tail on a hot dish. Thicken the gravy with the blended flour and strain over all.

Garnish with some freshly-cooked carrot tossed in butter.

BAKED STEAK AND ONIONS

1 *lb round steak cut thin*
paprika pepper
salt
2 *onions*
a little butter or margarine

Cut the steak into portion pieces and slice the onions. Sprinkle the latter with plenty of paprika pepper and some salt. Arrange half the onions in the bottom of a casserole. Lay the meat on top. Sprinkle with salt and cover with the remainder of the onions. Flake with butter. Cover with a lid and bake in a moderate oven $1\frac{1}{2}$-2 hours. No liquid is necessary.

Suggested oven temperature — 350° or " 3 ".

MEAT BALLS IN TOMATO SAUCE

$\frac{3}{4}$ *lb minced steak*
$1\frac{1}{2}$ *oz semolina*
$\frac{1}{2}$ *oz prepared suet*
$\frac{1}{2}$ *onion*
2 *cloves of garlic*
salt and pepper
1 *egg*
a little milk if necessary
$\frac{3}{4}$ *pint tomato sauce*

Combine the minced steak, semolina and suet. Add the finely-chopped onion and garlic. Season highly and bind with egg and milk. Divide the mixture and shape into 5 balls. Arrange in a casserole. Pour the tomato sauce over. Cover with a lid and bake in a moderate oven for $1\frac{1}{2}$ hours.

Suggested oven temperature — 350° or " 3 ".

Alternative sauces may be used if preferred, such as:

BARBECUE SAUCE: 6 *oz mushrooms*, $\frac{1}{2}$ *onion*, 1 *clove of garlic, salt, pepper*, $\frac{1}{2}$ *pint water*, 1 *dessertspoonful vinegar and* 1 *tablespoonful Worcester sauce.*

Slice the mushrooms and onion. Chop the clove of garlic finely. Season highly and add the water, vinegar and Worcester sauce. Pour over the meat balls and bake as before.

HAMBURGERS

1 *lb minced steak*
$\frac{1}{4}$ *onion — finely chopped*
1 *tablespoonful chopped parsley*
salt and pepper
1 *beaten egg*

Combine the minced steak, finely-chopped onion and parsley. Season well and bind with the beaten egg. Divide into four or five pieces and shape into cakes on a floured surface. Melt a little dripping in a frying pan and, when smoking hot, fry the hamburgers until brown on both sides. Reduce the heat and complete the cooking more slowly. The degree of cooking is a matter of taste, some preferring them slightly underdone and others enjoying them only when well cooked.

TOAD-IN-THE-HOLE

$^1/_2$ *lb sausages*
$^1/_2$ *pint Yorkshire batter*

Make the batter and put aside in a cool place.

Skin the sausages, split them lengthways and cut across, making four pieces. Arrange in a greased pie-dish or Yorkshire pudding tin. Pour over the batter and bake in a hot oven until well risen and brown — approximately $^3/_4$ hour.

Suggested oven temperature — 450° or " 7 ".

SHEPHERD'S PIE

Mince approximately $^1/_2$ lb left-over cooked meat such as the end of a joint, season highly and add 2-3 finely-chopped cloves of garlic. Either moisten with gravy or with a knob of melted butter and a little cream. Spread in a greased pie-dish. Cook and cream 4-5 potatoes and pile them on top. Smooth over with a knife dipped in milk and decorate by marking with a spoon or the point of a knife. Flake generously with butter or margarine and bake in a fairly hot oven until brown and hot through — approximately 30 minutes.

Suggested oven temperature — 450° or " 7 ".

A good shepherd's pie may also be made using freshly-stewed minced steak.

MEAT CAKES

$^1/_2$ *lb cooked meat*   1 *dessertspoonful*
$^1/_2$ *lb cooked potatoes*   *chopped parsley*

salt and pepper   1 *oz butter or*
                margarine
        egg and breadcrumbs

Mince the meat and rice the potatoes. Combine, season well and add the chopped parsley. Melt the butter and beat in. Divide the mixture into 5 or 6 portions and shape each into a round cake using a little flour to prevent the mixture sticking. Pass through beaten egg and breadcrumbs and fry in shallow or deep fat as convenient.

DURHAM CUTLETS

$^1/_4$ *lb cooked meat*   1 *gill stock*
$^1/_2$ *parboiled onion*   1 *dessertspoonful*
1 *oz butter or*   *chopped parsley*
  margarine   *salt and pepper*
1 *oz flour*   *egg and breadcrumbs*

Mince the meat and onion. Make a roux with the butter and flour. Add the stock and cook thoroughly until thick so that it will leave the sides of the pan. Beat in the meat, onion, parsley and seasoning and spread on a plate. Put aside to cool. Divide into 5 or 6 portions and shape into cutlets. Pass through beaten egg and breadcrumbs and fry in deep fat.

If wished, a short piece of macaroni may be stuck in the narrow end of each cutlet to represent the bone.

MEAT FRITTERS

$^1/_2$ *lb cooked meat* $^1/_2$ *teaspoonful baking*
$^1/_4$ *onion (parboiled)*   *powder*
1 *dessertspoonful*   *salt and pepper*
  chopped parsley   1 *egg*
3 *oz flour (light*   *milk*
  weight)

Mince the cooked meat and the onion. Add the chopped parsley, flour, baking powder and seasoning and mix to a stiff consistency with the beaten egg and milk. Using two spoons, form into egg-shaped portions and drop into a pan of hot deep fat. Fry gently for 10-12 minutes turning when brown on the under-side.

Serve piled on a hot dish accompanied by parsley or mustard sauce.

RISSOLES IN PASTRY

2 oz cooked meat	¹/₂ gill stock
¹/₄ boiled onion	salt and pepper
¹/₂ oz butter or	2 oz short crust
margarine	pastry
¹/₂ oz flour	egg and breadcrumbs

Mince the meat and onion. Make a panada with the butter, flour and stock. Add the meat, onion and seasoning. Roll out the pastry very thinly and cut into circles. Place a little mixture on each. Damp the edges and fold in two, fastening securely. Pass through beaten egg and breadcrumbs, and fry in deep fat.

SEA PIE

1 lb stewing beef	2 onions
1 dessertspoonful flour	water
1 carrot	6 oz suet pastry

Cut the meat into small pieces and toss in the seasoned flour. Cut the carrot and onion into thin slices. Choose a rather wide saucepan and arrange a layer of vegetables in the bottom. Place the meat on top and cover with the remainder of the vegetables. Season well and add sufficient water to cover. Simmer slowly for ¹/₂ hour.

Meanwhile, roll the pastry into a circle the size of the pan and lay on top of the stew. Continue the cooking until the meat is tender and the pastry well cooked — approximately 2 hours.

Care must be taken that the stew does not become dry and, if necessary,

the crust can be loosened from the sides of the pan and more water added.

When cooked, cut the pastry into 6-8 triangular wedges. Arrange the meat and vegetables on a hot dish and place the pastry neatly around.

STEAK AND KIDNEY PUDDING

1 lb round steak (cut thin)	1 dessertspoonful chopped parsley and thyme
¹/₃-¹/₂ ox kidney	
1 tablespoonful flour	salt and pepper
6 oz suet pastry	

Cut the meat into narrow strips suitable for rolling up. Core the kidney and cut in small pieces. Dip the steak and kidney into the seasoned flour, then roll up the strips of steak with a little kidney and a piece of fat inside each.

Use ²/₃ of the suet pastry to line a well-greased bowl. Fill with the steak and kidney, sprinkling the chopped herbs between the layers. Three-quarters fill with water. Cover with the remainder of the pastry and a good layer of greased paper. Set in a pan with boiling water to come half-way up the bowl. Cook steadily for 3 hours.

TO SERVE: Remove the greaseproof paper and wipe the bowl. Pin a folded table napkin round and serve accompanied by a jug of boiling water or hot gravy. The pudding will require filling up when the crust is cut.

It is not essential to roll the steak in the way described. It may simply be sliced, tossed in flour and combined with the pieces of kidney and chopped herbs.

STEAK AND KIDNEY PIE

1 lb round steak (cut thin)	1 tablespoonful chopped parsley and thyme

$^1/_3$-$^1/_2$ ox kidney $^1/_2$ onion (finely
1 tablespoonful flour   chopped)
salt and pepper   water
    6 oz flaky, rough puff or suet pastry

Cut the meat into strips suitable for rolling up. Skin and core the kidney and cut into small pieces. Toss the meat and kidney in the seasoned flour. Roll up the strips of meat with a piece of the kidney and a piece of fat inside each. Pack loosely into a pie-dish, leaving room for gravy and tending to pile the meat in the centre. Sprinkle the chopped herbs and onion through the rolls of meat. Two-thirds fill the pie-dish with water. Cover with the pastry, flake and scallop the edge, make a ventilation hole in the centre, brush with beaten egg and decorate with pastry leaves.

Bake in a fairly hot oven for 30 minutes to set the pastry. Complete the cooking at a reduced temperature.

Suggested oven temperature — 450º reduced to 375º or " 7 " reduced to " 3 ".

If it is feared the pastry will be too brown, the pie may be removed from the oven after the first 30 minutes and completely wrapped in wet greaseproof paper. Return to a cooler oven to complete the cooking.

A few potatoes or carrots, partly cooked and thinly sliced, may be included with the meat and kidney and will help to fill up the pie-dish if a big quantity of meat is not required.

Again the steak and kidney may be partially cooked before making into a pie; at the same time it is not really essential to roll the steak in the way described.

Before serving, fill the pie up with a little hot stock.

CORNISH PASTIES

$^1/_2$ lb short crust pastry

Filling:

$^1/_4$ lb round steak   a little finely-chopped
1 slice liver   onion
  (optional)   1 tablespoonful chopped
1-2 potatoes   parsley
        salt and pepper

Chop or mince the steak and liver. Slice or dice the potatoes. Add to the meat together with the onion, parsley and seasoning. Roll the pastry out thinly and cut into large rounds approximately the size of a saucer. Divide the meat mixture around. Damp the edges, then raise up and press together. Flute with the fingers. Brush with milk or beaten egg. Bake for 45-60 minutes — at first in a fairly hot oven to cook the pastry and then in a more moderate oven to cook the filling.

Suggested oven temperature — 450º reduced to 375º or " 7 " reduced to " 3 ".

Turnip and carrot may also be included in the filling for a Cornish pasty, while kidney may be used instead of the liver.

Alternatively, one large pasty may be made instead of smaller ones.

CURRIED BEEF

1 lb round steak   1 dessertspoonful
1 onion   chutney
1-2 oz dripping   1 tablespoonful chopped
1 tablespoonful curry   pickles
  powder   salt
1 tablespoonful $^3/_4$ pint stock or water
  flour   the juice of $^1/_2$ lemon
Garnish: 3-4 oz boiled rice

Cut the meat into small pieces. Chop the onion. Melt the dripping and fry the onion for a few minutes. Add the meat and fry all together until the meat is brown. Add the curry powder, flour, chutney, pickles and salt and cook gently for 5 minutes. Add the stock and stir until boiling point is reached. Cover with a lid and simmer gently until the meat is tender — approximately 1½ hours. Add the lemon juice.

Serve in a hot dish garnished with carefully-cooked dry rice.

A chopped apple may also be fried with the onion and a few raisins or sultanas included. The stock is frequently flavoured with 1 oz coco-nut.

FRIED STEAK AND ONION

2 *onions*   *dripping*
1 *lb rump steak (cut*   *salt, pepper and a little*
³/₄-1½ *inch thick)*   *sugar*

Slice the onions thinly. Beat the steak with a heavy rolling pin if this is thought necessary and either cut it into portion pieces or leave whole.

Heat a heavy frying-pan and melt a little dripping in it. When smoking hot, add the onions, cover with a plate and cook gently until soft and melting. Stir occasionally and season with salt, pepper and a pinch of sugar. If the onions are required more crisply cooked, they should be fried uncovered and stirred more frequently. Transfer the onions to a hot plate, draining away any surplus fat at the same time. Keep hot while the meat is being fried:

If necessary, wipe the pan with a piece of soft paper, It should contain the minimum of fat at this stage. Reheat and put in the steak when it is really hot. Brown on one side and turn and brown on the other, then keep turning until the meat is sufficiently cooked. This is a matter of taste, some preferring it slightly under-done and others well cooked. A one-inch steak will require approximately 10-12 minutes frying.

Serve the fried steak on a hot dish garnished with the fried onions. Place pats of butter on top of the meat or make a thin gravy in the frying pan.

GRILLED STEAK

Various steaks are suitable for grilling and their choice depends on the type of dish being prepared and on personal taste. They include:

RUMP STEAK which must be very tender and cut from beef which has been well hung.

SIRLOIN STEAK also called ENTRECÔTE, is sliced from the sirloin roast. This is a tender juicy cut and one with a full-bodied flavour. It is cut without the bone.

RIB STEAK or CONTREFILET is sliced from the rib roast. It also has a good flavour and is sliced without bone.

T-BONE STEAK is thick steak cut on the bone from the sirloin roast. It is sometimes referred to as a PORTERHOUSE STEAK.

ENTRECÔTE MINUTE is a ¼ inch slice of steak cut from the sirloin or rib.

THE FILLET or under-cut of the sirloin is also cut into various steaks suitable for grilling. All are tender and juicy, but without the fullness of flavour of sirloin or rib steaks:

CHATEAUBRIAND is a thick cut from the heavy end of the fillet. Again it is sometimes called a PORTERHOUSE STEAK.

TOURNEDOS are cut from the middle and tapering end of the fillet. They are oval in shape and quickly cooked — indeed while the " cook's back is turned ".

MEDALLIONS of FILLET of BEEF are similar, but round while FILETS MIGNONS refers to thin slices from the fillet.

For grilling, it is essential to have the grill and rack of the grill pan very hot.

The steak should be trimmed if necessary and brushed with oil or melted butter. Salt should not be used as it will prevent browning and tend to harden the meat. Lay it on the rack and brown quickly, first on one side and then on the other. Lower the heat and continue turning until the meat is sufficiently cooked. The time for grilling is regulated by the thickness of the steak and personal taste — some liking it while still pink in the centre and others preferring it well done.

Ten to fifteen minutes, however, should be ample for the average steak, or 3-4 minutes for an entrecôte minute.

Serve on a hot dish, pouring over any juice from the grill pan.

The simplest garnish for a grilled steak is maître d'hôtel butter. Alternatively, it may be accompanied by a béarnaise sauce. It is usual to serve fried or sauté potatoes as a garnish and accompaniment. Suitable vegetables to serve include fried onions, grilled tomatoes, mushrooms or boiled chestnuts.

MIXED GRILL

The ingredients for a mixed grill may be varied according to personal choice and may include steak or cutlets, sheep's kidneys, sausages, bacon, tomatoes and mushrooms. The chosen ingredients should be brushed with oil or melted butter, and the grill and rack of the grill pan should be very hot. The cooking should start with the item which takes longest to cook. This will probably be the piece of steak or cutlet, following on with the kidney and sausages and later still the tomatoes and mushrooms.

Serve piled in a hot dish and pour over the juices from the grill pan.

Garnish with maître d'hôtel butter, fried potatoes and watercress.

TOURNEDOS

"Tournedos" is the French name for small oval steaks cut from the fillet. They are cooked by grilling or frying and are generally served on a croûte of fried bread or buttered toast. They are used for entrées, the dish being named according to the sauce and garnish which accompanies it. Suggestions for sauces include béarnaise, Espagnole, horse-radish, reform and tomato sauces. Garnishes include baked mushrooms, tomatoes — either plain or stuffed — French beans, French fried onions, fried bananas, fried potatoes or potato croquettes.

STEAK AND KIDNEY —AUSTRALIAN STYLE

4 *portions of tender steak or 4 slices of fillet of beef*	*egg and breadcrumbs*
	2 tablespoonfuls sherry
seasoned flour	*a little stock or water*

Stuffing:

2 *sheep's kidneys*	1 *teaspoonful Worcester sauce*
1/4 *onion — finely chopped*	*salt and pepper*

Cut a pocket in each portion of steak. Then prepare the stuffing:

Skin and core the kidneys and cut into dice. Combine with the other ingredients and use to stuff the steaks. Using a strong thread, stitch the opening. Dip in seasoned flour, then pass through beaten egg and breadcrumbs. Fry in a little hot fat until brown on both sides, but without actually cooking the steak through.

Transfer to a shallow heat-proof dish. Pour the sherry and a little stock round. Cover and bake in a moderate oven for

15-30 minutes until the steak is tender. Avoid over-cooking.

Suggested oven temperature — 425° or " 6 ".

Remove the thread and serve on a hot dish with the gravy poured round. Creamed potatoes and stewed mushrooms make good accompaniments.

MUTTON AND LAMB

Cuts of mutton and lamb are fatter than beef and also have a larger proportion of bone. They are therefore not so economical. Unnecessary fat should be trimmed away and rendered down for use in the kitchen before the meat is cooked. Should the meat be cooked by roasting, the fat may be rendered down in the roasting pan at the same time.

Mutton and lamb should be well cooked.

PRINCIPAL JOINTS for ROASTING: saddle, leg, shoulder, loin and best end of neck. Breast of lamb, while one of the lesser cuts, may also be roasted.

PRINCIPAL JOINTS for BOILING: leg and shoulder.

PRINCIPAL CUTS for GRILLING and FRYING: cutlets from the best end of neck, loin and chump chops. Chops cut from the shoulder are also sometimes grilled or fried.

PRINCIPAL CUTS for STEWING: scrag end of neck, breast, flank, shanks, liver, kidneys and sweetbreads. Shoulder chops may also be stewed.

PRINCIPAL CUTS for BRAISING: leg, shoulder and breast.

BOILED MUTTON

A leg or shoulder of mutton is the best cut for boiling. Trim as necessary and put into a roomy saucepan of boiling water. Add salt and bring to the boil again. Boil for 5 minutes to seal the meat juices in and skim if necessary. Continue the cooking at simmering point allowing 20 minutes to the pound and 20 minutes over. One hour before the cooking is complete, add a mixture of carrot and turnip cut into fairly large pieces and a few whole or quartered onions. When the meat is tender, lift it onto a hot dish. It should be accompanied by a parsley or caper sauce made using milk and some of the broth from the saucepan. The sauce may either be used to coat the joint or served separately. Garnish with a few of the vegetables and serve the greater part separately. Boiled mutton should be served very hot as the fat is unpleasant if it is half cold.

ROAST MUTTON

The saddle, leg or gigot, loin and shoulder are the favourite joints of mutton for roasting.

Wipe and trim the meat, cutting away any superfluous fat. Rub the surface with seasoning and insert slivers of garlic into the fatty parts and near the bone if this flavouring is enjoyed. The aroma gently permeates the meat and is by no means strong. A spray of rosemary placed under the joint in the roasting pan is another good way of flavouring it.

If roasting a whole leg of mutton, it often happens that the shank end becomes overcooked and to prevent this, the tapering end may be wrapped in foil or several layers of paper to protect it a little.

Mutton is at its best when cooked slowly. In this way it retains its juiciness and flavour. Allow 20-25 minutes to each pound and 20-25 minutes over. Mutton should be well cooked.

Serve the joint on a hot dish accompanied by gravy, which may either be thin or slightly thickened. Particular care should be taken to see that it is not greasy. Red-currant, sloe, rowan or cranberry jelly should be served separately. Onion sauce is frequently served with a roast leg of mutton.

ROAST LAMB

Again the saddle, leg or gigot, loin and shoulder are the best joints for roasting, though if the lamb is very young, it is sometimes sold by the quarter — either fore-quarter or hind-quarter.

Prepare the joint as already described for mutton, and roast gently so that it will be juicy and well flavoured. Allow 20-25 minutes to each pound and 20-25 minutes over. Lamb should always be well cooked.

Serve it accompanied by a thin gravy and mint sauce or mint jelly.

STUFFED SHOULDER OF LAMB

Shoulder of lamb is difficult to carve if it is left on the bone and for this reason it is preferable to bone and roll it. At the same time, any unnecessary fat should be trimmed away. If wished, the roll may be stuffed and there is considerable choice in this matter. A simple breadcrumb stuffing, well flavoured with chopped herbs, is the usual choice, but apart from this any of the following are good:

RICE STUFFING: *2 oz rice, ¹/₂ onion, 2 slices lamb's liver, 1 oz raisins, 1 dessertspoonful chopped parsley, seasoning, 1 oz melted butter and 1 beaten egg.*

Boil and dry the rice in the usual way. Add the finely-chopped onion, chopped liver, raisins, parsley and seasoning. Mix with the melted butter and beaten egg. Use to stuff the boned shoulder of lamb.

This dish may be garnished with stewed prunes which have been stoned and the cavity filled with chutney.

MUSHROOM STUFFING: *4 oz mushrooms, ¹/₂ onion, 1 oz butter or margarine, 2-3 oz breadcrumbs, 1 dessertspoonful chopped parsley, seasoning and 1 beaten egg.*

Chop the mushrooms and onion finely and sauté in the melted butter. Add the breadcrumbs, parsley and seasoning and bind with the beaten egg.

CORIANDER SEEDS crushed and sprinkled inside a boned and rolled shoulder give an unusual and pleasant aromatic flavour to the meat.

The stuffed shoulder is roasted gently in the usual way, allowing a little longer cooking time than for a piece of unstuffed mutton or lamb.

Serve accompanied by a thin or slightly-thickened gravy, taking particular care to see that it is not greasy.

ROAST STUFFED BREAST OF LAMB

Breast of lamb, while a lesser cut and one which is inclined to be fat, can make a good and inexpensive joint if stuffed and roasted.

Choose meat which is as lean as possible and remove the bones. Spread with the stuffing, roll up and tie with string. Season the outside and roast slowly in a very moderately heated oven. For example a 2 lb piece of breast will require 1¹/₂-2 hours if cooked at a temperature of 325º or " 3-2 ". The slow cooking melts down the fatty tissue making the meat much more appetising and tender.

Any of the stuffings suggested for the stuffed shoulder of lamb are suitable, but a stuffing containing a proportion of meat in the form of sausage meat is, perhaps, a better choice:

SAUSAGE STUFFING: *2-4 oz stale bread, a little hot milk or water, ¹/₂ lb pork sausage meat, 1 tablespoonful finely-chopped onion, 1 dessertspoonful chopped parsley, seasoning, 1 oz melted butter or margarine (optional) and 1 beaten egg.*

Soak the bread in the milk or water until soft, then squeeze dry and flake with a fork. Combine with the sausage meat, onion, parsley, seasoning and melted butter. Bind with beaten egg.

A piece of stuffed breast of lamb is a suitable cut for braising.

FRIED BREAST OF LAMB

Boil or braise the breast of lamb and, when tender, remove the bones and press between two boards with a weight on top. When cold, cut into inch wide strips and pass through beaten egg and breadcrumbs. Put aside for the coating to dry then fry in shallow or deep fat. Serve with mint sauce or, if preferred, with a tartar sauce.

IRISH STEW

Irish stew is a traditional country dish. It has its origins in the cottage where cooking utensils were scarce and it was convenient to cook the meat, vegetables and potatoes together in the one pot hanging over the turf fire.

While mutton is probably the most frequently used meat for an Irish stew, it can also be made with beef — such as a piece of brisket, or with pork fillet, pork steak or griskin. Pork ribs are also good and are sometimes combined in the stew with a pig's kidney.

If mutton is the choice, the most suitable cuts are neck or breast, but for a superior dish, shoulder chops are excellent.

1-1 ¹/₂ lb neck of mutton	2 lb potatoes
	hot water
salt and pepper	1 tablespoonful chopped
1 onion	parsley

Cut the neck of mutton into portion pieces and trim away excessive fat. Season well. Slice the onions and potatoes. Arrange the meat in the bottom of a strong pan. Cover with the onions mixed with a proportion of the potatoes and finally layer with the remainder of the potatoes. Season well. Add sufficient water to cover the meat layer amply. Place the lid on the pan and cook gently for 1¹/₂-2 hours or until the meat is tender. Stir or shake the pan occasionally to prevent the stew sticking. It should not be watery when cooked for the potatoes should thicken the gravy. Serve on a hot dish, sprinkling generously with chopped parsley. To be at its best, it must be very hot and well seasoned.

Sometimes the meat is partially stewed before the onions and potatoes are added. In this way they are not so liable to be overcooked.

HOT POT

1 ¹/₂ lb neck of mutton	salt and pepper
2 sheep's kidneys	¹/₂ pint stock or water
1-2 onions	a little butter or
1 lb potatoes	dripping
chopped parsley	

Cut the neck of mutton into portion pieces, trimming away any unnecessary fat. Skin and core the kidneys and cut them into small pieces. Slice the onions and potatoes. Arrange the ingredients in layers in a hot-pot dish or casserole, seasoning each with pepper and salt. The last layer should be potato. Pour in the stock and flake with butter or dripping. Cover with a lid and cook in a moderate oven for 1½-2 hours.

Suggested oven temperature — 350° or " 3 ".

Half-an-hour before serving, remove the lid, baste the potatoes with the gravy and brown nicely. Serve sprinkled with chopped parsley.

Beef may be used instead of mutton for a hot-pot and a few mushrooms added if available. Traditionally, oysters were included in the recipe.

SPRING STEW

1 ½ lb middle neck of lamb	12 young carrots
salt and pepper	6-8 scallions (chopped)
1 oz dripping	8-12 baby new potatoes
½ oz flour	1 cupful green peas
1 pint hot water	2 oz sliced French
a bouquet garni	beans (optional)
chopped parsley	

Cut the lamb into portion pieces and sprinkle with seasoning. Heat the dripping in a saucepan and brown the meat on all sides. Drain off excessive fat, sprinkle in the flour and toss the meat through it. Continue the cooking until the flour is brown. Add the water and bouquet garni, cover and simmer gently for 30-40 minutes.

Lift the meat onto a plate, strain the gravy if necessary and skim off as much fat as possible. Return the meat and gravy to the pan and add the prepared vegetables. Simmer for another ³/₄-1 hour.

When the meat and vegetables are tender, remove the bouquet garni. Place the lamb in the centre of a hot dish,

arrange the vegetables round it and pour the gravy over all. Sprinkle with chopped parsley.

HARICOT MUTTON

1 ½ lb mutton	a piece of carrot and turnip
1 onion	
1 oz dripping	1-2 oz haricot beans
1 oz flour	(steeped overnight
salt and pepper	and ³/₄ cooked)
a bouquet garni	

Trim the meat and cut into portions. Suitable joints are the scrag end of neck, breast or shoulder, but the best dish of haricot mutton is made from neatly-trimmed mutton cutlets.

Slice the onion. Melt the dripping and fry the pieces of meat until brown on both sides. Remove and fry the onion until brown. Pour off excess fat, leaving about 1 tablespoonful in the pan. Add the flour and seasoning and brown gently. Stir in the stock and bring to the boil. Return the meat and onions together with the carrot and turnip cut into dice, the haricot beans and the bouquet garni. Cover the pan with a lid and simmer gently until the meat is tender — approximately 1-1 ½ hours depending on the cut of meat.

Arrange the pieces of mutton neatly on a hot dish, garnish with the vegetables and pour the gravy over. As with all mutton dishes, care should be taken to see that it is free from grease.

SAVOURY CHOPS

3-4 mutton chops	1 tablespoonful rice
1 onion	salt and pepper
1 carrot	½ pint stock
a piece of turnip	chopped parsley

Trim the chops free of unnecessary fat. Slice the onion and carrot thinly and cut the turnip into dice. Combine the vegetables with the rice and arrange in a casserole. Season and pour over the stock. Arrange the chops on top and again sprinkle with seasoning. Cover with a lid and cook slowly until the meat and vegetables are tender — approximately 1 1/2 hours.

Suggested oven temperature — 400° or " 5 ".

During the latter part of the cooking, remove the lid to brown the meat. Serve sprinkled with chopped parsley.

CORNISH CASSEROLE OF MUTTON

4 mutton chops   *2-4 leeks — according*
6-8 potatoes   *to size*
                    salt and pepper

Trim the chops. Peel and slice the potatoes fairly thinly, and shred the white part of the leek. Combine the two vegetables, sprinkle with seasoning and arrange in a casserole. Place the chops on top and season these also. Cover with a lid, and place in a fairly hot oven. Bake for approximately 1-1 1/2 hours or until the meat is tender, reducing the heat once the cooking has started.

Suggested oven temperature — 400° reduced to 350° or " 5 " reduced to " 3 ".

During the latter part of the cooking, remove the lid to brown the meat. Serve sprinkled with chopped parsley.

LAMB CUTLETS

Best end neck of lamb is the joint required for cutlets and it is best if the meat is from a small animal. The cut usually consists of 5-6 cutlets. Saw off the chine bone and, if necessary, make the rib bones shorter. Divide into cutlets and trim off the fat, leaving only a narrow rim. Also trim the skin from the inside of the bone of each cutlet and bare and clean the last inch of bone. Flatten slightly. The cutlets are now ready for cooking.

Generally, cutlets are grilled or baked, but if preferred, they may be dipped in beaten egg and crumbs and fried.

Cutlets are served with a sauce and garnish of vegetables, the dish taking its name from the garnish. Suitable sauces are Espagnole, reform and tomato, while suitable garnishes include any young spring vegetables such as peas, baby carrots or asparagus or a mixture of vegetables. Later in the year, French beans, mushrooms and Brussels sprouts are useful. Cutlets are frequently served on a border of creamed potatoes.

NOISETTES OF LAMB

Noisettes of lamb are also prepared from a piece of best end of neck. The joint should be chined, but the rib bones may be left a little longer than is suitable for cutlets. Remove the leaf of fat and the rib bones. Season the inside of the meat and roll up tightly, starting at the thick side. Tie firmly with string spacing these 1 1/2 inch apart and cut in slices midway between each tie.

Noisettes of lamb are either grilled, fried or baked and are accompanied by a sauce and vegetable garnish in the same way as cutlets.

PORK

Pork is eaten either fresh or cured, the flesh lending itself to salting, curing and smoking. Pork from a small animal is best and its quality should be judged by the smooth, thin rind, the pale pink flesh and the white fat.

It requires longer cooking then either beef or mutton and should always be well cooked.

PRINCIPAL CUTS for ROASTING are leg, loin, fillet, and ribs. Belly pork, while a lesser cut, may also be roasted.

PRINCIPAL CUTS for BOILING include pig's knees, feet, head and tail. Belly pork may be salted and, when boiled, makes a good accompaniment to a boiled chicken.

PRINCIPAL CUTS for GRILLING and FRYING: chops, pork fillet and the liver. While the following are all lesser cuts, all may be grilled or fried — pork steak, griskins and sliced belly pork.

PRINCIPAL CUTS for STEWING: pork steak, griskin, pig's kidney and liver. Pork fillet is sometimes used in a superior version of an Irish stew. Pork ribs may also be used for this purpose.

ROAST PORK

The favourite joints for roasting are the leg and loin. The latter may be stuffed, if wished.

To many, the great attraction of a roast of pork is the crackling, and care must be taken before and during the cooking of the joint to see that the rind blisters and crisps so that it is easy to carve and enjoyable to eat. To this end, choose pork with a thin rind and score it at intervals of a $1/4$ inch. The butcher will generally do this if asked. Brush the rind with oil or smear with dripping and sprinkle with salt and pepper. Sometimes it is advisable to do this the day prior to cooking the joint. If wished, insert slivers of garlic into the fat and near the bone.

Cook the joint in a moderate oven allowing 30 minutes to the pound and 30 minutes over. During this time, it is necessary to watch the progress of the crackling carefully — turning the joint if required and basting it occasionally. Crackling burns easily — in case one is tempted to turn up the heat of the oven to make it blister or even put the joint under the grill.

Roast pork is served accompanied by a thin or slightly-thickened gravy and apple sauce. Alternatively, a gooseberry sauce may be served.

ROAST STUFFED PORK FILLET

2 pork fillets

Stuffing:
2-3 oz breadcrumbs   1 $1/2$ oz butter,
salt and pepper   margarine or dripping
          1 teaspoonful dried sage
          $1/2$ onion — finely chopped

Make a long cut down the centre of the lean side of the pork fillet, follow this with long cuts to either side and continue in this manner until the fillet is opened out into a flat piece. Repeat the process with the second piece. Next prepare the stuffing:

Season the breadcrumbs and rub in the butter. Flavour with the sage and onion and draw the mixture together with the fingers. Arrange on top of one of the fillets turning in the tips, cover with the second fillet and tie firmly with fine string. Roast in a moderately-heated oven for approximately 1-1$1/4$ hours. While pork must be well cooked, overcooked pork fillet is apt to be dry and stringy. Alternatively, stuffed pork fillets may be cooked as a pot roast.

Remove the string and serve on a hot dish accompanied by a slightly-thickened gravy and apple sauce.

If only one pork fillet is required, it is sometimes stuffed and rolled. By this method it does not carve so satisfactorily, since it is sliced with the grain of the meat instead of across it.

ROAST STUFFED BELLY PORK

1 ¹/₂-2 *lb piece of belly pork from a young pig*
olive oil   *salt*
Stuffing :
2-3 *oz breadcrumbs*   1¹/₂ *oz dripping*
salt and pepper   1 *tablespoonful dried*
                                    sage
¹/₂ *onion — finely chopped*

Score the belly pork at intervals of a ¹/₄ inch and bone, if wished. Then cut a pocket in the thickness of the meat. Prepare the stuffing in the usual way and use to stuff the piece of meat. Brush the rind with olive oil and sprinkle with salt. Roast gently, giving the meat plenty of time to cook so that the greater party of the fatty tissue is melted away. The approximate time will be 1 ¹/₂-1 ³/₄ hours.

Serve accompanied by a slightly-thickened gravy and apple sauce.

Sometimes belly pork is boned, stuffed and rolled, but by this method the crackling cannot be crisped so satisfactorily.

ROAST PORK RIBS

When purchasing pork ribs, choose meaty ones and ask the butcher to chop the bones. Cut into pieces of convenient size and sprinkle with seasoning. Place in a roasting tin, cover the bottom of the tin with a little water and flake the meat with dripping. The steam from the water prevents the meat from shrivelling too much. Roast in a moderate oven for approximately 30-45 minutes. Turn once or twice during the cooking.

Alternatively, the side of pork ribs may be cut in two by the length. Lay sage and onion stuffing along one piece and use the second as a cover. Tie with string if thought necessary and roast in a moderate oven for approximately ³/₄-1 hour. Again, a little water in the tin is an advantage.

If wished, roast pork ribs may be served accompanied by apple sauce.

FRIED PORK CHOPS

Pork chops are cut from the loin or best end of the neck and are usually about ¹/₂ inch in thickness. Trim away unnecessary fat and sprinkle with seasoning and a little flour. Melt the trimmings in a frying-pan and fry the chops in this. Turn them several times and be careful to cook thoroughly. Alternatively, the chops may be browned in the fat and the cooking completed in the oven.

Serve accompanied by a slightly-thickened gravy and fried apple or apple sauce.

STEWED PORK CHOPS WITH CHESTNUTS

3-4 *pork chops*   *salt and pepper*
¹/₂ *oz butter or*   ¹/₄ *teaspoonful ground*
   margarine   *ginger*
1 *medium onion —*   ¹/₄ *teaspoonful curry*
   finely chopped   *powder*
¹/₄ *lb mushrooms*   ¹/₄ *teaspoonful mixed*
¹/₂ *oz flour*   *spice*
1 *tablespoonful*   1 *tablespoonful tomato*
   vinegar   *sauce*
1 *tablespoonful*   1 *cupful water*
   sugar   12 *skinned chestnuts*

Trim the chops and put in a pan with cold water to cover. Bring slowly to the boil and simmer for 3 minutes. Drain.

Now prepare the sauce:

Melt the butter and fry the chopped onion until soft and lightly brown. Slice the mushrooms and add to the onion. Fry for a few minutes to soften. Sprinkle in the flour and add the vinegar, sugar and other flavourings. Add the water and stir until boiling. Lay the chops in this together with the skinned chestnuts and simmer very gently until tender — approximately 40-45 minutes.

Alternatively, the chops and chestnuts may be laid in a casserole, the sauce spooned over and the cooking done in a moderate oven for 1 hour. Serve with creamed potatoes.

FRIED SAUSAGES

Prick the sausages with a fork. Melt a little dripping in a frying-pan, but avoid making it too hot before the sausages are put in otherwise it might cause them to burst. Fry the sausages gently, turning them frequently so that they are brown and crisp all over. Sausages should be well cooked.

Sausages may also be baked.

STUFFED SAUSAGES

1/2 lb sausages	4 rashers of bacon

Stuffing:

4 tablespoonfuls breadcrumbs	1 dessertspoonful chopped parsley
1 oz dripping or margarine	1 tablespoonful finely-chopped onion
salt and pepper	

Prepare the stuffing in the usual way. Then make a cut the length of each sausage. Open them out a little and fill the cavity with stuffing. Rind and stretch the bacon and wrap a rasher round each sausage. Bake in a moderately hot oven for approximately 20-30 minutes.

Suggested oven temperature — 425° or " 6 ".

PIG'S FEET

Prepare the pig's feet by first of all removing the hoofs. This is done by immersing the extremity of the foot in boiling water for a short time and then prising off the hoofs with a strong fork. Singe, if necessary, and wash and scrape throughly.

Pig's feet should be boiled in salted water flavoured with a bunch of herbs, a piece of carrot and onion. They should be cooked very slowly and given plenty of time, so that the flesh almost falls from the bones. The time will be approximately 2 hours. They may be served quite plainly with a cold vinaigrette or piquante sauce and crisp toast.

Alternatively, they may be left until cold, then cut in two, dipped in beaten egg and crumbs and grilled. During the grilling, baste with a little melted butter.

HAM AND BACON

A HAM is the hind leg of the pig, cut from the carcase at the fresh pork stage, trimmed and cured — generally dry cured. It will weigh approximately 10-16 lb.

GAMMON is also the hind leg of the pig, but it is cured while it is still on the side of bacon. It is generally brine-cured and is less expensive than ham.

Both may be cooked whole or in smaller cuts, while cuts of lean bacon also lend themselves to cooking by most of the recipes which follow:

BOILED HAM

Scrub the ham, if necessary and soak overnight in cold water. Next day rinse, place in a roomy pan and cover with cold water. Bring slowly to the boil, then draw to the side of the heat and cook gently, allowing 25-30 minutes to the pound according to the thickness of the ham. The water must not boil. If it does, the ham will be stringy and lack flavour. Flavouring vegetables and a bouquet garni may be cooked with the ham if wished and sometimes a pint of ale or cider is also added.

TO SERVE HOT: Lift the ham from the water as soon as cooked, remove the skin and trim. Coat it with brown breadcrumbs and put into a fairly hot oven for a few minutes to brown and crisp. Send to the table with a ham frill fastened round the knuckle.

In Ireland, cabbage is the traditional vegetable to serve with a boiled ham. It is cooked with the ham during the last 30 minutes and thus acquires a delicious flavour.

Various sauces are suitable to accompany a hot boiled ham, such as a simple parsley sauce, raisin and cider sauce, Madeira or Cumberland sauces.

TO SERVE COLD: Leave the ham to cool in the liquid, remembering it will continue to cook for a time and allowing for this in one's calculations. Remove from the water and skin. Trim the fat neatly and strew with browned breadcrumbs. To make these stick, it may be necessary to put the ham in the oven for a short time to melt the surface slightly. Fasten a frill round the knuckle of the ham and garnish with parsley.

Alternatively, the coatings recommended in the next recipe may be used instead of the browned breadcrumbs.

HAM — BOILED AND BAKED

Prepare and boil a ham or piece of ham in the usual way, but allowing 20-25 minutes per pound. The ham should be almost cooked, but not quite, at this stage.

Remove from the water, peel off the rind and cut a diamond pattern in the thickness of the fat. Spread with soft brown sugar, mixed to a stiff paste with ham liquor. Complete the cooking by baking in a moderate oven. Suggested oven temperature — 400° or " 6 ".

If wished, the ham may be basted occasionally with either pineapple juice or cider and served decorated with half cherries fastened in position with cloves. Pineapple slices heated in the juice round the joint while in the oven, make a pleasant accompaniment. Fasten a ham frill round the knuckle bone and serve accompanied by one of the usual sauces.

Alternative coatings may be used instead of the brown sugar:

Combine equal quantities of crumbs and soft brown sugar, and flavour with a spoonful of made mustard. Mix to a stiff paste with ham liquor, pineapple or cider and spread over the ham.

Yet another coating consists of the white of 1 egg combined with 1 tablespoonful made mustard and 3 teaspoonfuls sugar. Spread over the ham and sprinkle with fine breadcrumbs.

HAM BAKED IN A CRUST

Prepare a ham or piece of ham as for boiling and, if necessary, saw off the knuckle bone.

Next day, prepare a plain paste made with flour and water allowing 1 1/2 lb for a small ham. Roll it out, place the ham on top and wrap it in the paste, sealing it in completely. Place in a well-greased roasting tin and bake approximately 3 hours for a ham of medium size or allowing 20 minutes to the pound and 20 minutes over.

Suggested cooking temperature — 400° reduced to 375° or " 5 " reduced to " 3 ".

When the ham is cooked, remove the crust and skin, finish and serve as already described for a boiled ham.

The old name for the unleavened paste used to wrap round the ham, is a " huff " and its purpose is to keep in the juices and aroma. If the ham is to be served cold, it should be left to cool in the casing. The huff paste is not intended for eating, but was sometimes crushed and used to dress the ham instead of breadcrumbs.

VEAL

Veal is the flesh of the calf, the best coming from young animals of $2\frac{1}{2}$-3 months fed exclusively on milk. The flesh should be white or slightly pink and it should always be well cooked. As it is apt to be dry when cooked, care should be taken to avoid this.

The principal joints are:

THE LEG and FILLET: The best cuts, and largely used for cutting into escalopes.
THE LOIN may be cut into chops or roasted whole. Escalopes may also be cut from this piece.
THE SHOULDER and NECK are used for braising and stewing.
THE BREAST may be boned, stuffed, rolled and roasted. It may also be braised or stewed.
THE KNUCKLE is a favourite piece for flavouring white stocks.

ROAST LOIN OF VEAL

Bone the loin leaving a strip of skin sufficiently long to wrap round the fillet. Fill the cavity with a veal forcemeat, if wished, and tie securely. Season and lay some rashers of fat bacon on top of the joint. Place in a roasting tin and roast in a hot oven for 10 minutes, then baste and pour a cupful of boiling water into the tin. Continue the cooking, allowing 20 minutes to the pound and 20 minutes over.

Serve the joint on a hot dish accompanied by a slightly thickened gravy. It is frequently garnished with bacon rolls, while spinach is a favourite vegetable to accompany it.

The leg, fillet, shoulder and breast of veal may be roasted in the same way.

WHITE STEW OF VEAL

1 *lb veal taken from the shoulder or breast*
1-2 *onions*   *water*
a bouquet garni   1 $\frac{1}{2}$ *oz butter or*
salt and pepper   *margarine*
a squeeze of lemon   1 $\frac{1}{2}$ *oz flour*
         1-2 *egg yolks*
         2 *tablespoonfuls cream*

Cut the veal into convenient-sized pieces and, if wished, soak for an hour in boiling water to whiten. Drain and place in a saucepan with the sliced onion, bouquet garni, seasoning, the squeeze of lemon and sufficient water to cover. Bring to the boil and simmer gently until tender — approximately 1 $\frac{1}{2}$ hours. Strain off the liquid and make up, if necessary, to 1 $\frac{1}{4}$ pints. Make a roux with the butter and flour and add the veal stock gradually. Bring to the boil, stirring all the time. Cook thoroughly. Lastly stir in the combined yolks and cream, adding them by degrees. Do not boil again. Pour over the meat and onion in the pan and keep to the side of the heat until all is thoroughly hot.

Dish garnished with croûtes of fried bread.

A few sliced mushrooms may be added to a white stew of veal.

OFFAL

Offal is a term for internal meats and it includes the brains, heart, kidneys, liver, sweetbread, tongue and tripe of the ox, sheep, pig or calf.

All offal should be eaten fresh, no hanging being necessary.

KIDNEYS

Kidneys from the sheep or lamb are the most choice and are suitable for grilling. Calves' kidneys are also choice, while those from the ox or pig have a stronger flavour and are more suitable for stewing. They also make a good curry.

Kidneys should be skinned and the core carefully cut out with a sharp knife before cooking.

GRILLED KIDNEYS

Remove the skin from the required number of sheep's kidneys and split open on the rounded side, but without separating the two parts. Remove the core and any fat from the centre. Put on a skewer, so that they will remain open during the cooking — generally 2 kidneys may be fastened on one. Season with salt and pepper and brush with oil or melted butter. Grill in the usual way, turning them frequently. They will require approximately 8 minutes and should still be slightly pink in the centre when served.

Grilled kidneys may be served on toast with a pat of firm maître d'hôtel butter in the centre and accompanied by grilled bacon. It is usual to include grilled kidney in a mixed grill.

STEWED KIDNEY

Either ox or pig's kidney are suitable for stewing — the former requiring the longer cooking.

1 *ox kidney*	2 *oz dripping*
(*or 3-4 pigs' kidneys*)	1/4 *onion — finely*
2 *oz flour*	*chopped*
salt and pepper	3/4 *pint stock or water*
1/2 *teaspoonful mixed*	1 *dessertspoonful*
spice	*mushroom ketchup*

Garnish:

Wash the kidney and cut into thin slices, removing any fat and core at the same time. Ox kidney has a more delicate flavour if it is soaked in water and vinegar for an hour before cooking.

Drain and dry the kidney and toss the pieces in a mixture containing the flour, spice and seasoning. Melt the dripping in a saucepan and, when smoking hot, put in the pieces of kidney and the onion. Fry until well browned all over. Add the stock and ketchup and bring to the boil. Reduce the heat and simmer gently until tender — approximately 1½-2 hours for ox kidney and 1-1½ hours for pig's kidney.

Serve the stew on a hot dish garnished with boiled spaghetti or noodles.

A little bacon or sliced mushrooms may be included with advantage in this dish.

LIVER

The best liver is either from the calf or the lamb and it is very suitable for frying.

Ox liver is coarse both in texture and flavour and is only suitable for stewing.

The flavour is improved if it is steeped in salted water for an hour before cooking.

Pig's liver is superior to ox liver and may either be fried, stuffed and baked or stewed.

FRIED LIVER AND BACON

$^{1}/_{2}$ lb calfs' or lambs' liver — sliced	1-2 rashers of bacon per person
1 tablespoonful flour	a few slices of onion — cut very finely
salt and pepper	hot water

Garnish: *chopped parsley*

Rind the bacon and fry until crisp. Remove from the pan and keep hot. Dip the liver in the seasoned flour and fry quickly in the hot bacon fat. It will require 3-4 minutes. Remove the liver and keep hot. Fry the rings of onion until golden brown.

Serve the liver and bacon on a hot dish garnished with the onion. Then make a little gravy by adding a few spoonfuls of hot water and seasoning to the pan and bring to the boil. Pour over the liver and serve sprinkled with chopped parsley.

STEWED LIVER AND BACON

$^{3}/_{4}$ lb pigs' liver — sliced	salt and pepper
	1 onion — sliced
$^{1}/_{4}$ lb bacon	1 tablespoonful flour
$^{3}/_{4}$ pint stock or water	

Trim the liver. Rind the bacon and cut into small pieces. Fry in a saucepan until the fat begins to run. Remove. Dip the slices of liver in the seasoned flour and fry quickly until brown on both sides. Remove and fry the sliced onion. A little dripping may be required if the bacon is lean. Add the stock, bring to the boil and replace the bacon and liver. Simmer gently for approximately 1 hour.

A few sliced mushrooms may be added with advantage to this dish. They should be cooked in the fat, but not added to the stew until it is nearly cooked.

STUFFED LIVER AND BACON

$^{1}/_{2}$-$^{3}/_{4}$ lb pigs' liver — sliced	$^{1}/_{2}$ pint stock or water
	1 dessertspoonful Worcester sauce
$^{1}/_{4}$ lb streaky bacon	

Stuffing:

2-3 oz breadcrumbs	$^{1}/_{2}$ onion — finely chopped
1 $^{1}/_{2}$ oz butter or margarine	1 tablespoonful chopped parsley

salt and pepper

Trim the slices of liver and lay them on a greased tray. Prepare the stuffing in the usual way and arrange neatly on top. Rind and stretch the bacon and place a rasher over each portion. Pour sufficient stock or water into the tray to just cover the liver, but not sufficient to moisten the stuffing. Bake in a moderate oven for approximately 30 minutes, adding more stock if necessary. Care must be taken to avoid letting the liver become dry.

Suggested oven temperature — 400° or " 6 ".

Serve the slices of stuffed liver and bacon on a hot dish. Add the Worcester sauce to the liquid in the tray, bring to the boil and pour round the liver.

SWEETBREADS

Sweetbreads are obtained from the calf or the lamb. There are two types — one is elongated and, being found in the throat, is called the throat sweetbread. The other is rounder and lies near the heart. It is called the heart sweetbread. The latter is the better from a culinary point of view. Both are light and easily digested.

Sweetbreads should be very fresh and should be soaked in cold water for an hour or so immediately they come from the butchers. Then place them in a saucepan, cover with water and bring to the boil. Boil for 5 minutes. Change into cold water and, using the fingers, remove all fat and any membrane that will come away without destroying their shape. They are now ready for stewing or may be pressed until cold in preparation for frying.

STEWED SWEETBREADS

1 *pair of sweetbreads*	*salt and pepper*
1 *onion — quartered*	¹/₂ *pint stock*
3-4 *inches of lemon*	1 *oz butter or*
rind	*margarine*
a bouquet garni	1 *oz flour*
2-3 *tablespoonfuls cream*	

Garnish: *fried croûtes of bread and parsley*

Steep and blanch the sweetbreads as already directed. Then cut into suitable pieces. Place them in a saucepan and add the onion, lemon rind, bouquet garni, seasoning and stock. Bring to the boil and simmer gently until tender — approximately 1-1³/₄ hour. Remove the sweetbreads and make a sauce with the butter, flour and strained stock. Stir in the cream and return the sweetbreads. Heat thoroughly and serve garnished with fried croûtes of bread and parsley.

Stewed sweetbreads make a suitable filling for a vol-au-vent or patties.

FRIED SWEETBREADS

1 *sweetbread*	1 *egg*
a little lemon juice	1 *tablespoonful salad*
salt and pepper	*oil*
breadcrumbs	

Steep and blanch the sweetbread as already described. Then stew in stock or flavoured milk for ½ hour. When almost cooked, drain and press between two plates until cold. Cut into slices or neat pieces. Squeeze a little lemon juice over the pieces and season with salt and pepper. Beat the egg and add the salad oil. Dip the sweetbread in this and then in the breadcrumbs. Fry in deep or shallow fat until they are golden brown.

The fried sweetbreads may be served quite simply accompanied by crisply-fried rashers of bacon.

HEARTS

Hearts are usually stuffed and roasted and those generally used for this purpose are lamb's hearts. Calf's and ox hearts are only suitable for stewing.

Prepare the heart by cutting away the veins and arteries and wash well in plenty of cold water.

STUFFED ROAST SHEEP'S HEART

3 lamb's hearts

Stuffing:

3 *tablespoonfuls*	¹/₄ *onion — finely*
breadcrumbs	*chopped*
1 *oz dripping*	1 *dessertspoonful*
salt and pepper	*chopped parsley*

Trim the hearts and wash well. If thought necessary, steep for an hour in cold water.

Cut down one side of each heart and open out. Prepare the stuffing in the usual way and lay on one of the hearts. Cover with the second heart and tie securely with fine string. Roast gently in a saucepan, turning occasionally. The time required will be approximately ³/₄ hour.

Remove the string and serve on a hot dish accompanied by a slightly thickened brown gravy.

TRIPE

Tripe is the inner lining of the stomach of the ox, and it is usually sold partially prepared by the butcher.

There are several different kinds such as honeycomb, blanket, book and black tripe, but the honeycomb and blanket are the types usually preferred. All are light and easily digested.

STEWED TRIPE AND ONIONS

1 *lb prepared tripe*	*salt and pepper*
2 *onions*	³/₄ *pint milk*
1 *heaped tablespoonful flour*	

Garnish: *triangles of toasted bread*

Wash the tripe and put it into a saucepan of cold water. Bring to the boil and strain. Cut into neat pieces and slice the onion. Place in a saucepan, season and add the milk. Simmer gently for 1 hour. Blend the flour with a little extra milk and use to thicken the stew. Serve on a hot dish garnished with the triangles of toasted bread.

BRAINS

Calf's or lamb's brains are the best. They should be used while very fresh and should be steeped for 3-4 hours in cold water before use.

FRIED BRAINS

Steep the brains as already described, then poach very gently in water to which salt and a tablespoonful vinegar have been added. They will require 15-20 minutes. Cool in the water in which they have been cooked. Calf's brains should be sliced; lamb's brains may be left whole or cut in two. Sprinkle with seasoning and a little grated lemon rind. Coat with flour, then dip in beaten egg and breadcrumbs. Fry in deep fat.

Alternatively, fried brains may be coated with a frying batter. They should be served quite simply with crisply-fried rashers of bacon.

TONGUE

The most generally-favoured tongue is the tongue of the ox. It is, as a rule, salted and while this is usually done by the butcher, it may also be done quite easily at home.

TO PICKLE OX TONGUE

The pickle:

³/₄ *lb salt*	¹/₂ *oz saltpetre*
4 *oz soft brown sugar*	4 *pints water*

Put all the ingredients for the pickle into a saucepan, bring to the boil and boil for 15 minutes. Cool before use.

Meanwhile, wash the tongue thoroughly. When the pickle is quite cold, immerse the tongue in it — it should be completely covered. Cover and leave in a cool place to soak, allowing anything from 7 to 12 days as convenient or according to the degree of saltiness desired.

Other meats, such as brisket, silverside, or pig's head may be salted using this pickle.

BOILED TONGUE

If the tongue has been salted too much, steep it overnight in cold water. After soaking, wash well and place in a saucepan of cold water. Bring it slowly to the boil. Add a bouquet garni and a few flavouring vegetables. Cook very gently until the tongue is tender. The time required will vary according to the size of the tongue, but approximately 4-5 hours will be required. The tongue will prove better eating if the cooking is very slow and plenty of time is allowed.

When tender, remove and plunge into a basin of cold water to cool a little and make it easier to skin. Peel off the skin carefully and cut away excessive fat from the root. Also remove the little bones and any gristle to be found in the root. If the tongue is well cooked, this is very easy to do.

TO SERVE HOT: If the tongue is to be eaten hot, cover it with buttered paper and put it in the oven to heat through. Alternatively, heat through in the cooking liquor. Sprinkle it with browned crumbs and place on a hot dish garnished with sprays of parsley. Serve with a parsley or raisin and cider sauce. The following cream and butter sauce is particularly good with either boiled tongue, ham, salt beef or chicken.

CREAM AND BUTTER SAUCE: Put the contents of a small jar of cream into a saucepan. Add a nob of butter and seasoning. Bring to the boil and simmer for a few minutes. The sauce will thicken slightly and, as it is rich, only a little is required. Sometimes a teaspoonful of mayonnaise is added.

TO SERVE COLD in a ROUND: After boiling, lift the tongue into a basin of cold water. Then skin and trim the root. Remove all the little bones and any gristle. Roll it and pack tightly into a round cake tin. Place a plate on top and press heavily. Next day, turn out and serve garnished with parsley or cress.

DRESSED TONGUE

Boil the salt tongue as already described, then skin and remove the bones in the root. Trim neatly. Place the tongue on a board and fasten it at the root and tip ends, hammering fine skewers through it into the board. The tongue should be nicely arched. Leave until cold, then brush with glaze. Pipe attractively with coloured butter and fasten a frill round the root. Serve on a large dish garnished with parsley or cress.

A SIMPLE GLAZE: *Oxo cube, $^1/_2$ gill water and $^1/_4$ oz gelatine.*

Combine the ingredients and stir over a gentle heat until dissolved. Use when on the point of setting.

COOKED AND DRESSED MEATS

While Ireland does not boast the wealth of products that are associated with a charcuterie in France, yet cooked dressed meats, particularly pork, are important and there are many traditional dishes of this type. Besides, the modern delicatessen shops can now supply many items from the continent such as salame of all types, Parma ham and various liver sausages.

BRAWN

1 *pig's head—*	6 *cloves*
including the tongue	*a blade of mace*
2 *onions*	*a bouquet garni*
12 *peppercorns*	1 *teaspoonful whole allspice*

Ask the butcher to cleft the head in two and to remove the eyes.

Wash it thoroughly in plenty of running water. Remove the brains and use immediately for some other dish.

Put the head in pickle for 3 days. Alternatively, it may be put in a crock, the inside rubbed with salt to which a little salt petre has been added and the outside rubbed with salt only. Cover and leave for 3 days, rubbing daily. Wash well once more before proceeding.

Put the head and flavourings into a roomy saucepan. Barely cover with water and bring slowly to the boil. Simmer gently for 5-6 hours or until the flesh is so tender it leaves the bones easily.

Lift the head onto a large dish. Remove the tongue, skin it and cut into dice. Remove all the flesh from the bones and return these to the saucepan. Continue boiling without a lid to reduce the liquor. Now, using two forks, pull the meat apart. This should be done while it is still hot. The brawn will slice better if the meat is prepared in this way. Mix with the tongue adding more pepper, if necessary and pack loosely into a round plain mould or cake tin. Pour over a little of the strained liquor and put aside to set.

When firm, dip the mould in hot water and turn the brawn out.

BRAWN OF SHIN OF BEEF AND PIG'S FEET

2 *salted pig's feet*	3 *cloves*
2 *lb shin of beef*	*a bouquet garni*
8 *peppercorns*	6 *pints water*

Wash and scrape the pig's feet and cut the shin of beef into fairly large pieces. Remove the marrow from the bone and use for some other purpose. Put the feet, meat, bone and flavourings into a roomy saucepan and add the water. Bring to the boil and simmer gently for 4 hours. Remove the meat from the bones and mince or cut up finely. Pack loosely into a plain round mould or cake tin. Return the bones to the liquor in the saucepan and boil rapidly to reduce. Strain and use to fill up the mould. Put aside to set.

When firm, dip the mould in hot water and turn the brawn out.

PIG'S HEAD GALANTINE

1 *pig's head*	*a blade of mace*
12 *peppercorns*	*a bouquet garni*
6 *cloves*	1 *teaspoonful whole allspice*

Have the head cleft in two through the snout and wash it thoroughly in plenty of running water. Remove the brains and put the head into a pickle for 3 days. Wash once more before proceeding: —

Put the head and the flavourings into a roomy saucepan and cover with water. Bring to the boil and simmer gently for approximately 4-5 hours or until the bones can easily be removed. Lift onto a large dish and bone, keeping the outer skin whole.

Skin and slice the tongue and insert these pieces into the fatty parts of the cheek. Cut off the ears and put the two halves together, skin side in and having half a snout to each end. Tie firmly in a strong cloth and press heavily until cold. Glaze, if wished.

BATH CHAPS

A Bath Chap consists of the lower half of a pig's cheek and part of the tongue cured in much the same way as bacon. It is sold cooked and dressed in crumbs. It is usually served cold, but may also be heated in the oven and served in the same way as boiled ham

WHITE PUDDINGS

White puddings are a form of thick sausage. The filling is made of toasted oatmeal and lard flavoured with onion and highly seasoned. This mixture is packed into sausage skins and boiled, after which they may be hung up for use as required.

Nowadays, they are generally purchased at this stage and the most usual method of cooking them is to cut the pudding into slices, dip in egg and breadcrumbs and fry in bacon fat. They are served with fried bacon.

BLACK PUDDINGS

Black puddings are another form of thick sausage. They were made on the farms at the time a pig was killed, the blood being mixed with lard and oatmeal to make the filling. These, too, were boiled and hung up for use as required.

Nowadays, black puddings are usually purchased ready for use. They are generally sliced, fried and served hot with bacon and perhaps creamed potatoes.

COLD MEAT GALANTINE

¹/₂ lb lean beef	*1 dessertspoonful finely*
4 oz fat bacon	*chopped onion*
6 oz pork sausage meat	*1 teaspoonful finely*
³/₄ cupful breadcrumbs	*chopped gherkins*
1 dessertspoonful	*¹/₄ teaspoonful mixed*
chopped parsley	*spice*

salt and pepper

1 egg

a little stock or water

Decoration: *meat glaze and coloured butter*

Mince the meat and rinded bacon twice, if necessary. Add the sausagemeat, breadcrumbs and flavourings. Moisten with the beaten egg and a little stock or water. Form into a neat roll and tie firmly in a greased cloth. Put in a saucepan of boiling salted water and simmer gently for 1³/₄ hours. Lift out and remove the cloth. Rinse and use to re-tie the galantine. Press between two dishes until cold.

Then remove the cloth, brush with glaze and decorate attractively by piping with coloured butter. Serve garnished with parsley or cress.

RAISED PORK PIE

³/₄ lb hot water crust

Pie filling:

1 lb fresh pork	*pepper*
1 teaspoonful salt	*a pinch of dried sage*

Jellied stock:

1 lb bones or pig's foot	*a bouquet garni*
1 onion	*salt*

3 pints water

Commence by making the jellied stock:

Put the bones and flavouring into a saucepan and add the water. Bring to the boil and simmer very slowly for 7-8 hours. When well reduced, strain and put aside until the next day. Alternatively, it may be jellied by dissolving ¹/₂ oz gelatine in 1 pint stock. This is a much quicker method, but the flavour is·not so good.

Now prepare the filling:

Cut the pork up finely, season well and flavour with the sage.

Prepare the hot water crust and cut into two pieces — one for the pie-case and one for the lid. Working quickly, knead the larger piece and shape and raise with the hands into a hollow pie-case. Fill with the meat, pressing the mixture well down. There should be a rim of pastry left all the way round. Roll out the smaller piece of pastry for the lid. Damp the edges and lay it on top of the pie, pressing the two edges together. Trim with scissors and snip around, making cuts ¹/₄ inch apart. Double one piece in and one out to make a fancy edge. Make a ventilation hole in the top of the pie and fasten a double strip of paper around. Brush with egg and bake in a moderate oven for approximately 1¹/₂ hours.

Suggested oven temperature — 400° or " 5 ".

When ready, fill with jellied stock and serve cold.

Alternatively, individual pies may be made. These are sometimes shaped round a jam-jar.

A pork pie may also be made in a cake tin, using short crust pastry.

RAISED MUTTON PIES

1 lb raised pie crust

Filling:

³/₄ lb lean mutton   *a little grated nutmeg*
salt and pepper   *a little gravy*

Any scraps of mutton may be used for these pies providing they are not too fat. Cut it into small pieces and season with salt, pepper and a little nutmeg. Moisten with water or gravy.

Prepare the raised pie crust, mixing it as hot as possible. Put aside ¹/₃ of the pastry and keep warm for making into lids later. Divide the larger portion into six pieces and form each into a little pie-case. This may be done either with the fingers and thumb or around a jam-pot or tumbler. Fill them with the meat. Roll out the pastry which has been kept warm and cut into rounds. Damp the edges and use to cover the pies. Decorate the edges and make a ventilation hole in the top. Brush with egg and bake in a moderately hot oven for 30-40 minutes.

Suggested oven temperature — 425° or " 6 ".

Before serving, fill up with gravy.

RAISED VEAL AND HAM PIE

¹/₂ lb raised pie crust

Filling:

¹/₂ lb veal   *salt and pepper*
2 oz ham   *a little grated lemon rind*
1 teaspoonful chopped   *jellied stock (see recipe*
parsley   *for raised pork pie)*

Cut the veal into small pieces. Remove the rind from the ham and cut into dice. Combine and add the flavourings. Moisten with a little water.

Prepare the raised pie crust and turn it out as hot as possible on to a floured flavourings. Moisten with a little water. surface. Knead lightly and cut off approximately ¹/₃ for the lid. Keep this portion warm. Shape the large piece to form a pie-case and fill with the meat mixture. Roll out the pastry for the lid, damp the edges and use to cover the pie. Decorate the edges and fasten a double band of greaseproof paper around the pie. Make a ventilation hole in the top and brush with egg. Bake in a moderate oven for approximately 1 ¹/₂ hours.

Suggested oven temperature — 400° or " 5 ".

When baked, fill up with the jellied stock and serve cold.

POULTRY, GAME AND RABBITS

CHICKENS

Young birds or cockerels generally weigh from $2^1/_2$-$4^1/_2$ lb and are easily recognised by testing the end of the breast bone with the thumb. While young the tip of this bone is pliable and gristly and as the bird ages, the bone develops and hardens. Apart from this, choose a bird which is plump and fresh.

Poussins are baby chickens from 4-8 weeks old and they may either be served whole or split in two according to their size. Like the young cockerels, they may be roasted, fried or sautéed and, while very tender, it is generally conceded that they have not such a full flavour.

The preparation of a chicken for cooking is as follows:

The chicken should be plucked if possible while it is still warm. It should then be hung up by the feet in a cool, airy place for 2-4 days. The exact time required for hanging depends on the age of the bird and the weather. It should not be drawn until just prior to cooking.

Before drawing, however, it is probably necessary to singe away any hairs or down left after the plucking. This may be conveniently done over a gas jet or the flame from a little methylated spirits burning in an old tin. Any quills that remain should also be removed.

The bird is now ready for drawing and it is best to begin by protecting the working surface with paper. In addition have a bowl of water for the giblets, and water to rinse the fingers. Begin by cutting off the head, leaving approximately three inches of the neck. Slit the skin of the neck at the back and remove the crop and windpipe. Push two fingers into the opening and loosen the internal organs by breaking the ligaments which attach them to the carcase. Now make a slit across the skin between the tail and the vent.

Insert a finger and gently loosen all round. Draw out the gizzard, intestines, liver with the gall-bladder attached and the heart. The lungs which lie close to the ribs must not be forgotten. Wipe the bird with a damp cloth — washing is not usually necessary. Keep the gizzard, cutting it open and removing the bag of stones from the inside, and the liver, removing the gall-bladder and any green parts nearby; also retain the heart. Rinse these pieces and put aside with the neck.

The sinews of very young chickens are not necessarily removed, but it is advisable as the bird becomes older. The sinews, if allowed to remain in a mature bird, spoil the drumstick for eating. There are several methods of removing them, but perhaps the surest is to make a slit on the inside of the leg and, using a skewer, pull them out one by one — in all there are seven ligaments. Now chop off the feet. This should be done one inch below the joint if the bird is to be roasted. Scald this piece of the leg and peel off outside skin. Scald the feet also and skin. They make an excellent addition to the other giblets.

ROAST CHICKEN — ENGLISH STYLE

A chicken for roasting is generally stuffed in the breast and for this purpose a simple parsley and breadcrumb stuffing is excellent — two to three ounces of crumbs are ample. Alternatively, use a chestnut or forcemeat stuffing. The stuffing is packed into the breast cavity and in doing this see that the final shape is good. Secure the stuffing by folding the neck skin firmly to the underside. Fold the pinions to the back also. Enlarge the vent and push the

tail through. Now press the legs well in against the body so that the bird is compact and plump in appearance. Using a trussing needle threaded with fine twine, pass the needle along one wing, take a stitch through the neck skin on the underside and down the second wing. Finally stitch through the body cavity, passing the needle between the thigh and drumstick of the leg on either side. This brings the string back to the starting point where it can be tied firmly. Tie also at the rump end, lapping a piece of fine twine round the tail and the two legs and tying tightly. Place slices of fat bacon over the breast and cover with greased paper. Place in a roasting tin with a little dripping and roast in a moderately hot oven.

Suggested oven temperature — 400° or " 6 ".

The time will depend on the age and size of the bird. A small, young chicken will take $3/4$ hour, an older bird 1-1 $1/2$ hours. During the cooking, baste and turn the bird from time to time so that it browns evenly.

When nearly cooked remove the paper and bacon to give the breast a final browning. Sometimes it is dredged with flour, basted and returned to the oven to froth.

When the bird is ready, lift it onto a hot dish and remove the trussing string. Garnish with watercress and bacon rolls.

Serve accompanied by gravy, made using giblet stock, and bread sauce.

BOILED FOWL

A fowl for boiling is trussed as follows: Draw the sinews. Insert the fingers through the opening made for drawing the bird and loosen all the outside skin from the flesh of the thighs. Press the leg joints inside. They should be completely out of sight and are spoken of as " pocketed ". Push the tail inside also and draw the skin over so as to close the opening.

Complete the trussing in the same way as has been described for a roast chicken.

Rub the entire surface with a piece of cut lemon in order to keep the flesh an attractive white colour. Have ready a pan of freshly-boiling water. Put the fowl into this placing it breast down. Add salt and the giblets. Bring to the boil and simmer very gently until tender. The time will largely depend on the age and size of the bird and might be anything from $1\frac{1}{2}$ to 3 or 4 hours. To test for tenderness, pierce with a skewer between the thigh and body.

When cooked, lift and drain well before placing on a hot dish. Remove the trussing string and coat with parsley, egg or celery sauce. Garnish with bacon rolls and hard-boiled egg. The sauce has a particularly good flavour if a proportion of the liquid used is that from the pan in which the chicken has been cooking. Indeed a fowl may well be very fat so that this stock is greasy and the fat floating on top should be used in the sauce also.

FRICASSÉE OF CHICKEN

1 *chicken*	1 $\frac{1}{2}$ *oz butter or*
1 *onion*	*margarine*
a piece of carrot	1 $\frac{1}{2}$ *oz flour*
a bouquet garni	*salt and pepper*

1 $\frac{1}{2}$ *gills concentrated chicken stock*
1 $\frac{1}{2}$ *gills milk*

Garnish: *croûtons of fried bread, sautéed mushrooms and bacon rolls*

Prepare the chicken for boiling and simmer gently in a small amount of water to which has been added the quartered onion, carrot, bouquet garni and seasoning. When almost cooked, remove and carve into portions. Return the carcase and trimmings to the liquor in the pan and boil rapidly to reduce and concentrate the stock. Now make a sauce with the butter, flour, stock and milk. Add the joints of chicken and complete the cooking. Serve neatly, coating the chicken with the sauce and then garnish with croûtons of fried bread, sautéed mushrooms and bacon rolls.

COLD ROAST CHICKEN WITH MUSHROOM DRESSING

1 *roasting chicken of*	*a spray of thyme*
3-3 $\frac{1}{2}$ *lb*	*salt and pepper*
1-2 *cloves of garlic*	*a knob of butter*

Mushroom dressing:	French dressing:
6-8 *oz mushrooms*	2 *dessertspoonfuls olive*
salt and pepper	*oil*
1-2 *tablespoonfuls*	1 $\frac{1}{2}$ *teaspoonfuls*
olive oil	*lemon juice*
2 *glasses port or*	1 *teaspoonful sugar*
burgundy	*and seasoning*
	chopped parsley

Garnish: *watercress and tomatoes*

Chop the garlic with a pinch of salt and work into a knob of butter. Put inside the chicken together with a spray of thyme. Truss for roasting and butter the outside of the bird. Sprinkle with seasoning. Roast in a moderately hot oven for approximately 1-1 $\frac{1}{4}$ hours or according to size.

Suggested oven temperature — 400° or " 6 ".

Turn the bird occasionally so that the skin is brown and crisp all over.

Meanwhile prepare the mushroom dressing:

Slice the mushrooms, season and sauté for a few minutes in the olive oil. Reduce the wine by half and add to the mushrooms. Add the French dressing also.

When the chicken is cooked and only just cold, carve it into neat joints. Marinade in the mushroom dressing for 20-30 minutes then dish, spooning the dressing over. Serve garnished with cress and sliced tomatoes moistened with French dressing.

SAUTÉED OR FRIED CHICKEN

There are several methods of frying a chicken, but in each case it is essential that it should be young and tender.

If using poussins, cut the birds into halves, season the pieces and dust with a little flour. Fry in a frying pan allowing approximately half-an-inch of butter, butter and oil or bacon fat for this purpose. In the first instance cook the pieces of chicken until they are brown, then reduce the heat, cover the pan and continue cooking until they are tender. Allow from 30-35 minutes cooking time according to size.

If a young roasting chicken of 3-3½ lb is to be fried it should be cut into joints, preferably cutting the legs in two. Toss in seasoned flour and dip in the beaten egg and breadcrumbs. Then put aside for an hour so that the crumbs may dry. Heat some bacon fat, butter or butter and oil in a heavy frying pan. When hot add the pieces of chicken and brown on all sides. Reduce the heat and cook slowly until tender, allowing approximately 35-45 minutes.

Yet again, the chicken may first of all be boiled until almost cooked. When cold carve into joints and either dip into batter or egg and crumbs before frying in deep fat.

Serve the fried chicken quite plainly accompanied by a tossed salad.

Alternatively, it can be garnished with fried bananas, hot rings of pineapple and crisp rashers of bacon and accompanied by a velouté or suprême sauce made with chicken stock.

CHICKEN MARYLAND is probably the best known dish incorporating fried chicken. For this the garnish always includes fried banana and cornfritters.

CHICKEN SALAD

1 *chicken*	1 *oz butter or margarine*
1 *onion*	1 *oz flour*
a piece of carrot	½ *pint concentrated*
a bouquet garni	*chicken stock*
¼ *lb streaky bacon in*	2-3 *tablespoonfuls*
a piece	*whipped cream*
	salt and pepper

Garnish: 6-8 *oz green grapes, tomatoes, chicory or lettuce*

Boil the chicken in a small amount of water, to which the flavourings have been added. Leave to cool in the cooking liquor. Boil the bacon also.

Carve the chicken and bone the joints. Cut the flesh into neat, but not too small cubes. Rind the bacon and dice also. Meanwhile return the carcase and the trimmings to the stock and boil to reduce and concentrate.

Make a sauce with the butter, flour and strained stock. Cool and fold in the whipped cream. Correct the seasoning and add the chicken and bacon. Arrange in a neat mound on a serving dish and garnish with pitted grapes, tomatoes and chicory quarters or lettuce leaves.

CHICKEN GALANTINE

1 *fowl or large*   1 *onion*
  chicken (undrawn) 1 *carrot*
             a bouquet garni

Farce:
³/₄ lb pork sausage *a little finely-chopped*
  meat   *onion*
       2-3 oz cooked ham
1 *tablespoonful* 1 *egg*
  chopped parsley *2-3 oz cooked tongue*

Chaudfroid:
¹/₂ pint béchamel sauce ¹/₂ pint aspic jelly
  a little extra aspic jelly for glazing

Garnish: *cucumber, radishes, tomato and fine cress*

Singe the bird and pick out any ends of feathers. Remove sinews if this is considered necessary. The bird should not be drawn, however, as it will be firmer to work on if left as it is.

The boning may be done as follows:

Turn the bird onto the breast and make a slit down the centre of the back. With the point of a sharp knife, work down one side, raising the flesh as cleanly as possible from the bones. Disjoint the leg and wing and continue removing the flesh from the carcase until the breast bone is reached. The process is then repeated on the other side so that the carcase can be removed. Now bone out the legs and the wings to the first joint or as far as possible.

Draw the carcase and retain the heart, liver and gizzard. Put the bones, giblets and flavouring into a roomy saucepan with water to cover and simmer gently.

Spread the bird on a board skin side down, and arrange the flesh so as to have it of an equal thickness all over, and as oblong a shape as possible. Sprinkle with seasoning.

Now prepare the stuffing:

Combine the sausage meat with the parsley, onion and beaten egg and spread half of this mixture over the chicken. Cut the tongue and ham into strips and lay these over the sausage meat. Sometimes hard-boiled egg is also used, as well as pistachio nuts and truffles if these are available. Cover with the remainder of the sausage meat and fold in two sides of the oblong on to the farce. Roll up to form a neat galantine. Stitch securely and tie in a cloth. Put into the prepared stock and simmer gently for 1¹/₂-3 hours according to the age of the bird.

When cooked, lift out, remove the cloth, rinse and re-roll the galantine. Press between two dishes with a weight on top.

When cold, remove the cloth and stitches and place the galantine on a cooling wire placed over a dish.

Combine the béchamel sauce with the liquid aspic jelly (just before setting) and when it shows signs of thickening, use to coat the galantine. Allow to set and give another coating if necessary. Again allow to set. Decorate prettily with cucumber, radishes, tomato and cress moistened with aspic jelly, and, when set, give a final glazing with a little cold but liquid aspic.

Dish, garnishing further with chopped aspic if wished and salad material.

DUCKS AND DUCKLINGS

Ducklings are young birds up to three months old and weighing 3¹/₂-4 lb. Ducks usually weigh from 4¹/₂ to 6 lb. The age and tenderness of the bird can best be judged by the flexibility of the breast bones — otherwise choose one which is plump, without being over-fattened.

ROAST DUCK

A duck is stuffed in the body cavity, generally with a sage and onion or herb stuffing. The liver is often diced and mixed through it. Truss the bird and roast for approximately 1 hour or according to the size and age of the fowl.

Suggested oven temperature — 400° or "6".

Serve accompanied by a brown gravy, made using giblet stock and apple sauce or an orange salad.

COLD DUCK WITH LEMON

1 *duck*	*seasoning*
butter	*a spray of rosemary*

Stuffing:

2 oz breadcrumbs	*3 rashers of bacon*
2 oz finely-chopped mushrooms	*a little finely-chopped onion*
the liver of the duck	*chopped parsley*
2 chickens' livers	*salt and pepper*
	1 egg

Glaze:
1 pint aspic jelly
Garnish: curled celery or a potato salad
prunes stuffed with chutney
shredded red and green peppers tossed in French dressing or tomato salad

Prepare the stuffing first:

Add the chopped mushrooms to the breadcrumbs. Dice the livers and the rinded bacon and add together with the chopped onion, parsley and seasoning. Bind with the beaten egg. Use to stuff the body cavity of the duck. Spread the butter over the breast and legs and season lightly with salt and pepper. Set in a roasting tin with the rosemary underneath and roast in a moderately-heated oven for approximately 1 hour or according to the size of the bird.

Suggested oven temperature — 400° or "6".

When cold, carve the duck into neat joints, cutting the legs in two. Remove the bones from the leg joints and the wing. Fill the cavity left with stuffing. Arrange the stuffing on the portions of breast also. Place the pieces of duck on a wire cooler and glaze with aspic jelly used at setting point.

Serve garnished with the curled celery or potato salad, the stuffed prunes and pepper or tomato salad and accompanied by the following lemon compote.

LEMON COMPÔTE:

4-5 lemons	*3 oz sugar*
3/4 gill water	

Grate a little rind from one lemon. Remove the peel and white pith from all the lemons and cut the flesh into neat slices. Arrange in a glass dish. Sprinkle with the grated rind. Boil the sugar and water together for a few minutes to form a syrup. Cool a little and pour over the lemons. Use very cold.

PHEASANT

A pheasant requires to be well hung before being cooked. The time depends largely on the weather, but may be anything from 7 to 10 days or even longer. Connoisseurs agree that the ideal period is until the pheasant begins to decompose. When the pheasant has reached this point, it should be plucked and dressed, reserving the best of the tail feathers to use as a garnish later.

A young pheasant suitable for roasting can be distinguished by the pliable nature of the upper beak.

ROAST PHEASANT

Pheasant is often accused of being

dry, but if roasted in the following way, it should be juicy and good:

Put a knob of butter inside the bird, season, truss and wrap in well-buttered foil. Place the pheasant on a roasting tin lying on one side and cook in a moderately-heated oven for approximately 45-60 minutes according to size.

Suggested oven temperature — 375º or " 5 ".

During this time turn the bird on-to the other side. For the last 15 minutes cook it breastuppermost and with the foil folded back in order to brown it nicely, but taking care not to lose the juices.

Dish garnished, if wished, with the tail feathers.

A good gravy can be made by transferring the juices in the aluminium foil to a small saucepan. Add seasoning and 2-3 teaspoonfuls of white wine and bubble together for a few minutes.

Serve the roast pheasant accompanied by bread sauce, fried buttered crumbs and game chips as wished. A thick slice of fat bacon cut in match stick pieces and cooked until crisp is another pleasant accompaniment.

HARE

A young hare is called a leveret and is recognisable by its size and the softness of pad, claw and ear which should tear easily, and its teeth which are small and sharp. It should be skinned, paunched and dressed at once, unlike an old hare which should be hung from 7-10 days.

After hanging the hare should be skinned. To do this cut off the legs at the first joint, then make a slit through the fur only, along the underside. Carefully loosen the skin to either side drawing it away from the hind legs and

finally pulling it right off. Continue drawing the skin off the body towards the shoulders, and skin the fore-legs or wings. Cut off the head — though many authorities skin this also, claiming that it makes very good gravy.

The hare is now ready for paunching:

Make a slit along the underside and remove the stomach, intestines, liver and kidneys. The blood is used in the cooking later, and will generally be found behind the diaphram in the rib cavity. This should, therefore, be broken with care and the blood collected in a bowl.

A young hare may be roasted or the saddle only cooked in this way and the legs used for some other dish such as jugged hare or a steamed pudding — made after the style of a steak and kidney pudding with suet pastry.

An older hare is best cooked by some slow, moist method in order to ensure tenderness. Of these methods the best known is jugged hare — a traditional English dish. Originally the " jug " was cooked in a special, tall stewpot with a lid. A 7 lb stone jam jar can be used as a substitute and the authentic method of cooking was to seal this with a bladder and to set the jug in a deep pan of boiling water to cook slowly for 3-4 hours. Nowadays, it is more often cooked in a casserole in the oven, but continues to be known as jugged hare.

JUGGED HARE

1 hare	*the juice of ¹/₂ lemon*
2 oz flour	*1 inch cinnamon stick*
¹/₂ lb bacon	*stock or water*
2 onions	*2 glasses of port or*
6 cloves	*red wine*
a bouquet garni	*1 tablespoonful red-*
a strip of lemon rind	*currant jelly*
	salt and pepper

Forcemeat balls:

the liver of the	*1 dessertspoonful*
hare	*chopped mixed herbs*
3 oz breadcrumbs	*a grating of lemon rind*
1 ½ oz suet	*1 dessertspoonful*
1 dessertspoonful	*chopped onion*
chopped parsley	*salt and pepper*
	1 egg

Cut the hare into neat pieces. Then toss in some of the flour. Rind the bacon and cut into 1 inch pieces. Put into a roomy saucepan and fry. Now add the hare, the onions stuck with the cloves and the other flavourings tied in muslin. Put the lid on the pan and cook slowly for 20 minutes, shaking the pan occasionally. Blend the remainder of the flour with a little stock or water and add it to the contents of the saucepan together with enough stock to cover the hare. Add the lemon juice, seasoning and 1 glass of port. Stir until simmering point is reached, then transfer to a casserole. Cover and cook in a moderate oven until the hare is tender. It should be cooked for approximately 3-4 hours.

A little before serving remove the muslin bag and add the second glass of port, the red currant jelly and the blood — though this may be omitted if preferred. Cook a little longer, being careful the gravy does not boil again as the blood would cause it to curdle. Serve garnished with forcemeat balls. These are made as follows:

Parboil the liver and chop finely. Add the breadcrumbs and other ingredients and season highly. Bind together with the beaten egg. Form into balls and bake in a tin with a little dripping until brown.

Frequently the pieces of hare are marinaded for 2-3 hours before cooking.

This improves the flavour and tenderness of the dish. A suitable marinade is as follows:

1 glass red wine (which may be used later in the jug)
2 tablespoonfuls olive oil
a little onion
2 bay-leaves
salt and pepper

RABBIT

Rabbit is at its best from October to February. It is paunched immediately it is killed. It is generally used while fresh, but if it is necessary to keep it for a day or two, the skin should not be removed until about to be cooked. Tie the two hind feet together and hang the rabbit up in a cool, airy place. A young rabbit is recognisable by sharp white teeth and sharp claws and the ears, which should tear easily. If the kidneys are buried in fat, the rabbit is certain to be in good condition.

WHITE STEW OF RABBIT

1 rabbit	*1 ½ oz flour*
1 onion	*1 ½ gills rabbit stock*
a bouquet garni	*1 ½ gills milk*
1 ½ oz butter or	*salt and pepper*
margarine	

Garnish: *bacon rolls*

Joint the rabbit and steep overnight in cold water to which a little vinegar has been added.

Next day, drain and put the pieces of rabbit into a saucepan together with salt, the quartered onion and bouquet garni. Barely cover with cold water and bring slowly to simmering point. Skim if necessary and cook gently until the rabbit is tender — about 1 ½ hours. Then remove the pieces of meat and strain the liquor. Make a sauce with the butter, flour and a combination of liquor from the saucepan and milk. Season nicely and return the pieces of rabbit. When hot again, serve the rabbit coating it with the sauce. Garnish with bacon rolls.

FRIED RABBIT

1 *rabbit*	*a bouquet garni*
1 *onion*	*salt and pepper*
	egg and breadcrumbs

Joint the rabbit and steep overnight in cold water to which a little vinegar has been added.

Next day, drain and put the pieces of rabbit, the quartered onion and the bouquet garni into a saucepan. Add seasoning and barely cover with cold water. Bring slowly to simmering point. Skim, if necessary, and cook gently until the rabbit is tender — about 1 1/2 hours. Drain and put aside to cool. Flour the joints of meat and pass through beaten egg and breadcrumbs. Fry in deep fat. Serve garnished with watercress accompanied by tartar sauce.

CASSEROLE OF RABBIT

1 *rabbit*	1 *onion (chopped)*
1 *large tablespoonful*	1 *small carrot (sliced)*
flour	2 *cloves*
salt and pepper	*approximately* 3/4 *pint*
2-4 *oz bacon*	*stock or water*
a little dripping	

Joint the rabbit and blanch overnight in cold water to which a little vinegar has been added.

Next day drain and dry the pieces of meat. Toss in the seasoned flour. Rind the bacon and cut in short lengths. Fry. Remove and add dripping as required to fry the rabbit. Fry the onion. Arrange the onion, bacon and rabbit in a casserole. Add the sliced carrot, cloves and sufficient stock to cover. Cook until the rabbit is tender — about 2 hours.

Suggested oven temperature — 350° or " 3 ".

VEGETABLES AND SALADS

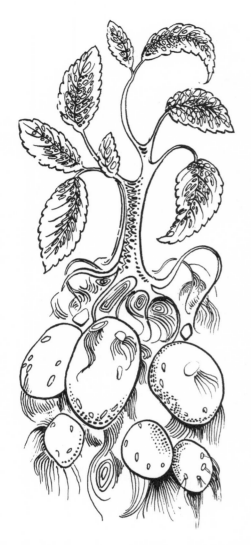

COOKING VEGETABLES BY BOILING: By far the most common basic method of cooking vegetables is by boiling in salted water. Use as little water as is reasonable and cover the pan with a lid to prevent evaporation. The addition of baking soda is not recommended, since it tends to flavour the vegetables and also diminishes the vitamin content. An exception might be considered if the vegetables are old and difficult to cook. Vegetables should be boiled for as short a time as possible — the determining factor being the size of the pieces and the age of the vegetable. As soon as they are tender, drain free from water and, if to be served without any other elaboration, toss in melted butter before dishing.

COOKING FROZEN VEGETABLES: The instructions on the packet should be followed carefully, remembering that the cooking time of frozen vegetables is much shorter than the time required for fresh vegetables. A very small quantity of water is required, while it is necessary to add seasoning and to serve the cooked vegetables tossed in butter.

COOKING DRIED VEGETABLES: Dried vegetables such as butter and haricot beans or peas require overnight steeping before cooking. Sometimes the addition of a pinch of baking soda is advisable to assist in softening them. Next day, drain and put in a saucepan with fresh cold water to cover. Add salt and simmer slowly until tender. The time will vary according to the age of the dried vegetables, but they will usually require two hours cooking or longer. Drain and serve tossed in butter. Dried peas are improved by the addition of a little sugar and also a spray of mint.

WELL-COOKED vegetables make an important contribution towards the success of any meal and to cook them is not difficult. Its very simplicity is perhaps the stumbling block as we occupy ourselves in the kitchen with more interesting work.

Vegetables should, ideally, be used while fresh from the garden and served as soon as possible after the cooking is completed, as many of them spoil if they have to be kept warm.

111

Haricot beans have a good flavour if cooked with a chopped onion and a bunch of herbs.

ARTICHOKES

There are two different types of artichokes common in this country — the globe and the Jerusalem artichokes. The first is a true artichoke and the latter only called an artichoke because its flavour approximates to that of the globe.

THE GLOBE ARTICHOKE is a form of thistle and it is the bud of the plant which is eaten. The base or fond of the plant is the part which is prized together with the fleshy tip of each scale of the bud. The globe artichoke is generally served as a separate course — plainly boiled and accompanied by melted butter or Hollandaise sauce, or served cold with a French dressing.

JERUSALEM ARTICHOKES are tubers resembling rough potatoes. They are a winter vegetable being at their best during December, January and February. They are good plainly boiled and served with a white or parsley sauce, besides making an excellent soup.

Jerusalem artichokes tend to discolour quickly once they are peeled and for this reason a little vinegar or lemon juice is often added to the steeping water and they should be cooked immediately following preparation. Some authorities recommend peeling after boiling. The water in which they have been cooked has a good flavour and will even set in a jelly. It is, therefore, a useful addition to the sauce to accompany them, or to soups.

ASPARAGUS

Asparagus is a choice vegetable at its best in the spring. There are many varieties — white, violet and green. The latter is the cheapest and often has the most pronounced flavour.

The two favourite methods of serving asparagus are plainly boiled and served hot with melted butter or Hollandaise sauce, or cold with mayonnaise.

The boiling of asparagus requires care and a special narrow pan is recommended so that it may be cooked " standing ". In this way the stems are in the boiling water and the tender tips are cooked by steam. It requires approximately 20-30 minutes cooking time.

BEETROOT

Beetroot is a useful vegetable with a long autumn and winter season. It is generally used cold for salads and hors-d'oeuvres, but also makes an interesting hot vegetable.

Beetroot is usually boiled and care must be taken in the preliminary preparation not to cut or scrape the skin or cut the leaves or fibous rootlets closely, otherwise it will bleed and lose its colour. Start the cooking in boiling salted water and simmer gently until tender. On an average beetroot will require $1\frac{1}{2}$ to 2 hours to cook, or perhaps longer if they are very large. For this reason the use of a pressure saucepan is often preferred since it reduces the cooking time.

When tender, drain, trim the root and gently rub off the outer skin.

Beetroot may also be wrapped in well-greased paper and baked in a moderate oven.

If beetroot is to be served hot it is either sliced or cut into dice and served with a well-flavoured white sauce. The following three recipes are perhaps better still:

BEETROOT WITH A CLEAR SAUCE: *Approximately 2 cupful diced cooked beetroot hot water to cover, salt, pepper, 1 dessertspoonful arrowroot, 1 oz butter or margarine and a little vinegar (optional).*

Put the diced cooked beetroot into a saucepan and add sufficient hot water to cover. Season and simmer gently until thoroughly hot. Blend the arrowroot with a little cold water and use to thicken the contents of the saucepan. Stir in the butter and cook all thoroughly. A little vinegar may be added for extra piquancy.

SWEET-SOUR BEETROOT: *approximately 2-3 cupfuls diced cooked beetroot, 3 oz sugar, 1 level tablespoonful cornflour, salt, pepper, 1/4 pint mild vinegar and 1 oz butter or margarine.*

Dice the freshly-cooked beetroot. Combine and blend the sugar, cornflour, seasoning and vinegar. Cook gently until clear. Add the beetroot and continue cooking for 20-30 minutes. Just before serving, stir in the butter.

BEETROOT WITH CAPERS: 2-3 *cupfuls diced cooked beetroot, 2 tablespoonfuls vinegar, 1 tablespoonful sugar, salt, pepper, a knob of butter and 1 tablespoonful capers.*

Put the diced beetroot into a saucepan and add the vinegar, sugar and seasoning. Simmer gently until thoroughly hot, then stir in the butter and capers. Cook a little longer and serve very hot.

BROAD BEANS

Broad beans are a summer vegetable. They may be cooked at three stages and are at their best while very young, when they are prepared by slicing in the same way as French beans. As the furry lining of the pod develops, this is no longer a suitable method and they

are then shelled and boiled in the usual way. They may, if wished, be served with a white sauce. Later still, the actual skin of the bean becomes tough and it is necessary to remove it. This is done by blanching in boiling water for a few minutes and then peeling.

BRUSSELS SPROUTS

Brussels sprouts are a winter vegetable at their best around Christmas. Choose, if possible, the smaller sprouts and those of even size. Before cooking, trim the stalk and remove the outer leaves. If the sprout is large, a slit or cross in the stem enables the heat to penetrate so that it cooks evenly. Wash well and cook in boiling salted water for 10 minutes or until tender. Generally, they are served tossed in melted butter.

BRUSSELS SPROUTS WITH CHESTNUTS: Allow roughly twice as many sprouts as chestnuts and cook each separately, remembering that the chestnuts take longer to cook. Drain well and combine. Serve tossed in melted butter.

CABBAGE

Cabbage can be obtained throughout the year in one of its many forms, all of which are moderately priced. During the spring and summer, spring greens or pamphrey (as they are called in Ireland) are in season. They are followed by winter cabbage, which is available from October to January, and savoys, which are even hardier and are available from November to February.

Finally, there are curlies which are at their best after Christmas.

As a rule, these vegetables are cooked by boiling. Before cooking, however, all discoloured or tough leaves should be removed and the cabbage cut into quarters, the hard core and all tough stalks being cut away. Wash as required and shred finely with a sharp knife. Cook in a small amount of boiling salted water. The pan should be covered to prevent evaporation, and overcooking should be avoided. Drain thoroughly, and serve tossed in melted butter. All types of cabbage require plenty of seasoning, particularly pepper.

A typically Irish method of serving greens is to toss them after draining into a frying-pan in which there is a layer of bacon fat. The two are stirred together over gentle heat until thoroughly hot and the fat has been absorbed by the greens. Some would say that this method of treating cabbage accounts for the Irish name for spring greens — " pan-fry " or pamphrey.

In Ireland, too, cabbage is the popular vegetable to serve with boiled ham or bacon and in this case, the two are often cooked together, the cabbage absorbing the flavour of the ham. It is better still if the ham is only partly cooked by boiling and finished by baking in the oven. The ham water can then be used to better advantage for cooking the greens.

CREAMED CABBAGE: Combine freshly-cooked cabbage with sufficient white sauce to give a creamy mixture and serve very hot.

CABBAGE AU GRATIN: Combine freshly-cooked cabbage with a cheese sauce. Transfer to a heat-proof dish, sprinkle with grated cheese and brown in a hot oven.

CABBAGE AND CELERY: Cook equal quantities of shredded cabbage and celery together in boiling salted water. Drain and serve tossed in melted butter.

CARROTS

Carrots are available throughout the year, but are at their best when young and small in the spring and early summer. At this stage they should be well scrubbed and cooked whole. Serve tossed in butter and chopped parsley or mint.

Larger carrots should be washed and scraped or thinly peeled with a potato peeler. Either cut into slices, sticks or dice and cook in boiling salted water. Serve tossed in butter and chopped parsley or with a white or parsley sauce.

MASHED CARROTS: Cut the prepared carrots into rings and boil until tender. Drain, add a knob of butter and mash until smooth. A combination of equal quantities of carrots and parsnips may also be mashed together.

CONSERVATIVELY COOKED CARROTS: Cut the prepared carrot into rings, sticks or dice and put into a saucepan with a spoonful of water, a knob of butter, seasoning and a pinch of sugar. Cover with a tight-fitting lid and cook gently until tender — about 20 minutes. When ready the liquid should have evaporated and the carrots be glazed with the butter. Sprinkle with parsley and a little pepper and serve very hot.

CAULIFLOWER

Cauliflower is available during the late spring, summer and autumn and is preceded by its hardier relative, broccoli, which is in season in the early spring.

It is usually broken into sprigs, the best of the inner leaves shredded and both boiled until tender — about 15 minutes. Serve with a white sauce or a sauce flavoured and coloured with paprika.

CAULIFLOWER AU GRATIN: Cook the cauliflower sprigs and leaves as already described. After draining, arrange in a heat-proof dish and coat with a cheese sauce. Sprinkle with extra grated cheese and brown in a hot oven.

CAULIFLOWER AND MUSHROOMS AU GRATIN: Combine cooked cauliflower sprigs with approximately 4-8 oz sliced mushrooms sautéed with 2-3 rashers of chopped bacon. Arrange the mixture in a heat-proof dish and coat with a cheese sauce. Sprinkle with extra grated cheese and brown in a hot oven.

CELERIAC

Celeriac is a variety of celery grown for its root which somewhat resembles a rough turnip. It has a similar flavour to celery and is less stringy.

To prepare celeriac, wash and slice thickly. Remove the skin and cut into sticks or cubes. Boil in salted water and serve with a white or cheese sauce.

CELERY

Celery is in season throughout the autumn and during the early winter. To prepare it, scrub the stalks, remove the leaves and shorten the green tops down to the white part. The trimmings are useful for flavouring purposes. Cut the stalks to an even length, or alternatively, cut into one inch pieces. This is perhaps the better method if there is any tendency to stringiness. Boil in salted water and serve with a white or cheese sauce.

CHESTNUTS

Chestnuts may be used for either sweet or savoury dishes, but in either case, the basic preparation is the same:

Make a slit in the shell of each nut and put into a pan of water. Bring to the boil and boil for a few minutes. Draw to the side of the heat, remove one or two nuts at a time and peel off the outer and inner skins. Alternatively, make a slit in each nut and bake in the oven until tender. Remove the outer and inner skins. The latter is the better method if very dry chestnuts are required for any purpose.

If the chestnuts are to be used as a vegetable, they are usually boiled and served whole and may take the place of potatoes. They may also be mixed with boiled Brussels sprouts.

CHICORY

The name "chicory" gives rise to some confusion for it refers to a vegetable the French call "endive". In this country the word endive indicates a curly-leafed salad plant.

Chicory is generally imported from Holland and Belgium and is in season during the autumn, winter and early spring. It is a plant which has been blanched by growing in the dark and there is usually very little waste in its preparation. It may be used raw in salads or cooked.

STEWED CHICORY: Melt a knob of butter in a saucepan, add a little lemon juice, salt and 3 tablespoonfuls water. Arrange the prepared chicory in the pan, flake with butter and cover with a tight-fitting lid. Cook gently for 30 minutes or until the chicory is tender.

BRAISED CHICORY: Melt a knob of butter in a heat-proof dish. Arrange the prepared chicory in the dish and sprinkle with salt and a little lemon juice. Flake with more butter, cover with a lid and cook gently in a moderate oven for approximately 45 minutes.

Chicory is usually served with the

liquor in which it was cooked, poured around. It may also be served with melted butter, hot cream or a white sauce.

ENDIVE

Endive has a characteristic curly leaf and it is principally used as a salad plant in place of lettuce. It has a more bitter flavour. Endive may also be cooked in the same way as spinach.

FRENCH AND RUNNER BEANS

French beans and runner beans are somewhat similar, but the former are smaller and more tender. If they are picked while young, it is sufficient to " top and tail " each bean and to cook whole. Otherwise the two vegetables are prepared in a similar way: After washing, remove the " tops and tails " and any stringy threads from the length of the bean. Slice diagonally and as thinly as possible. Cook in boiling salted water for approximately 15-20 minutes and serve tossed in melted butter.

HARICOT BEANS

Haricot beans are the dried seeds of various kinds of dwarf and climbing beans. They should be soaked overnight in water to soften and, next day, boiled gently in salted water until tender. The time will vary according to the age of the bean, but will take approximately two hours. Serve tossed in melted butter.
BAKED BEANS: *6 oz haricot beans (steeped overnight and boiled until tender), 1 sliced onion, 1 tablespoonful golden syrup, 1 dessertspoonful treacle, 2-3 rashers of bacon, $^1/_4$ teaspoonful made mustard, salt, pepper and water to cover.*
Combine the cooked beans with the sliced onion and arrange in a casserole. Add the golden syrup and the treacle. Rind the bacon and cut into one inch pieces. Add together with the mustard, seasoning and enough water to cover all. Place the lid on the casserole and bake in a slow oven for 2-3 or 4 hours, as time permits — the longer the better the flavour of the dish. If the beans become dry, add a little more water.
HARICOT BEANS WITH ONION: Steep 6 oz haricot beans in water overnight. Next day, drain and put to cook in fresh salted water. Add 1-2 sliced onions and a bouquet garni and cook all gently until the beans are tender. Drain, remove the bay-leaf and serve tossed in melted butter.

KOHL-RABI

Kohl-rabi is a member of the cabbage family and it is the swollen stem of the plant which is eaten. It is somewhat similar in shape to a turnip and is cooked in the same way.

LEEKS

Leeks have the mildest flavour of any of the onion family and are in season throughout the winter. To prepare them, trim off the roots, the greater part of the green leaves and the outer covering.
If large, cut down the middle and wash carefully to remove any grit. They may be stewed in stock or milk or boiled. Serve with melted butter or white sauce.
LEEKS WITH BACON: Cut a few rashers of bacon into 1 inch pieces and fry gently. If the bacon is lean, add a knob of butter. Prepare some leeks and cut into $^1/_2$ inch pieces. Add these to the bacon, season with salt and pepper and

cook gently for approximately 30 minutes or until the leeks are tender.

LEEKS WITH CREAM AND CHEESE: Boil the leeks in the usual way. Sprinkle some grated cheese in the bottom of a heat-proof dish. Arrange the leeks on top. Pour over a little thick cream and sprinkle generously with more cheese. Each layer should be seasoned. Brown in a hot oven.

MARROWS

A marrow suitable for cooking should be young and tender. When at their best, they are not more than 5 to 6 inches long and are known as "courgettes". Indeed, these may be so tender that it is unnecessary to peel them and, since the seeds have not developed, they may be cooked whole or in slices.

An older marrow must be peeled, sliced, the seeds removed and the flesh cut into neat pieces. While it may be boiled and served with white or cheese sauce, it is better cooked conservatively in its own juices as follows:

SAVOURY MARROW WITH HERBS: *Approximately $1/3$ marrow, 1-2 oz butter or margarine, 1 finely-chopped shallot or piece of onion, salt, pepper, 1 tablespoonful chopped parsley and 1 teaspoonful chopped thyme.*

Cut the marrow into neat pieces. Melt the butter, add the shallot and cook together without browning. Add the marrow, seasoning and a spoonful of water if considered necessary. Cover with a tight-fitting lid and cook gently until the marrow is almost tender. Add the chopped parsley and thyme and complete the cooking.

MUSHROOMS

Mushrooms freshly gathered from the field have the best flavour and are in season during August and September. Cultivated mushrooms are available throughout the year. They quickly acquire a foreign flavour and can even be spoilt by taking on the flavour of such a simple thing as the paper bag in which they are sold.

Field mushrooms should be washed and peeled before use, but the cultivated mushrooms are generally so perfect that washing alone suffices.

FRIED MUSHROOMS: Mushrooms for frying may either be left whole or sliced. If whole, sprinkle the underside of each cap with seasoning, flake with butter and fry gently in bacon fat or butter in a covered pan.

GRILLED MUSHROOMS: Wash the mushrooms and trim the stem level with the cap. Season and brush the rounded side with oil or melted butter. Place rounded side up on the grill pan and cook for 4-5 minutes. Turn over and put a flake of butter into each hollow. Season and complete the cooking under the grill. In serving, be careful not to lose the juice from the centre of each mushroom.

BAKED MUSHROOMS: Lay the mushroom caps in an oven-dish, hollow side up. Season and put a flake of butter into each. Cover with buttered paper or a lid and bake in a moderate oven for approximately 10 minutes. Alternatively, a little cream may be poured around the mushrooms before baking.

STEWED MUSHROOMS: *$1/2$ lb mushrooms, 1 oz butter or margarine, salt, pepper, $1/2$ pint milk and 1 oz flour.*

Slice the mushrooms and cook in the melted butter for a few minutes. Add seasoning and the milk and simmer together for 7-10 minutes. Do not overcook or the mushrooms will lose their flavour. Thicken with the flour blended with a little extra milk.

ONIONS

The onion is an indispensable flavouring agent and vegetable. It is inexpensive and available throughout the year.

The mildest and best is the Spanish onion. If the flavour is considered to be too strong, the onion may be blanched in boiling water before cooking by any of the following methods:

BOILED ONIONS WITH WHITE SAUCE: If possible, choose medium-sized onions suitable for cooking whole. Otherwise, the large ones must be cut in two or quartered. Boil in salted water until tender. The time will vary according to the size of the onion, but allow approximately $1^1/_2$-2 hours. Drain thoroughly, if necessary returning them to the pan to dry out over a gentle heat so that no liquid remains to spoil the sauce. Arrange in a hot dish and coat with a white sauce.

FRIED ONIONS: Slice the onions. Heat some dripping in a frying pan, add the onions and turn constantly until brown. Alternatively, the pan may be covered with a plate and the onions cooked more slowly until completely tender and brown.

FRENCH FRIED ONIONS: Slice the onions into rings, dip in milk, toss in seasoned flour and fry immediately in deep fat.

PAPRIKA ONIONS: Boil the onions whole and when almost tender, drain and cut in two. Sprinkle the flat surface with brown sugar, salt and paprika pepper. Flake with butter and complete the cooking in a moderate oven.

PARSNIPS

Parsnips are a winter vegetable at their best after the first frosts. They have a thin skin which may be scraped off or thinly peeled with a potato peeler. They are generally sliced, boiled and served mashed and are particularly good if combined with an equal quantity of boiled carrot. Alternatively, they may be mashed with a few boiled potatoes. In mashing them, add a good lump of butter and season well.

PARSNIP CROQUETTES: *1 lb cooked parsnips, 1 oz butter or margarine, a little finely-chopped onion, 1 oz flour, salt, pepper, 1 gill milk, 1 oz breadcrumbs, egg and breadcrumbs for coating.*

Sieve the parsnips. Melt the butter, add the onion and cook gently without browning. Add the flour and seasoning and stir together for a few minutes over the heat. Draw the pan aside and add the milk. Cook thoroughly to form a stiff panada. Add the parsnips and breadcrumbs. Cool. Turn on to a floured surface, divide into 5 or 6 portions and shape into croquettes. Pass through beaten egg and breadcrumbs and fry in deep fat.

PEAS

Green peas are a very popular vegetable available fresh during the summer months and throughout the year as a quick frozen vegetable.

To be at their best, they must be eaten while young and it is important to remember that they quickly harden once they have been shelled.

They are generally boiled in salted water, perhaps flavoured with a spray of mint and served tossed in melted butter. A pinch of sugar is often included in the seasoning.

PIMENTO OR SWEET PEPPERS

Sweet peppers range in colour from green to orange or red. They are hollow and are prepared by cutting away the stem and scooping out the seeds and veiny interior.

SAUTÉED SWEET PEPPERS: Choose peppers in a variety of colours and remove the seeds. Shred or cut into rings. Melt a knob of butter in a saucepan. Add the peppers and cover with a tight-fitting lid. Cook gently until tender — approximately 15-20 minutes.

Sometimes the shredded peppers are blanched in boiling water before cooking.

STUFFED PEPPERS: Cut the pepper in two by the length and remove the seeds and some of the inner membrane. Parboil for 10 minutes. Drain. Stuff with any savoury mixture or use the following:

To sautéed sliced mushrooms and onion add breadcrumbs or boiled rice and moisten with a little gravy. Use to fill the blanched peppers, flake with butter and heat through in a moderate oven.

POTATOES

The social history of Ireland is linked in no small measure with the history of the potato. It is not a native plant, but was introduced from America some time during the last fifteen years of the sixteenth century and is said to have been grown at Youghal by Sir Walter Raleigh.

As its cultivation became common it gradually ousted other crops and in the eighteenth and early nineteenth centuries became the staple food, debasing the diet of the peasants. It was because of this that the great potato famines of 1845 and 1846 were so serious. Following the famines there was a general reaction against everything connected with it. Indeed, so hurtful is the peasant's memory of this terrible time that useful sources of wild food are now neglected, such as wild berries, edible seaweeds, shell fish, mushrooms, eels, hares and rabbits — all available in plenty.

More recent history is more cheerful and Northern Ireland has now made a mark in the world with the quality of the potatoes grown, with the seed potatoes which are exported and for the raising of many new varieties.

Potatoes are available throughout the year as new, not so new and old and they lend themselves to a great variety of uses. Undoubtedly, the truly Irish way of cooking potatoes is to boil them in their jackets and those living within reach of the sea considered it necessary to boil them in sea-water — a reminder that fresh water should be well salted.

In the homes of the rich and middle classes, these plainly-boiled potatoes reached the table served in a wooden bowl or on a folded napkin in a beautifully-ornamented silver dish-ring or potato-ring.

Such rings are now highly prized and are often used for fruit and flower arrangements.

TO BOIL NEW POTATOES

New potatoes should be scraped and not peeled and if they are fresh from the ground, this is easy to do. If the skin is tough, it may be peeled either before or after cooking.

Put the new potatoes on in boiling, salted water and boil steadily until tender. The time will vary from 15 to 20-25 minutes according to the size of the potato and for this reason it is advisable to choose those of equal size. Drain, cover with a clean cloth and return to the heat to dry out. Serve tossed in melted butter and chopped parsley or mint.

A spray of mint is often added to the water in which new potatoes are cooked.

TO BOIL OLD POTATOES

Choose potatoes of equal size and either scrub and boil in their skins or peel before cooking. Potatoes boiled in their jackets undoubtedly have the better flavour. As they are prepared, drop into a basin of cold water until required for cooking. Transfer to a saucepan, cover with cold water and add salt. Bring to the boil and boil steadily until tender — approximately 20-30 or 35 minutes according to the size and variety of the potato. Drain, cover with a clean cloth and return to the heat to dry out.

Potatoes boiled in their jackets may be served as they are — preferably on a clean napkin, or alternatively, they may be peeled before dishing.

Potatoes which prove difficult to boil without breaking may be cooked as follows:

Cover with cold salted water and bring to the boil. Boil gently until barely cooked — that is for approximately 15 minutes. Drain, cover with a clean cloth, put the lid on the pan and complete the cooking over a very gentle heat.

The liquor from boiled potatoes is a useful addition to gravy and many soups.

MASHED POTATOES

Boil peeled potatoes in the usual way and dry thoroughly. Pound with a potato masher until free from lumps. Meanwhile melt a lump of butter in some hot milk and gradually beat this into the potatoes using a fork or a wooden spoon. Season well and continue to beat until light.

Alternatively, the potatoes may be put through a potato ricer or sieved before creaming.

Sometimes it is convenient to serve mashed potatoes in a heat-proof dish, flaked with butter and toasted in a hot oven.

POMMES MOUSSELINE is the French version of creamed potatoes. The great point of difference is that they are more softly creamed with melted butter and plenty of boiling milk. A little grated nutmeg is also added with the other seasoning.

CHEESE POTATOES

Cream 6-8 potatoes in the usual way and beat in 2 oz grated cheese with the melted butter and hot milk. This mixture may either be served appetisingly arranged in a vegetable dish or transferred to a heat-proof dish After forking up attractively, sprinkle it with grated cheese and brown under the grill or in a hot oven.

CHAMP

Champ or thump is the Irish method of serving mashed potatoes. It can be made in great variety with parsley, chives, scallions, peas or young nettles. It is a favourite meal for a fast day and is served in mounds, each with a hollow in the centre into which is put a large lump of butter. The champ should be eaten from the outside, dipping each mouthful in the melting butter. A glass of milk or buttermilk completes the meal.

Champ is also a Hallowe'en dish and in the country, it is an old custom to place the first two portions on the top of the flat pier at the farm gate for the fairies.

In old cottages where there is a clay floor there is sometimes a large " pot-hole " or hollow into which the iron pot is set while the potatoes are beetled with a long handled masher or beetle. This was often the work of the man of the house — his wife adding the hot milk.

For champ the peeled potatoes are boiled in the usual way and, while they are cooking, the chopped scallions, nettle tops or peas are cooked in the milk. When the potatoes are drained, dried and mashed free of lumps, the milk and second vegetable are beaten in together with salt and pepper. Chopped chives and parsley are generally added without cooking. Serve very hot with a generous lump of butter in the centre of each portion.

Sometimes beaten egg is added to champ.

COLCANNON

A Scottish dish.

1 *cupful cooked potatoes*	1 *oz butter or dripping*
1 *cupful cooked cabbage*	1 *egg*
	salt and pepper
	a few browned crumbs

Mash or sieve the potatoes and chop the cabbage until fine. Melt the butter in a saucepan. Add the potato and cabbage. Beat in the whisked egg and season highly. Grease a plain mould or basin generously and coat with the browned crumbs.

Press in the potato and cabbage mixture and bake in a moderate oven until firm. Cool a little before unmoulding.

Colcannon may also be made with other additions such as a chopped boiled, onion, cooked carrot or turnip. Sometimes the mixture is made softer with hot milk and served piled in a vegetable dish.

BAKED POTATOES

Choose medium or large potatoes and scrub thoroughly. Prick, sprinkle with salt and place on a baking tray. Bake slowly in a moderate oven for 2 hours or as required.

Suggested oven temperature — 350° or " 3 ".

When the potatoes are tender, press in the hollow of the hand so that they open on one side. Dish on a folded napkin with plenty of butter served separately or with pats inserted into the potato.

ROAST POTATOES

Wash and peel the required number of potatoes. Parboil for 10 minutes and drain. Place in a baking tin with melted dripping and roast in a moderate oven until nicely browned all over. They should be turned as required during the cooking. Drain free of fat and sprinkle with salt before serving.

If the roast potatoes are to accompany a joint, they may be cooked in the same pan, putting them in the required time before the meat will be ready. Roast potatoes cook in approximately 45-60 minutes.

An alternative way of roasting potatoes is as follows. It is a superior method resulting in very even browning:

Parboil the potatoes and, after draining, dip each one in melted butter or dripping. Arrange, without any more fat, on a baking sheet, sprinkle with salt and roast in a fairly hot oven.

Potatoes are not necessarily parboiled before roasting and sometimes too, they are dusted with flour to help them brown nicely.

FRIED POTATOES

There are many different varieties of fried potatoes, the name altering according to the manner in which they are cut. Different cutters are also sold, which make the preparation simpler and ensures evenness, which is essential to obtain uniform browning. The following are a few of the best known varieties of fried potato:

POTATO CHIPS, FRENCH FRIED POTATOES or " POMMES FRITES " are the most generally useful. The potatoes are cut into sticks approximately 1/4 inch square and 2-2 1/2 inches long.

POMMES PONT NEUF are rather larger, being cut approximately 1/3 inch square and 2-2 1/2 inches long. They are suitable to serve as an accompaniment to grilled meat.

Wash the chips well and dry in a clean cloth. Place in a frying basket and lower carefully into hot fat. Fry gently until cooked, but not coloured. Remove the basket of potatoes and reheat the fat to smoking point. Return the potatoes and cook until crisp and golden brown. Drain, sprinkle with salt and serve piled in a hot dish.

POTATO STRAWS, POMMES PAILLES and POMMES ALLUMETTES are cut much finer, like match-sticks or approximately 1/3 inch square. Only one frying is necessary.

GAME CHIPS or POTATO CRISPS are served with roast game and chicken, or with cocktails. The potatoes are cut into very thin slices — this is most successfully done if a mandoline is used. Wash in cold water to remove the surface starch and dry thoroughly. Fry in very hot fat until golden. Drain and serve sprinkled with salt.

Potato crisps will keep successfully if stored in an air-tight tin.

SAUTÉ POTATOES

Use cooked potatoes and cut into slices about 1/4 inch in thickness. Fry in shallow fat until nicely browned on both sides. Sprinkle with seasoning and chopped parsley and serve piled in a hot dish.

POTATO CROQUETTES

1/2 lb cooked potatoes	salt and pepper
1 oz butter or	1 egg yolk
margarine	

egg and breadcrumbs

Sieve the potatoes. Melt the butter in a saucepan and add the sieved potato. Season and add the egg yolk or half a whole egg well beaten. Mix all well together and turn on to a plate to cool. Divide into portions and shape into croquettes. Coat with egg and roll in breadcrumbs. Fry in hot fat until nicely browned. Avoid frying too many at one time, as the fat is cooled down so much that they tend to burst before they are golden. After frying, drain well and serve on a hot dish garnished with parsley.

DUCHESS POTATOES

1/2 lb cooked potatoes	1 egg yolk
1 oz butter or	1-2 tablespoonfuls milk
margarine	salt and pepper

a little grated nutmeg
beaten egg to brush

Sieve the potatoes. Melt the butter in a saucepan and add the prepared potato, together with the egg yolk and sufficient milk to bind all together. Season with salt, pepper and grated nutmeg and beat well.

Put this potato purée into a forcing bag with a large star pipe and pipe onto a greased tray into oblong shapes or swirls. Brush lightly with beaten egg and brown in a hot oven. Avoid making the duchess potatoes too small or overcooking them in the oven, otherwise the eating qualities of the dish is spoiled.

POMMES ANNA

approximately 1¹/₂ *lb*   *2 oz melted*
  potatoes   *butter*
              salt and pepper

Peel the potatoes and cut into thin slices, preferably using a mandoline. If a very neat appearance is desired, the potatoes may be trimmed into cylindrical shapes so that each slice has the same diameter—about the size of a penny.

Do not wash or store in water since the surface starch assists in forming the potatoes into a cake. Butter a charlotte mould or small cake tin generously. Arrange the sliced potatoes in circles, overlapping one another to cover the bottom of the tin. Place over a gentle heat and fry until golden on the under side. Then fill the mould with layers of sliced potato, reversing the overlap in each layer and adding seasoning as the work progresses, together with a little melted butter. When the mould is full, bake in a moderate oven until the potatoes are tender — approximately 1¹/₂-2 hours.

Suggested oven temperature — 400° or " 5 ".

Half-way through the cooking, remove from the oven and press the potatoes down in order to form a firm cake.

When ready, unmould onto a hot dish. It should have the appearance of a brown cake.

POMMES SAVOYARD

approximately 1¹/₂ *lb potatoes of uniform size*
1 small onion   *stock (or water)*

salt and pepper   1-1¹/₂ oz grated cheese
      a little butter or margarine

Butter a shallow oven dish generously. Peel and slice the potatoes thinly, but still retaining the shape of the whole potato. Arrange in the dish with the slices upright. Chop the onion finely and sprinkle between the potatoes. Add sufficient stock to cover the bottom of the dish amply. Sprinkle the cheese on top and flake the surface with butter. Bake for 1¹/₂-2 hours, adding a little more stock should this be necessary.

Suggested oven temperature—375° or " 3 ":

POMMES BOULANGÈRE

approximately 1¹/₂ *lb*   *2-3 cloves of garlic*
  potatoes   *3 oz grated cheese*
2-3 onions   *stock (or water)*
              salt and pepper

Butter an oven dish generously. Peel and slice the potatoes and onions thinly. Chop the garlic in a little salt. Then arrange in layers — potato, onion, garlic and cheese, seasoning as the work progresses. The last layers should be potato and cheese. Pour over sufficient stock to cover the bottom of the dish amply and flake with butter. Bake in a moderate oven for approximately 1¹/₂-2 hours or until the potatoes are tender.

Suggested oven temperature — 375° or " 3 ".

Serve in the dish in which it has been cooked, sprinkling with chopped parsley.

PURPLE SPROUTING BROCCOLI

Purple sprouting broccoli is one of the best vegetables available in the late winter and early spring. It is a member of the broccoli family and throws out tender purple-tipped shoots from the central stem. The shoots or stems should be tied in bunches and boiled quickly until tender. Dress with melted butter or a white or cheese sauce.

RED CABBAGE

Red cabbage is at its best in the autumn after the first frosts. It is generally pickled, but also makes an excellent hot vegetable.

RED CABBAGE with APPLES: *6 cups shredded red cabbage, 2 oz butter or bacon fat, 1/2 finely-chopped onion, 2 chopped apples, 3 tablespoonfuls brown sugar, salt, pepper, 3 tablespoonfuls vinegar and 1 tablespoonful caraway seeds (optional).*

Prepare the cabbage and melt the fat in a saucepan. Add the finely-chopped onion and sauté together for 10 minutes. Add the apple, sugar, seasoning, vinegar, caraway seeds and cabbage and cook together for 25 minutes or until tender. Stir occasionally.

SLOKE

Sloke is an edible seaweed found along parts of the coast or Ireland, as well as in Wales. It is described, very justly, as sea spinach and tastes extraordinarily like that vegetable. It, therefore, qualifies for inclusion in this chapter.

Sloke is brown when gathered, but turns a dark green when cooked. The cooking is a tedious process and it is generally sold prepared. All that is necessary is to heat it with a lump of melted butter and to season it with pepper. Sometimes a little lemon juice or vinegar is added. It is served like a vegetable, often with roast mutton or boiled bacon.

It may also be eaten cold with cold meat.

SPINACH AND SPINACH BEET

Spinach is available throughout the entire year in one of its many forms, but is at its best during the spring and summer. It is a bulky vegetable and approximately 2 lb is required to make a dish for four. The leaves need careful washing to rid them of grit and, if they are at all coarse, the centre rib should be removed.

CREAMED SPINACH: Put the prepared spinach into a saucepan with only the water which clings to the leaves. Cover the pan with a lid and cook until tender. Drain and press well. Either chop until fine or sieve and return to the pan. Add 1 or 2 spoonfuls of white sauce or cream and season highly with salt, pepper and a little sugar.

SWEET CORN

There is a saying in America that you may walk down the garden to cut the corn, but you must run back. Indeed, it is only at its best if cooked shortly after being picked. To judge its quality, press the grains with the nail. If the cob is in prime condition, the milky contents should ooze out immediately.

CORN ON THE COB: Remove the outer husk and the silk, but leave the innermost layer. Either boil the cobs for 20 minutes in salted water or bake in the oven for half-an-hour. Send to table on a napkin accompanied by pats of butter.

TOMATOES

Tomatoes are available throughout the year, but the best tomatoes are those which are just ripe and freshly picked. They are generally more acceptable uncooked, but may be fried, grilled, baked or stuffed or used in many composite dishes. Tomatoes are often improved if a little sugar is included in the seasoning, while chopped basil is to tomatoes as mint is to lamb.

TO SKIN TOMATOES: Immerse in boiling water for 10-20 seconds, or according to their ripeness, remove from the water and skin. The skin may also be removed by searing in the flame from a gas ring.

FRIED TOMATOES may be prepared in various ways:

Cut the tomatoes in two, season with salt, pepper and sugar and sprinkle with chopped basil or dust with the dried herb. Fry in butter or bacon fat.

Alternatively, peel and slice the tomatoes thickly. Either dip the pieces in seasoned flour, batter or pass through egg and crumbs and fry.

Small tomatoes may be fried whole.

GRILLED TOMATOES: Leave the tomatoes whole or cut in two. Brush with oil or melted butter. Season and cook under the grill.

BAKED TOMATOES: Whole or half tomatoes may be baked. Season appropriately and sprinkle with chopped basil or use the dried herb. Flake with butter or margarine, cover with a buttered paper and bake in a moderate oven until soft, but not broken.

TURNIPS

Young garden turnips come into season in the late spring and early summer and the leaves may be cooked and eaten as well as the root. Throughout the winter, the older turnip or swede makes a useful and inexpensive vegetable.

Turnips have a thick woody skin, which should be removed before cooking. Small turnips may be boiled whole or cut into fairly large pieces while the older turnips are also cut into blocks

for boiling. Serve garden turnips dressed with melted butter and chopped parsley or with a white sauce. Swedes may be served in the same way, but are more often mashed. A proportion of boiled potato mashed with them is an improvement — giving a drier purée.

SALADS

Salads vary tremendously from a simple affair of one vegetable, with appropriate dressing, to an elaborate combination of vegetables and fruit. All depend, however, for their success on the attention given to a few basic points.

In the first instance the ingredients should be of choice quality. Vegetables to be used raw should be fresh, well washed and dried with equal care, for the presence of water in any salad spoils it and prevents the dressing clinging. Vegetables enjoyed because of their crispness should be really crisp, and in this connection, the great advantage of a refrigerator as a means of refreshing and crisping green salad plants and celery should be exploited to the full.

The quality and suitability of the salad dressing is important too, be it a simple boiled dressing, mayonnaise or some variant of the classic French dressing.

Finally, the success of a salad depends largely on the originality and good taste of the cook, both in her choice of ingredients and in their presentation. As in other things, simplicity combined with quality should be a guiding principle.

Many of the following salads are suitable to be used in a mixed hors-d'oeuvre.

GREEN SALAD

This is sometimes also spoken of as a tossed salad.

Generally, it consists of well-washed, dry, crisp lettuce tossed, at the moment of serving, in French dressing. If the leaves are large, they should be torn into smaller pieces with the fingers and they should be kept covered in the refrigerator until required. In this way one can ensure complete crispness. Sometimes chopped chives or scallions may be added with advantage.

The seasoning included in the French dressing may also be varied to suit the dish which the salad is to accompany. For example, a little mustard may be added if the salad is to accompany roast beef or a grilled steak; sometimes the addition of garlic is welcomed, especially if the salad is to be eaten with lamb or beef; chopped herbs may be included or lemon juice used instead of vinegar if a very mild dressing is required.

A tossed green salad is a good accompaniment to many hot dishes as well as cold, notably roast chicken, lamb and beef. While it is essentially simple, attention to detail is of great importance.

Endive, chicory and watercress salads may be prepared in the same way.

TOMATO SALAD

Peel the tomatoes by immersing them in boiling water for 10-20 seconds, or according to their ripeness, remove from the water and skin.

Cut into slices, and marinade in French dressing sweetened with a little sugar and flavoured with chopped basil, parsley, chives, scallions or a scraping of onion juice. Dish simply and chill before serving.

If wished, tomato salad may be garnished with thinly-sliced rings of onion. An onion salad in its own right may be made in the same way.

TOMATO AND ORANGE SALAD

Combine an equal quantity of orange sections and quarters of peeled tomatoes. Marinade in French dressing sweetened with a little sugar and flavoured with a grating of lemon, chopped parsley or chives. Dish piled in a salad bowl and chill before serving.

GREEK SALAD

Use equal quantities of:
> *large tomatoes*
> *cucumber*
> *green peppers*
French dressing.

Peel the tomatoes and cut into eight or more wedges. Peel the cucumber and cut roughly into pieces.

Cut the pepper in two, remove the seeds and shred. Combine the vegetables and marinade with French dressing. Pile in a salad bowl, and chill in the refrigerator before serving.

POTATO SALAD

Potato salad is best if made from freshly-boiled potatoes. They should be cooked until only just tender so that they may be neatly sliced or cubed. Season well and toss while still warm in mayonnaise or a boiled dressing. In this way the dressing penetrates and flavours the potato.

Potato salad is also often made using two dressings. In the first instance the prepared potatoes are tossed while still warm in French dressing. Later, when they are cold, they are tossed in mayonnaise or a boiled dressing. Serve, piled in a dish and garnished with watercress or chopped parsley.

Cubed apples, celery or chopped gherkins may be incorporated in a potato salad with advantage.

WINTER SALAD

Use equal quantities of:
cooked beetroot, cooked potato, celery and apple salad dressing or mayonnaise.

Reserve a few slices of beetroot and some of the green from the inner stalks of celery for a garnish. Cut the remainder of the beet into dice. Cube the potato and apple also and slice the sticks of celery. Combine the vegetables, sprinkle with seasoning and toss in the salad dressing. Arrange neatly in a serving dish and garnish with the slices of beetroot and the pretty foliage from the celery.

Other cooked vegetables may be included in a winter salad such as cooked cauliflower sprigs, carrot or cooked haricot beans.

Chopped walnuts are an excellent addition.

BEETROOT SALAD

A beetroot salad should be made some time before it is required so that the beet may have time to absorb the dressing and mellow in flavour.

Slice the cooked beetrot thinly and season well with salt and freshly-ground pepper. Lay in a deep dish and pour over the following dressing:

Combine 3-4 tablespoonfuls vinegar, 1 tablespoonful olive oil, 2-3 finely-chopped cloves of garlic and 1 tablespoonful sugar.

Use sufficient to cover the beetroot and turn it in the mixture from time to time. Chill in the refrigerator before serving. If preferred, finely-chopped onion may be used instead of the garlic.

CUCUMBER SALAD

Cucumber may be peeled or not according to taste. Slice thinly and sprinkle with salt and pepper. Dress immediately with a French dressing.

Alternatively, the sliced cucumber may be sprinkled with salt and put aside for half-an-hour. Drain away the juice and toss the cucumber in French dressing made without salt.

Sometimes cucumber is cut into dice instead of thin slices.

CUCUMBER AND PINEAPPLE SALAD

Cubed cucumber combines well with pineapple pieces in a salad. Toss the mixture in either mayonnaise or a French dressing.

ORANGE SALAD

To be served with roast duck.

Grate a little of the zest from one of the oranges and set aside while the fruit is peeled and freed of all pith. Slice thinly or cut into sections free of membrane. Arrange in a glass dish, sprinkle with sugar and grated rind. Dress with a French dressing and put aside in a cool place before serving.

Garnish, if wished, with curled celery.

MUSHROOM SALAD

Choose firm white mushrooms for a salad and, after washing and drying, slice thinly. Toss in a French dressing made with oil, lemon juice, pepper and a little garlic if wished. The salt should not be added until the time of serving.

Garnish, if wished, with anchovy fillets.

COLE-SLAW

For this salad use the firm heart of a

white cabbage. Cut it in quarters, remove the centre stalk and shred as finely as possible. Put the prepared cabbage into ice-cold water and set aside for a time or even overnight. Drain and dry thoroughly. Diced apple, celery, a little finely-chopped onion, chopped walnuts or shredded carrot may be added, as wished, before tossing the mixture in mayonnaise or a cooked dressing.

If preferred, the shredded cabbage may be blanched for a minute in boiling water before using in the salad.

JELLIED BEETROOT

1 *packet of raspberry jelly made up to* 1 *pint*
with vinegar and boiling water
1-2 *cooked beetroot*
salt and pepper

Make up the jelly square with the vinegar and water. Dice the cooked beetroot and season with salt and pepper. Add to the jelly and put aside until showing signs of setting. Stir and pour into a suitable mould. When set, draw through hot water and turn out.

This salad looks particularly attractive if made using a border mould, when the centre may be filled with a contrasting salad mixture.

COLD STUFFED TOMATOES

Allow 1 tomato per person and 1 tablespoonful cubed cheese and a little mayonnaise or cooked dressing for every portion.

Remove a lid from the rounded end of each tomato and scoop out the pulp. Invert onto a plate to drain completely. Season the inside of the tomatoes with salt and pepper and fill with the cubed cheese tossed in salad dressing. Replace the lid and serve garnished with green salad material.

RICE SALAD

6 *oz Italian or Patna rice*	6-8 *anchovy fillets*
2-4 *cloves of garlic salt*	3 *tablespoonfuls cooked peas*
4-6 *tomatoes*	*mayonnaise or salad cream*

Cook and dry the rice and put aside to cool.

Chop the garlic very finely with the salt. Skin the tomatoes, remove the seeds and cut into shreds. Cut the anchovy fillets into small pieces. Add the garlic, tomatoes, anchovies and peas to the rice, season highly and toss the mixture in mayonnaise. Serve piled in a dish garnished with anchovies, peas, tomato or cress.

Alternatively, rice salad may be made with the addition of tinned pimento cut in shreds instead of the tomato. Shredded green and red peppers make another attractive, alternative addition.

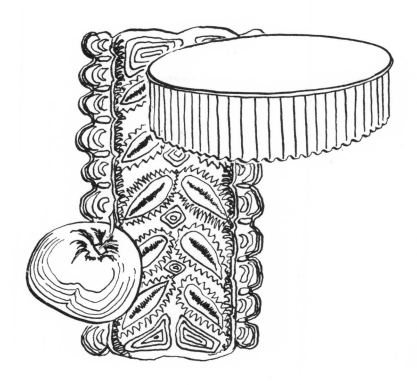

HOT AND COLD PUDDINGS

STEWED FRUIT

Generally 4 oz granulated sugar is allowed to each pound of fresh fruit though this may vary slightly. Dried fruit requires rather less, bulk for bulk, and it should be steeped over night in boiling water. The amount of water also varies according to the natural juiciness of the fruit and the purpose for which it is required.

Broadly, speaking, there are three methods of stewing fruit. The choice will depend on circumstances and personal preference:

1. A syrup of sugar and water is prepared. The fruit is laid in this and gently poached until tender but still retaining its shape.
2. The fruit, sugar and water are put in a pan and cooked gently together. By this method the fruit is more apt to pulp.
3. The fruit, sugar and water are put in a heat-proof dish, covered with a lid and cooked in a moderate oven for 20-30 minutes or until tender.

Additional flavourings may be added to fruit while it is being stewed such as cloves, cinnamon stick, or a strip of the zest of a lemon. Mixtures of fruit are also good, e.g. damsons combined with pineapple pieces, rhubarb with a little chopped preserved ginger or, a mixture of summer fruits such as raspberries, currants and gooseberries.

BAKED APPLES

Choose large apples of equal size. Wipe, core and make a cut in the skin round the centre of each apple. Rub with butter paper and place on a tin or heat-proof dish.

The centre of the apple may be filled in various ways, e.g. with sugar and cloves; a mixture of butter, sugar and grated lemon rind or ground cinnamon; dates or raisins and sugar.

Pour a little water around and bake in a moderate oven until tender. The actual time will vary from 30 minutes to an hour or longer, depending on the size of the apples and the oven temperature, but very slow cooking greatly improves the eating qualities of the dish.

FRUIT SALAD

Almost any kind of fruit may be used in a fruit salad such as apples, pears, oranges, bananas, grapes, apricots, peaches, melon, pineapple, raspberries, strawberries or currants. A proportion of tinned fruit may also be used, granadilla or passion fruit being particularly good.

In winter, dates, a little chopped preserved ginger or nuts make interesting additions. The salad may either be made from a great variety of fruits or merely using two or three.

The fruit should be peeled, pipped and cut into convenient-sized pieces.

The dressing for a fruit salad may consist of a heavy syrup flavoured if wished with cinnamon stick, lemon or orange rind and coloured by infusing the skins of purple grapes in it or by

using red colouring. Sometimes fruit juice, a sweet wine or liqueur are added.

Alternatively, the fruit may be layered with icing or castor sugar and set aside for some hours to give it time to dissolve and form a syrup with the fruit juice.

Fruit salad should be served very cold accompanied by cream.

GOOSEBERRY FOOL

1 *lb gooseberries*	*¹/₄ pint cream*
4 *oz granulated sugar*	or *a mixture of custard*
¹/₂ gill water	*and cream*

Top and tail the gooseberries. Wash and stew with the sugar and water until pulped. Sieve. Whip the cream and combine with the fruit. Serve in small glasses.

Other fruits such as strawberries, raspberries and apricots also make a good fruit fool. The two former should be used without cooking.

BAKED RICE PUDDING

1¹/₂ *oz Carolina rice*	1 *pint of milk*
1 *oz sugar*	*a knob of butter*
	nutmeg

Butter a pie-dish generously and into it put the rice and sugar. Pour in the milk, add a knob of butter and grate a little nutmeg over the top. Bake in a slow oven for 2-3 hours.

Suggested oven temperature — 325° or " 2 ". Baked sago and tapioca puddings are made in a similar way.

BAKED SEMOLINA PUDDING

1 *pint milk*	1 *egg*
1¹/₂ *oz semolina*	*flavouring such as*
1 *oz sugar*	*vanilla, orange,*
	lemon or nutmeg

Heat the milk in a saucepan, sprinkle in the semolina stirring all the time and cook gently for approximately 10 minutes stirring occasionally. Add the sugar and flavouring and allow to cool. Stir in the egg yolk. Whisk the egg white stiffly and fold into the mixture. Pour into a buttered pie-dish. Bake in a moderate oven for approximately 20-30 minutes.

Suggested oven temperature — 400° or " 6 ".

A baked ground rice pudding may be made in a similar way.

CORNFLOUR MOULD

1 *pint milk*	1 *oz sugar*
1¹/₂ *oz cornflour*	*colouring and flavouring as wished*

Heat three-quarters of the milk in a saucepan and use the remainder to blend the cornflour. Add to the hot milk stirring well, and bring to the boil. Boil gently until the cornflour is thoroughly cooked. This will take a minimum of three minutes. Add the sugar, colouring and flavouring as wished and pour into a wet mould. Cover and put aside to cool and set. When required turn out into a glass dish and serve accompanied by stewed fruit and cream.

BAKED CUSTARD

2 *eggs*	*a pinch of salt*
1 *oz sugar*	1 *pint of milk*
	nutmeg

Beat the eggs, sugar and salt together but avoid a froth. Heat the milk until nearly boiling and pour it slowly over the eggs. Strain into a greased pie-dish. Grate a little nutmeg over the top, place in bain-marie and bake in a moderate oven until set and lightly browned — approximately 1-1¹/₂ hours.

Suggested oven temperature — 350° or " 3 ".

Note: A richer custard may be made by adding 1-2 extra yolks or a third egg.

JUNKET

1 *pint milk*	*flavouring, e.g. vanilla,*
1 *teaspoonful rennet*	*coffee, chocolate,*
1 *oz castor sugar*	*colouring if wished.*

To finish: *whipped cream*

Heat the milk to blood temperature. Stir in the rennet, sugar, flavouring and colouring if used. Pour into warm glasses and leave in a warm place to set. Once set, put in a cool place until required. Serve with a little lightly-whipped cream poured over the top.

The junket may be decorated according to the flavour, i.e. with a grating of nutmeg, a sprinkling of instant coffee or a little grated chocolate.

CARRAGEEN MOSS JELLY

¹/₄ *oz carrageen moss*	2 *strips lemon rind*
1 *pint milk*	1 *oz sugar*

Trim and wash the moss. Steep in water for 10-15 minutes. Put into a saucepan with the milk and lemon rind. Bring it very slowly to the boil and cook until the carrageen coats the back of a wooden spoon. Add the sugar and when dissolved strain into a wet mould. Turn out when set and serve with stewed fruit.

CARRAGEEN MOSS BLANC-MANGE

¹/₄ *oz carrageen moss*	¹/₂ *oz sugar*
1 *pint milk*	1 *egg*
	2 *strips of lemon rind*

Cook the carrageen moss as in the previous recipe. Separate the yolk from the egg white. Beat the yolk with the sugar. Strain in the carrageen mixture stirring well. Fold in the stiffly-beaten egg white and pour into a glass dish.

Put in a cool place to set. Serve with stewed fruit and cream.

BREAD AND BUTTER PUDDING

2-3 *slices of thin*	$^1/_2$ *oz candied peel*
bread and butter	$^3/_4$ *pint milk*
$1^1/_2$ *oz sugar*	1-2 *eggs*
2 *oz sultanas*	*nutmeg*

Butter a pie-dish generously. Cut the bread and butter into small squares and layer in the pie-dish with the sugar and fruit. The last layer should be bread arranged buttered side uppermost. Heat the milk and pour over the beaten egg. Add the custard to the contents of the pie-dish, grate a little nutmeg over the top and leave to soak for $^1/_2$-1 hour. Bake in a moderate oven until the custard is set and the top browned and crusty — approximately 40-45 minutes.

Suggested oven temperature — 400° or " 6 ".

SPICED BREAD PUDDING

$^1/_4$ *lb stale crusts*	$^1/_2$ *teaspoonful mixed*
$1^1/_2$ *oz chopped suet*	*spice*
$1^1/_2$ *oz sugar*	$^1/_2$ *teaspoonful ground*
$1^1/_2$ *oz raisins*	*cinnamon*
$1^1/_2$ *oz currants*	*a little pepper*
$^1/_2$ *oz chopped peel*	$^1/_2$ *teaspoonful baking*
1 *egg (optional)*	*soda*
a little milk	

Soak the crusts in cold water, if necessary, overnight. Squeeze dry and crumble with a fork. Add the dry ingredients except the baking soda. Mix the baking soda with a little milk. Add the beaten egg and use to mix all to a fairly soft consistency.

Spiced bread pudding may be steamed or baked. If the latter, the mixture should be made more moist.

Steam $2^1/_2$ hours.
Bake $^3/_4$ hour.
Suggested oven temperature — 425° or " 6 ".

CABINET PUDDING

3-4 *sponge cakes*	$^1/_2$ *pint milk*
or 1 round of sponge	$1^1/_2$ *oz sugar*
cake	*sherry (or almond*
a few ratafia biscuits	*essence)*
or macaroons	*cherries and raisins to*
2 *eggs*	*decorate*

Line the bottom of a plain mould with paper and butter generously. Decorate with raisins and cherries. Cut the sponge cake into cubes and crush the biscuits. Combine and turn loosely into the mould. It should not be more than half full. Prepare a custard with the eggs, milk and sugar. Flavour with sherry (or almond essence) and pour into the mould. Leave to soak for $^1/_2$ hour. Steam gently until set — approximately 1 hour.

Serve hot accompanied by a whipped egg sauce.

SUMMER PUDDING

thin slices of bread
juicy stewed fruit such as blackcurrants, raspberries or blackberries and apples mixed

Line a basin or china soufflé case with slices of bread. Have the stewed fruit at boiling point and pour into the centre. Any trimmings of bread can be layered through the fruit. Finish with a circle of bread on top. Cover with a small plate and place a weight on top. Leave overnight in a cool place. Turn out onto a glass dish and serve with a custard sauce or cream.

ROLY-POLY

6 *oz suet pastry*	2-3 *tablespoonfuls*
	stiff jam

132

Roll the pastry into an oblong shape about $^1/_4$ inch in thickness. Spread the jam to within $^1/_2$ inch of the edge. Turn in the edges of the two long sides and roll up, damping the last edge of pastry. Dip a pudding cloth in boiling water, flour it well and tie the roly-poly in this. Plunge the pudding into a saucepan of fast-boiling water and boil for $1^1/_2$-2 hours. Remove the cloth and turn the roly-poly onto a hot dish.

Alternatively the roly-poly may be steamed in a straight-sided jam jar.

DELAWARE PUDDING

6 oz suet pastry
Filling:

1-2 apples	*2 oz demerara sugar*
2 oz currants	*$^1/_2$ teaspoonful mixed*
1 oz chopped candied	*spice*
peel	*the rind and juice of*
	$^1/_2$ lemon
	1 oz melted margarine

Chop the apples finely and combine with the other ingredients. Divide the pastry into 3 or 4 graduated pieces and roll out into circles. Put the smallest round of pastry into the bottom of a greased and sugared pudding bowl. Cover with a third of the filling and repeat, making the last layer pastry. Cover the basin with greased paper and steam for $2^1/_2$-3 hours.

Serve with a lemon sauce.

TREACLE PUDDING

$^1/_2$ lb flour or 4 oz	*2 oz castor sugar*
flour and 4 oz	*1 egg (optional)*
crumbs	*2 oz treacle (or mixture*
3 oz chopped suet	*of golden syrup and*
1 teaspoonful ground	*treacle)*
ginger	*$^1/_2$ teaspoonful baking*
$^1/_2$ teaspoonful salt	*soda*
milk (about 1 gill)	

Measure the dry ingredients except the baking soda into a bowl. Beat the egg and stir in the treacle. Moisten the baking soda with the milk. Add to the egg and treacle and use to mix all to a heavy dropping consistency. Turn into a greased pudding bowl. Cover with greased paper and steam for $2^1/_2$ hours. Serve with syrup sauce.

GINGER PUDDING

$^1/_2$ lb flour	*1 tablespoonful soft*
$^1/_2$ teaspoonful baking	*brown sugar*
soda	*3 oz margarine*
1 large teaspoonful	*2 large tablespoonfuls*
ground ginger	*golden syrup*
	buttermilk

Measure the dry ingredients into a bowl, crushing the lumps from the baking soda. Rub in the margarine. Mix to a stiff consistency with the golden syrup and buttermilk. Turn into a greased pudding bowl and steam for $2^1/_2$ hours.

Serve with syrup or a sweet white sauce.

GOLDEN PUDDING

$^1/_4$ lb flour	*2 oz soft brown sugar*
1 teaspoonful baking	*1-2 eggs*
powder	*2 tablespoonfuls golden*
$^1/_4$ lb crumbs	*syrup*
$^1/_4$ lb chopped suet	*milk*

Measure the dry ingredients into a bowl. Beat the eggs and stir in the golden syrup. Use together with milk as necessary, to mix all to a heavy dropping consistency. Pour into a greased bowl. Cover with greased paper and steam $2^1/_2$ hours.

Serve with lemon sauce.

MARMALADE PUDDING may be made in the same way substituting marmalade for the golden syrup. Serve with a sauce made with marmalade.

STEAMED CHOCOLATE PUDDING

4 oz butter or margarine	2 oz chocolate
4 oz castor sugar	1 tablespoonful water
2 eggs	4 oz flour
1/2 teaspoonful vanilla flavouring	1/2 teaspoonful baking powder

Cream the butter and sugar and gradually beat in the lightly-whisked eggs. Add the vanilla essence. Break the chocolate into small pieces and melt in the tablespoonful of water. Cool. Add alternately with the flour and baking powder. Turn into a well-greased mould, cover with greased paper and steam for 1 1/2 hours. Turn out and serve coated with chocolate sauce.

STEAMED COFFEE AND WALNUT PUDDING

4 oz butter or margarine	5 oz flour
4 oz castor sugar	1/2 teaspoonful baking powder
2 eggs	2 oz walnuts
1 tablespoonful coffee essence	a little milk if necessary

Cream the butter and sugar and gradually beat in the lightly-whisked eggs. Add the coffee essence. Stir in the flour and baking powder adding these in three or four portions. Lastly, add the chopped walnuts and a little milk if necessary. Turn the mixture into a greased mould, cover with greased paper and steam for 1 1/2 hours.

Serve accompanied by fudge sauce.

STEAMED ORANGE PUDDING

4 oz butter or margarine	the rind of one orange
4 oz castor sugar	5 oz flour
2 eggs	1/2 teaspoonful baking powder
	a little milk if necessary

Cream the butter and sugar and gradually beat in the lightly-whisked eggs. Add the grated orange rind. Stir in the flour and baking powder adding them in three or four portions. If necessary, add a little milk to keep the consistency slack. Turn into a greased mould, cover with greased paper and steam 1 1/2 hours.

Serve with orange sauce.

MADELEINES

2 oz butter or margarine	3 oz flour
2 oz castor sugar	1/4 teaspoonful baking powder
1 egg	a little milk

To finish: *raspberry jam and coco-nut*

Cream the butter and sugar and gradually beat in the lightly-whisked eggs. Stir in the flour and baking powder adding milk as necessary to keep the consistency slack. Divide into five greased dariole moulds. Bake in a fairly hot oven for approximately 20 minutes.

Suggested oven temperature—425° or " 6 ".

To Finish — heat the raspberry jam and use to brush the puddings. Roll in coco-nut and decorate with cherry and angelica.

Serve with raspberry jam sauce.

EVE'S PUDDING

3 oz butter or margarine	4 oz flour
3 oz castor sugar	1/2 teaspoonful baking powder
2 eggs	1 lb stewed apples

Cream the butter and sugar and gradually beat in the lightly-whisked eggs. Stir in the flour and baking powder.

Spread the stewed apples in the bottom of a pie-dish and cover with the cake mixture. Bake in a moderate oven for approximately 1 hour.

Suggested oven temperature — 375° or "5".

RHUBARB CRUMBLE

3/4 cup rolled oats *1/2 teaspoonful baking*
1/4 cup flour *powder*
3 oz butter or margarine
2 oz soft brown sugar

Filling:
approximately 1 lb prepared rhubarb
1 tablespoonful flour
3 tablespoonfuls soft brown sugar

Measure the rolled oats, flour and baking powder into a bowl. Cut and rub in the butter. Add the soft brown sugar. The mixture should resemble crumbs.

Combine the prepared rhubarb with the flour and soft brown sugar and arrange in a pie-dish. The dish should be approximately two-thirds full.

Sprinkle the crumb mixture over the top and bake in a moderate oven for 40-45 minutes.

Suggested oven temperature — 400° or "5".

DUTCH·APPLE CAKE

1/2 lb flour *4 oz butter or*
1 teaspoonful baking *margarine*
powder *2 oz castor sugar*
pinch of salt *milk*

Apple mixture:
3-4 apples
2 tablespoonfuls sugar
1 teaspoonful ground cinnamon

Measure the flour, baking powder and salt into a bowl. Rub in the butter. Add the sugar and mix to a stiff dough with the milk. Press into a deep pie-plate.

Peel and core the apples and slice into neat liths. Stick neatly into the foundation mixture and sprinkle with the

sugar and the ground cinnamon. Bake in a moderate oven for approximately 40 minutes.

Suggested oven temperature — 400° or "6".

FRUIT PIE

6 oz short crust or rich short crust pastry
Filling: *approximately 1 lb fruit and 4 oz granulated sugar*
Frosting: *white of egg and a little castor sugar*

Prepare the fruit as necessary and layer with the sugar in a pie-dish. The dish should be well filled. Roll out the pastry and use to cover the pie. Decorate the edge attractively. Bake in a quick oven for approximately 30-40 minutes.

Suggested oven temperature — 450° or "7".

Remove from the oven and brush over the top with slightly-beaten egg white. Dredge with castor sugar and return to the oven for a few minutes until nicely browned.

SPICED APPLE CAKE

Spiced pastry:
5 oz flour *2 1/2 oz butter or*
1/2 teaspoonful ground *margarine*
cinnamon *1 dessertspoonful castor*
a pinch of salt *sugar*
beaten egg to mix

Filling:
2 large apples *2 tablespoonfuls soft*
1/4 lb chopped dates *brown sugar*
2 tablespoonfuls water
1/2 teaspoonful ground cinnamon

Prepare the filling first:

Peel, core and slice the apples finely. Add the remainder of the ingredients and stew together to a smooth dry pulp. Cool.

Now prepare the pastry:

Measure the flour, spice and salt into a bowl. Cut and rub in the butter.

Add the sugar and mix all to a stiff paste with the beaten egg. Turn on to a floured surface and divide into two pieces of roughly two-thirds and one-third. Roll out the larger piece and use to line a 7 inch sandwich tin. Fill with the apple mixture and cover with the remainder of the pastry. Bake in a fairly hot oven for approximately 40-45 minutes.

Suggested oven temperature — 425º or " 6 ".

Turn out and use the underside as the top of the cake.

Serve thickly dusted with pink castor sugar.

SWISS TART

3 oz rich short crust pastry
Filling:

5-6 *apples*	6 *oz granulated sugar*
¹/₂ *gill water*	*the juice of* ¹/₂ *lemon*

Meringue:

2 *egg whites*	4 *oz castor sugar*

Decoration: *a little red-currant jelly*

Use the pastry to line a 6 inch flan ring and bake it blind for approximately 25-30 minutes.

Suggested oven temperature — 425º or " 6 ".

Make a syrup with the water, sugar and lemon juice. Peel, quarter and core the apples and poach carefully in the syrup. Use to fill the flan case, piling the apple high in the centre.

Whisk the egg whites until stiff. Place the bowl over a pan of hot water and gradually whisk in the sugar. Continue whisking until the mixture is very thick. Pipe in stars to cover the top of the flan. Dust with sugar and bake in a cool oven until set and golden brown — about 20 minutes.

Suggested oven temperature — 325º or " 2 ".

A final decoration may be given to the meringue by piping a bead of red-currant jelly on each point.

AMERICAN FRUIT PIE

6 oz rich short crust pastry
Filling:

1 *oz chopped candied peel*	1 *finely-chopped apple*
2 *oz sultanas*	1 *teaspoonful grated lemon rind*
2 *oz raisins*	2 *egg yolks*
2 *oz currants*	2 *oz castor sugar*
1 *oz chopped almonds*	

Meringue:

2 *egg whites*	2 *oz castor sugar*

Use the pastry to line a 9 inch heat-proof plate. Prick well and bake in a moderately-heated oven until just beginning to colour.

Suggested oven temperature — 425º or " 6 ".

Combine the ingredients for the filling and spread over the pastry. Whisk the egg whites until stiff, beat in half the sugar adding it gradually and fold in the remainder lightly. Use to cover the fruit mixture, spreading the meringue lightly and attractively. Dust with castor sugar and bake for approximately ¹/₂ hour in a cooler oven.

Suggested oven temperature — 325º or " 2 ".

Serve with a lemon sauce.

APPLE AMBER

4 oz rich short crust pastry
Filling:

4-5 *apples*	3-4 *oz granulated sugar*
the rind and juice of	
1 *lemon*	2 *egg yolks*
1¹/₂ *oz butter or margarine*	

Meringue:

2 *egg whites*   3 *oz castor sugar*

Use the pastry to line a pie-dish and decorate the rim. Peel and slice the apples and stew to a pulp with the rind and juice of the lemon, the butter and sugar. Beat the mixture until smooth, or sieve and then add the egg yolks. Pour into the pastry case when cold and bake in a moderate oven for 30-40 minutes.

Suggested oven temperature — 425° or "6".

Make a meringue with the egg whites and the sugar and pile attractively on top. Dust with sugar and return to a cool oven until set and golden — about 20 minutes.

Suggested oven temperature — 325° or "2".

If wished, the meringue may be decorated with cherry and angelica.

Note: Other fruits, stewed to a pulp may be used instead of apples. Should a very juicy type be chosen a few bread or cake crumbs may be added to adjust the consistency.

FRENCH APPLE TART

3 *oz rich short crust pastry*

Filling:

4-5 *apples*	1 *oz butter or margarine*
the rind of ¹/₂ *lemon*	4 *oz granulated sugar*

Decoration:

1 *apple*	*sugar to dust*
a knob of butter —	*a little red-currant*
melted	*jelly*

Prepare the filling first:

Reserve the best apple for the decoration. Peel and slice the remainder and stew to a pulp with the grated lemon rind, the butter and sugar. Cool.

Use the pastry to line a 6 inch flan ring. Prick and fill three parts full with the apple pulp. Peel, quarter and core the apple reserved for the decoration and cut into neat liths. Arrange these slices in a circle around the top of the flan overlapping them neatly and covering the apple pulp entirely. Brush with melted butter and sprinkle with sugar. Bake in a moderate oven until the pastry is cooked and the apples golden brown — approximately 30-40 minutes.

Suggested oven temperature — 425° or "6".

Before serving, the centre may be decorated further with a little red-currant jelly.

GATEAU JALOUSIE

4-6 *oz puff pastry*

2-3 *tablespoonfuls raspberry jam or a cup of stewed apple*

a little egg white and castor sugar

Cut the pastry into two pieces one a little larger than the other. Roll the smaller piece to an oblong about 4 inch wide and ¹/₁₀ inch thick. Trim the edges and place on a damp baking sheet. Damp the edges and run a narrow strip of pastry round the four sides. Spread the centre with jam or stewed apple. Roll the second piece of pastry to an oblong a little larger than the base. Fold in two by the length and cut with a sharp knife across the fold. The cuts should be ¹/₄ inch apart and 1 inch in from the edges. Open out and lift on-to the base. Press the edges together and flake with a knife. Bake in a hot oven for approximately 25 minutes.

Suggested oven temperature — 450° or "7".

Remove from the oven when brown and brush with a little beaten egg white and sprinkle immediately with castor sugar.

Return to the oven for a few minutes to set the glaze.

CUSTARD TART

6 oz short crust pastry
Custard filling:

¹/₂ pint milk	*1 oz castor sugar*
1 dessertspoonful	*2 egg yolks*
cornflour	*1 egg white*
	nutmeg

First prepare the custard filling for the tart. Blend the cornflour with a little of the milk and heat the remainder. Add the cornflour to the hot milk and stir carefully until boiling. Cook for a few minutes. Put the yolks and the white of egg into a bowl with the sugar and work them together with a wooden spoon until creamy. Then pour the milk and cornflour slowly onto them, stirring all the time. Cover and put aside to cool.

Use the pastry to line a flan ring or a deep pie-plate. Prick. Fill with the custard, grate a little nutmeg over the top and bake in a moderate oven until the pastry is thoroughly cooked and the custard a golden brown. This will take approximately 30-40 minutes.

Suggested oven temperature — 400° or " 5 ".

SYRUP TART

8 oz short crust pastry
Filling:

3-4 *tablespoonfuls*	*a little grated lemon*
golden syrup	*rind*
2 *tablespoonfuls*	*a squeeze of lemon*
breadcrumbs	*juice*

Use approximately ²/₃ of the pastry to line a heat-proof plate. Combine the ingredients for the filling and spread over the pastry. Roll out the remainder of the pastry and cut into narrow strips about ¹/₄ inch wide. Lay across the tart in a trelliswork pattern. Damp the edges and lay a final strip around the outer rim. Flake or pinch around the edge as in decorating shortbread. Bake in a moderately hot oven for approximately 30-35 minutes.

Suggested oven temperature — 450° or " 7 ".

Lower the heat once the pastry has set.

NORFOLK TREACLE TART

4 oz rich short crust pastry
Filling:

4 *tablespoonfuls*	2 *tablespoonfuls*
golden syrup	*cream*
¹/₂ *oz butter or*	1 *egg*
margarine	
	a little grated lemon rind

Use the pastry to line a flan ring and prick well. Warm the golden syrup and the butter gently together. Stir in the cream, the beaten egg and a little grated lemon rind. Pour into the flan case and bake in a moderate oven for approximately 30 minutes or until the pastry is crisp and the filling set.

Suggested oven temperature — 400° or " 5 ".

BUTTERSCOTCH TART

4 oz rich short crust pastry
Filling:

2 *oz butter or*	¹/₂ *pint milk*
margarine	2 *egg yolks*
6 *oz soft brown sugar*	1 *teaspoonful vanilla*
2 *oz flour*	*flavouring*

Meringue:

3 *egg whites*	4 *oz castor sugar*

Use the pastry to line a heat-proof plate and decorate the edge. Prick and bake in a fairly hot oven until light brown and crisp.

Suggested temperature — 425º or "6".

Meanwhile prepare the filling:

Melt the butter, add the brown sugar and cook together to brown and develop a butterscotch flavour. Cool. Stir in the flour and milk. Bring to the boil stirring all the time and cook for a few minutes. Add the yolks and the vanilla flavouring and pour into the pastry case. Make the meringue from the three egg whites and the castor sugar and pile lightly on top. Dust with castor sugar and brown lightly in a slow oven.

Suggested oven temperature — 325º or "2".

LEMON MERINGUE PIE

4 oz rich short crust pastry

Filling:

1 *oz cornflour*	2 *oz castor sugar*
1/4 *pint water*	1 *oz butter or*
rind and juice of 1	*margarine*
large lemon	2 *egg yolks*

Meringue:

3 *egg whites*	4 *oz castor sugar*

Line a heat-proof plate with the pastry and decorate the edge. Prick and bake in a moderate oven until a light golden brown colour.

Suggested oven temperature — 425º or "6".

Meanwhile prepare the filling:

Blend the cornflour with the water and add the lemon rind and juice. Bring to the boil stirring all the time, and cook for 3-4 minutes. Cool a little and add the sugar, butter and egg yolks. Spread over the pastry. Whisk the egg whites until dry and stiff. Whisk in three teaspoonfuls of sugar gradually and lightly fold in the remainder. Pile the meringue on top of the pie. Dust with sugar and

return to a cool oven until set and golden —about 30 minutes.

Suggested oven temperature—325º or "2"

APPLE CHARLOTTE

4 apples	*the rind and juice of*
4 oz granulated	1 *lemon*
sugar	*thin slices of bread*
a little water if	*2-3 oz melted butter or*
necessary	*margarine*

Stew the apples to a thick pulp with the sugar and the grated rind and juice of a lemon. Add water only if necessary.

Butter a plain mould and dust with sugar. Remove the crusts from the bread and cut into fingers about 1¹/₄ inch wide and the length equal to the depth of the mould. Dip in melted butter and use to line the sides, overlapping slightly. Cut two rounds of bread for the top and bottom of the mould. Dip in melted butter and put the round for the bottom in position. Fill the mould with the stewed apple and place the last round of bread on top. Bake in a fairly hot oven for approximately 40 minutes or until well browned.

Suggested oven temperature—450º or "7".

Cool a little before unmoulding and dust with castor sugar.

Note: Sometimes it is considered an improvement to add two egg yolks to the apple mixture before using it to make up the apple Charlotte.

BREAD AND JAM FRITTERS

6 slices of bread cut from a sandwich pan
butter and raspberry jam

Batter:

6 *oz flour*	¹/₄ *teaspoonful baking*
¹/₄ *teaspoonful*	*soda*
salt	*water*

Butter the slices of bread and make into decker sandwiches using three slices of bread and two layers of jam to each round. Remove the crusts and cut each round into three oblong sandwiches. Combine the flour, salt and baking soda crushing the lumps from the latter. Mix to a creamy batter with water. Dip the jam sandwiches in this and drop into hot deep fat. Fry until golden brown, turning when necessary. Drain and toss in castor sugar.

FRUIT FRITTERS

Apples, bananas, oranges, tangerines, pears and strawberries are among the fruits suitable for fritters and often a variety is used.

Batter:

6 *oz flour*	$^1/_4$ *teaspoonful baking*
$^1/_4$ *teaspoonful*	*soda*
salt	*water*

The fruit should be prepared according to type and either cut into rings or segments.

Combine the flour, salt and baking soda, crushing the lumps from the latter. Mix to a creamy batter with water. Dip the pieces of fruit into this and fry in hot deep fat. Drain well and toss in castor sugar.

BAKED LEMON PUDDING

1 *oz butter or*	*the rind and juice of*
margarine	1 *lemon*
6 *oz castor sugar*	2 *eggs*
	2 *oz flour*
	1 *gill milk*

Melt the butter and beat in the sugar, lemon rind and juice. Separate the yolks from the egg whites and add to the first mixture. Beat well. Add the flour alternately with the milk and lastly fold in the stiffly-beaten egg whites.

Pour into a greased pie-dish and leave for approximately $^1/_2$ hour before baking.

Set the pie-dish in a larger dish of cold water and bake in a very moderate oven for 45 minutes.

Suggested oven temperature — 375° or " 3 ".

The mixture should separate into a light cake layer with a lemon curd mixture underneath.

PINEAPPLE MERINGUE PUDDING

1 *tin pineapple*	$1^1/_2$ *oz flour*
pieces	$^1/_2$ *pint milk*
$1^1/_2$ *oz butter or*	$1^1/_2$ *oz castor sugar*
margarine	2 *egg yolks*

Meringue:

2 *egg whites*	3-4 *oz castor sugar*

Drain the pineapple and measure $^1/_4$ pint of the juice. Make a roux with the butter and flour. Gradually stir in the milk and the pineapple juice. Bring to the boil and cook for 3-4 minutes. Stir in the pineapple pieces, sugar and yolks. Pour into a greased pie-dish and bake in a moderate oven until set — about 30 minutes.

Suggested oven temperature — 425° or " 6 ".

Make a meringue with the egg whites and the sugar and pile attractively on top. Dust with sugar and return to a cool oven until set and golden — about 20 minutes.

Suggested oven temperature — 325° or " 2 ".

QUEEN OF PUDDINGS

$^1/_2$ *pint milk*	*the grated rind of* 1
1 *oz butter or*	*lemon*
margarine	1 *oz castor sugar*
2 *oz breadcrumbs*	2 *egg yolks*
	2 *tablespoonfuls raspberry jam*

Meringue:

2 *egg whites*   3 *oz castor sugar*

Heat the milk and butter and pour over the breadcrumbs. Leave to soak for a short time. Stir in the grated lemon rind, sugar and yolks. Pour into a greased pie-dish and bake in a moderate oven until set—about 30 minutes.

Suggested oven temperature—425° or " 6 ".

Spread the raspberry jam over the top. Whip the egg whites until stiff, fold in the sugar and pile on the top of the pudding. Dust with castor sugar and return to a slow oven until the meringue is dry and lightly browned.

Suggested oven temperature—325° or " 2 ".

BAKED CHOCOLATE MERINGUE PUDDING

1/2 *pint milk*	1 *oz sugar*
1 1/2 *oz grated chocolate or chocolate powder*	1 *teaspoonful vanilla flavouring*
1 *oz butter or margarine*	2 *tablespoonfuls cream (optional)*
2 *oz breadcrumbs*	2 *egg yolks*

Meringue:

2 *egg whites*   3 *oz castor sugar*

Heat the milk, grated chocolate and butter together. Pour over the breadcrumbs and leave to soak for a short time. Stir in the sugar, vanilla, cream and egg yolks. Pour into a greased pie-dish and bake in a moderate oven until set—about 30 minutes.

Suggested oven temperature—425° or " 6 ".

Whisk the egg whites until stiff. Fold in the sugar and pile on top of the pudding. Dust with sugar and return to a cool oven until the meringue is dry and lightly browned.

Suggested oven temperature—325° or " 2 ".

PEAR CONDÉ

2 *oz Carolina rice*	1 *tablespoonful granulated sugar*
1 *pint milk*	
1/2 *gill unsweetened condensed milk*	
5-6 *half pears (tinned or stewed)*	

Glaze:

1/2 *pint pear juice*	*pink colouring*
2-3 *teaspoonfuls arrowroot*	

Decoration: *whipped cream, cherry and angelica.*

Cook the rice in the milk until thick. Add the sugar and fold in the stiffly-beaten unsweetened condensed milk. Divide into individual glasses. Put aside to cool and firm.

Arrange a half pear on top of each portion. Thicken the pear juice with the blended arrowroot. Cook thoroughly, and colour pink. Use to glaze the pears. When cold, pipe with rosettes of whipped cream and decorate with cherry and angelica.

CARAMEL CUSTARD

1/2 *pint milk*	2 *eggs and* 1 *egg yolk*
1 *oz castor sugar*	*vanilla flavouring*

Caramel:

2 *oz granulated sugar*	*a pinch of cream of tartar*
1/4 *gill water*	

Begin by making the caramel:

Put the sugar and water into a small, strong saucepan and stir until dissolved. Stir in the cream of tartar. Remove the spoon. Wash down the sides of the pan with a pastry brush dipped in water. Bring to the boil and boil gently until a rich golden brown. Use immediately to line a plain mould.

Heat the milk and sugar. Beat the eggs a little, but without making them frothy. Add the hot milk. Add vanilla flavouring and strain into the prepared mould. Set in a larger tin of cold water and bake in a moderate oven until set.

Suggested oven temperature — 350° or " 3 ".

Preferably leave until cold before turning out onto a glass dish. Any caramel remaining in the mould or in the saucepan should be melted down with a little water and poured round.

OMELETTE SOUFFLÉE

2 *yolks*	2-3 *egg whites*
1 *teaspoonful castor sugar*	¹/₂ *oz butter or olive oil*
	a little warm jam

Beat the yolks and the sugar together. Whisk the egg whites until very stiff and fold in the yolks. Melt the butter in an omelet pan and when gently heated, pour in the egg mixture. Cook slowly until nicely browned on the underside. Cook the upper side under a gently-heated grill or in the oven. When set and showing signs of shrinking at the edges, turn onto a sugared paper. Make an incision in the centre. Spread with a little jam and fold in two.

Dust with sugar and serve immediately.

CHOCOLATE SOUFFLÉ (HOT)

2 *oz chocolate*	1 *oz castor sugar*
1 *gill milk*	2 *eggs*
³/₄ *oz butter or margarine*	1 *teaspoonful vanilla flavouring*
³/₄ *oz flour*	¹/₂ *pint chocolate sauce*

Break up the chocolate and dissolve in milk.

Melt the butter, add the flour and cook together for a few minutes. Add the milk and cook thoroughly, stirring all the time. Cool a little and add the sugar, flavouring and the two yolks, beating them well in. Lastly fold in the stiffly-beaten egg whites. Turn the mixture into a prepared soufflé tin and steam gently for approximately 25 minutes.

When set, turn out and coat with chocolate sauce.

Alternatively, the mixture may be baked in a soufflé case in a moderate oven for 20 minutes.

Suggested oven temperature — 400° or " 6 ".

SPONGE FLAN WITH PEARS

Sponge:

2 *eggs*	2 *oz castor sugar*
	2 *oz flour*

Decoration for sides of the sponge flan:
a little toasted coco-nut
1 *tablespoonful apricot jam*
Filling:

1 *medium tin of pears*	2-3 *teaspoonfuls*
¹/₂ *pint pear juice*	*arrowroot*
	pink colouring

Prepare the sponge mixture in the usual way and bake in a sponge flan tin for approximately 20 minutes.

Suggested oven temperature — 400° or " 6 ".

Heat the apricot jam and brush over the sides of the flan. Finish with a coating of toasted coco-nut.

Drain the juice from the pears and use a little to soak the sponge flan. Arrange the half pears attractively in the centre. Thicken half a pint of the juice with the blended arrowroot, cooking the mixture thoroughly. Colour pink and use to glaze the pears.

If wished, finish with a piping of whipped cream.

COLD CHOCOLATE SPONGE

3 *gills unsweetened condensed milk*	*a little vanilla flavouring*

1 *tablespoonful cocoa* 4 *tablespoonfuls*
1 *dessertspoonful*   *castor sugar*
  coffee essence $^1/_2$ *oz gelatine*
     2 *tablespoonfuls water*

Whisk the unsweetened condensed milk until thick. Whisk in the cocoa, coffee essence, and sugar vanilla flavouring. Dissolve the gelatine in the water and, when hot enough to sting the little finger when tested, whisk into the chocolate mixture. Pour into a glass dish and put aside to set.

Decorate by piping with whipped cream and with a little chocolate vermicelli.

COLD LEMON SPONGE

1 *packet lemon*   *the rind and juice of*
  jelly $^1/_2$ *lemon*
$^1/_2$ *pint boiling*   3 *gills unsweetened*
  water   *condensed milk*

Melt the jelly in the boiling water. Add the grated lemon rind and juice and put aside to cool. When on the point of setting, whip the tinned milk until thick and gradually beat in the jelly. Pour into a mould when light and thick. When set pass through hot water and turn out.

If wished, the mould may first be decorated with a little plain coloured jelly.

LEMON EGG JELLY

2 *lemons* $^1/_2$ *oz gelatine*
$^1/_2$ *pint water*,   2 *eggs*
    4 *oz granulated sugar*

Grate the lemons and squeeze the juice. Measure the latter and make up to a $^1/_4$ pint with water. Put the rind, juice, water, sugar and gelatine into a saucepan. Stir until dissolved, then bring to the boil. Cool a little. Beat the eggs, then pour on the gelatine mixture, stirring

all the time. Strain and mould. When set pass through hot water and turn out. Pipe with whipped cream if wished.

PRUNE AND BANANA MOULD

6 *oz prunes*   1 *packet wine or*
2 *inch cinnamon*   *raspberry jelly*
  stick   1-2 *bananas*

Steep the prunes overnight in boiling water. Next day, add the cinnamon stick and stew gently until tender. Strain off the juice and stone and chop the prunes. Make up the jelly square with prune juice and boiling water as necessary to give one pint. Add the prunes and the sliced bananas and mould. When set, pass through hot water and turn out. Pipe with whipped cream if wished.

NORWEGIAN CREAM

3 *eggs* $^1/_4$ *oz gelatine*
2 *oz castor sugar* $^1/_2$ *gill water*
   the rind and juice of 1 *orange*

To decorate:
2-3 *tablespoonfuls*   *whipped cream*
  raspberry jam

Separate the yolks from the egg whites. Add the sugar to the former and whisk together until creamy and light. Gradually beat in the orange rind and juice. Dissolve the gelatine in the water. Whisk the egg whites until stiff. When the gelatine is hot add it to the yolk mixture. Fold in the egg whites and when beginning to set, pour all into a glass dish. Put aside to set.

Sieve the raspberry jam and spread over the top of the pudding. Decorate with whipped cream.

APPLE SNOW

approximately 6 *small*   *raspberry jam*
  sponge cakes

Custard:

$1/2$ *pint milk*	2 *egg yolks*
rind of $1/2$	1 *dessertspoonful*
lemon	*castor sugar*

Snow:

2 *baked apples*	2 *oz castor sugar*
2 *egg whites*	*juice of 1 lemon*

Split the sponge cakes and sandwich with raspberry jam. Cut up as for trifle and arrange in a glass dish.

Prepare the custard in the usual way and use to soak the sponge cake.

Sieve the baked apples and add the lemon juice. Whisk the egg whites until very stiff and gradually beat in the apple and sugar adding these alternately. Pile lightly on top of the sponge foundation and decorate with a sprinkling of green cake decoration.

RASPBERRY SNOW

1 *sponge cake*	2 *tablespoonfuls*
1 *tin of raspberries*	*raspberry jam*

Custard:

$1/2$ *pint milk*	1 *dessertspoonful*
2 *egg yolks*	*castor sugar*
	vanilla flavouring

Snow:

$1/2$ *packet raspberry*	2 *egg whites*
jelly	

Split the sponge cake and sandwich with raspberry jam. Cut as for trifle and combine with the raspberries. Arrange in a glass dish. Make the custard in the usual way and use to soak the sponge.

Make up the raspberry jelly with boiling water to give half a pint. Put aside until beginning to thicken. Whisk the egg whites until stiff and gradually beat in the jelly. Continue whisking until the mixture will stand in peaks. Pile attractively on top of the sponge foundation and put aside in a cool place until set.

TRIFLE

1 *sponge cake*
raspberry jam
a few ratafia or macaroon biscuits
sherry or a mixture of sherry and brandy used in
  the proportion:
  1 *gill sherry*
  3 *tablespoonfuls brandy*

Custard:

$1/2$ *pint milk*	2 *egg yolks*
1 *dessertspoonful*	*vanilla*
castor sugar	*flavouring*
$1/2$ *pint whipped cream*	
a few almonds blanched and split	

Split the sponge cake, spread with raspberry jam and cut into suitable pieces. Crush the biscuits roughly. Combine with the sponge and pile in a glass dish. Dabble with sherry so as to distribute the flavour evenly. The foundation should be light and moist without being sodden.

Make the custard in the usual way and use to give the final soaking to the sponge. Cover and put aside until cool. The trifle is all the better for prolonged soaking at this stage.

Decorate by piling lightly-whipped cream in the centre.

Stick the split almonds over the surface and sprinkle with a few ratafia biscuits.

Sometimes trifle is decorated with spun sugar.

MERINGUE BASKETS

4 *egg whites*	*vanilla flavouring*
$8^1/2$ *oz icing sugar*	
fruit salad	
whipped cream	

Whisk the egg whites until stiff. Place the bowl over a pan of hot water and gradually beat in the sieved icing sugar. Continue whisking until the mixture will hold its shape. Whisk in the vanilla flavouring.

Transfer the meringue to a bag fitted with a large star pipe.

Pipe onto prepared trays to form round baskets. Make the base in the form of a spiral, beginning in the centre and finish round the edge with one or two rows of stars. Dust with sugar and dry off in a slow oven.

Suggested oven temperature — 300° reduced to 200° or "$1/4$".

When required, fill with fruit salad and decorate with whipped cream. If wished, the basket may be completed with a handle of angelica.

PAVLOVA

3 *egg whites*   6 *oz castor sugar*
1 *small teaspoonful vinegar*
Lemon cream filling:
3 *egg yolks*   *the grated rind and juice*
3 *oz castor sugar*   *of 1 lemon*
whipped cream
toasted flaked almonds and cherries

Line a baking tray with greaseproof paper. Grease. Hold under the cold tap for a moment and shake off any surplus water.

Whisk the egg whites until very stiff. Whisk in three teaspoonfuls castor sugar adding them one at a time and beating well between each addition. Fold in the remainder of the sugar together with the vinegar. Turn the meringue on-to the prepared tray and shape into a round cake about $1\frac{1}{2}$ inch deep.

Dust with sugar and bake in a slow oven for approximately $1\frac{1}{4}$ hours.

Suggested oven temperature — 325° for $3/4$ hour and "off" for half-an-hour or

"1" for $3/4$ hour and "$1/2$" for half-an-hour.

When the meringue is nearly baked prepare the lemon filling:

Beat the yolks with the sugar until creamy and light. Beat in the lemon rind and juice and transfer all to a small saucepan. Cook gently, stirring all the time until the mixture thickens.

Spread the lemon mixture on top of the cake of meringue and swirl lightly-whipped cream on top. Sprinkle with a little toasted flaked almonds and decorate with whole cherries.

Note: Pavlova may be made with other fillings instead of the lemon cream mixture. For example, fruit salad, sliced strawberries and sugar or fresh raspberries would all be suitable.

PEACH VACHERIN

3 *egg whites*   6 *oz castor sugar*
a pinch of salt
Filling:
1 *tin sliced peaches*   *whipped cream*
Decoration: *cherries, angelica leaves and flaked almonds*

Line three baking trays with greaseproof paper and on each draw a circle round a small sandwich tin. Grease.

Whisk the egg whites with a pinch of salt until very stiff. Gradually beat in the castor sugar. Transfer to a forcing bag fitted with a rose pipe. Pipe out to give three circles — two in the form of a spiral and one trellised and finished round the edge with stars. Decorate the trellised layer with quarters of cherries and angelica leaves arranged at intervals on the border of stars and sprinkle in between with flaked almonds. Dust all three layers with sugar and bake in a very moderately-heated oven until dry and a light golden brown.

Suggested oven temperature — 300º reduced to 200º or "¹/₄".

When required put together with the fruit (drained free of juice) and whipped cream.

APPLES ROSEBERRY

1 lb apples	8 oz castor sugar
1¹/₂ gills water	1 gill cream
¹/₂ stick of cinnamon	2 egg whites
1 orange	pink colouring
1 lemon	¹/₂ oz gelatine
	¹/₂ gill water

Decoration: ¹/₂ pint jelly

Decorate the bottom of a mould with a thin layer of a pink jelly — the colour should be fairly strong. Put aside to set.

Stew the apples with the water, cinnamon stick and the grated rind of the orange and lemon. Sieve. Measure and make up to half a pint if this should be necessary. Add the juice of the orange and lemon and the sugar. Lightly whisk the cream. Stir in the apple mixture and fold in the stiffly-beaten egg whites. Lastly add the gelatine dissolved in the water. Colour pink and mould when beginning to show signs of setting.

When set, pass through hot water and turn out.

Decorate with a little chopped jelly and whipped cream.

Note: The egg whites may be omitted if wished.

CHARLOTTE RUSSE

¹/₂ pint pink jelly	1 packet boudoir biscuits
Filling:	
2 eggs	2 tablespoonfuls water
1 gill milk	1 gill cream
2¹/₂ oz castor sugar	3 tablespoonfuls sherry
¹/₄ oz gelatine	(or other flavouring if preferred)

Line the bottom of a plain mould with a thin layer of jelly. When set, decorate the sides with the boudoir biscuits. These may either be left plain or dipped in melted jelly or sherry to soften them a little before use. In addition they may require trimming so that they fit well.

Make a custard with the yolks, milk and sugar. Dissolve the gelatine in the water and add to the custard before it is quite cold. Add the sherry or any other flavouring preferred. Fold in the stiffly-beaten egg whites and the lightly-whipped cream. Mould when this begins to thicken. Put aside to set.

Dip the mould into hot water and unmould on to a glass dish. Decorate with a little chopped jelly round the base.

LEMON SOUFFLÉ (COLD)

2 eggs	¹/₄ oz gelatine
1 lemon	¹/₄ gill water
	2 oz castor sugar
	whipped cream to decorate

Separate the yolks from the egg whites. Whisk the yolks with the grated lemon rind and the sugar until creamy and light. Gradually beat in the lemon juice. Dissolve the gelatine in the water and, when hot, add to the lemon mixture. Fold in the stiffly-beaten egg whites and pour into a prepared 4¹/₂ inch soufflé case.

When set remove the paper band and decorate the top with whipped cream, or as wished.

MILANAISE SOUFFLÉ

3 eggs	8 oz castor sugar
the rind and juice of	¹/₂ pint cream
2¹/₂ lemons	¹/₂ oz gelatine
	¹/₂ gill water

Separate the yolks from the egg whites.

To the yolks add the rind and juice of the lemons and the sugar. Place the bowl over a pan of hot water and whisk until creamy and light. Remove from the heat and cool. Half whip the cream. Fold into the lemon mixture. Dissolve the gelatine in the water and add when hot. Lastly, fold in the stiffly-beaten egg whites and, when beginning to thicken, pour into a prepared 6¼ inch soufflé case.

When set remove the paper band and decorate the top as wished.

CHOCOLATE PROFITEROLES

choux pastry   *whipped cream*
Chocolate sauce:
4 oz dark chocolate   *1 teaspoonful arrowroot*
¼ pint water   *1 teaspoonful vanilla*
1 tablespoonful castor   *flavouring*
  sugar   *2 tablespoonfuls cream*
              ½ oz butter

Put the choux pastry out in teaspoonfuls onto a greased tray. Bake for approximately 20 minutes in a moderately hot oven.

Suggested oven temperature — 425° or " 6 ".

When cool fill with whipped cream and pile in a glass dish.

Dissolve the chocolate in the water. Add the sugar and simmer very gently for 15 minutes. Thicken with the arrowroot blended with a little extra water.

Add the vanilla flavouring, cream and butter. Cool a little and use to coat the pyramid of choux pastry. Serve sprinkled with toasted flaked almonds and piped with extra cream if wished.

BABA AU RHUM

6 oz flour   *½ gill warm water*
¼ teaspoonful salt   *2 eggs*
1 teaspoonful castor   *2½ oz butter or*
  sugar   *margarine*
½ oz yeast   *¾ oz castor sugar*
              1½ oz currants
Syrup:
4 oz granulated sugar   *the thinly-peeled rind*
1 gill water   *of ½ lemon*
              1 glass sherry
              1 glass rum
Decoration: *whipped cream*

Measure the flour, salt and sugar into a bowl. Cream the yeast with the warm water. Whisk the eggs. Use the yeast, eggs and warm water to mix the flour to a very soft dough. Beat well.

Melt the butter and pour on top of the dough. Sprinkle with the remainder of the sugar. Cover and put in a warm place to prove. This will take approximately 30 minutes.

When double its original size knock back. Add the currants and divide around greased dariole moulds.

Prove again for 5-10 minutes or until the yeast begins to work. Bake in a fairly hot oven for approximately 20 minutes.

Suggested oven temperature — 425° or " 6 ".

Prepare the syrup:

Put the sugar, water and lemon peel in a saucepan and boil quickly for 10 minutes. Strain and add the sherry and rum.

Immerse the baba in this syrup and when well soaked serve piped with whipped cream.

SAVARIN AU RHUM

Use the yeast mixture given for the baba but omit the currants. Bake in a ring mould with a rounded base. When cooked baste it with rum syrup and serve with fruit piled in the centre and piped with whipped cream.

REFRIGERATOR ICE CREAM

Basic mixture:

2 *eggs*
1 *gill cream*
2 *tablespoonfuls icing sugar*
flavouring as required

Set the temperature control of the refrigerator to its coldest point about half-an-hour before beginning to make the ice cream and chill the ingredients, a mixing bowl and whisk.

Separate the yolks from the egg whites. Whisk the egg whites until stiff. Whisk the cream and beat in the yolks and the sieved icing sugar. Add the flavouring and fold in the egg whites. Pour into the ice tray of the refrigerator. Cover with aluminium foil and freeze as quickly as possible. No stirring is necessary.

Suggested flavourings include vanilla, coffee, chocolate or a mixture of coffee with chopped nuts and broken meringue or macaroons. An ice flavoured with peppermint essence and served with hot chocolate sauce is also good.

LEMON WATER ICE

$^1/_2$ *lb granulated sugar*
1 *pint water*
the grated rind of 2 lemons
the juice of 4 lemons
2 *egg whites*

Put the sugar, water and the grated lemon rind into a saucepan and boil together for 10 minutes. Strain and cool. Add the lemon juice and freeze.

The freezing can be done by one of two methods:

(a) Using an ice cream freezer or churn. When the mixture is half frozen the stiffly-beaten egg whites should be folded in and the freezing continued until the mixture is stiff.

(b) Using the ice drawer of the refrigerator.

Set the temperature control of the refrigerator to its coldest point about half-an-hour before beginning to make the ice. Freeze the syrup as quickly as possible until beginning to set round the edges. Turn the mixture into a chilled bowl and whisk. Fold in the stiffly-beaten egg whites and return the mixture to the ice drawer. Cover with foil and complete the freezing as quickly as possible.

BAKED ALASKA

a rectangular piece of sponge cake approximately $^1/_2$ inch bigger in both length and width than the block of ice cream
1 *"family size" block of ice cream*
1 *tin or packet of frozen strawberries or raspberries*
Meringue:
5 *egg whites*   5 *oz castor sugar*
Decoration: *cherries and diamonds of angelica*

Soak the sponge cake with the fruit juice. Place an a heat-proof dish.

Whisk the egg whites until stiff and fold in the sugar. Place the block of firm ice cream on the sponge. Arrange the fruit on top and quickly cover all with a $^3/_4$ inch layer of meringue. Leave the surface rough. Dust with icing sugar and decorate with bold pieces of cherry and diamonds of angelica. Brown in a hot oven for 2 minutes.

Suggested oven temperature — 500° or " 9 ".

148

SAVOURIES AND SANDWICHES

CHEESE SCONES

1/2 *lb flour*	2 *oz grated cheese*
1 *teaspoonful baking powder*	*seasoning of salt, pepper and mustard*
2 *oz butter or margarine*	1 *egg (optional)* *milk to mix*

Measure the flour and baking powder into a mixing bowl and cut and rub in the butter. Add the grated cheese and season highly. Mix to a soft dough with the beaten egg and milk. Turn onto a floured surface, roll out and cut into scones. Brush with egg, if wished, and bake in a hot oven for 15 minutes.

Suggested oven temperature — 475° or " 9 ".

CHEESE PUFFS

4 *oz flour*	1 *oz butter or margarine*
2 *teaspoonfuls baking powder*	4 *oz well-flavoured cheese*
seasoning of salt, pepper and mustard	1 *egg* *milk*

Measure the flour, baking powder and seasoning into a bowl and rub in the butter. Grate the cheese and add. Whisk the egg until light and use with the milk to mix all to a rather sloppy consistency.

Divide around 15 or 16 well-greased patty tins and bake in a fairly hot oven for 15 minutes.

Suggested oven temperature — 425° or " 6 ".

Serve hot, split diagonally with a slice of butter inserted in the cut.

CHEESE BISCUITS

2 *oz flour*	2 *oz grated cheese*
1/2 *teaspoonful baking powder*	*seasoning of salt, cayenne and mustard*
1 *oz fine breadcrumbs*	2 *oz butter or margarine*

Measure the flour, baking powder, crumbs and grated cheese into a bowl. Season highly and add the butter. Gradually work the fat into the other ingredients as in making shortbread. Turn on to a floured surface. Roll out fairly thinly and cut into small, fancy shapes. Bake in a very moderately-heated oven until lightly coloured.

Suggested oven temperature — 375° or " 3 ".

These cheese biscuits are useful as a base for cheese canapés.

CHEESE AND ALMOND SABLES

6 *oz flour*	*salt and pepper*
4 *oz butter or margarine*	1/2 *teaspoonful paprika pepper*
1 1/2 *oz ground almonds*	1 *egg yolk*
3 *oz grated cheese*	*a little water*

149

To finish:

Egg to gild
poppy seeds, caraway seeds, sesame seeds,
chopped or whole almonds or other nuts such
as cashew nuts, pea-nuts or pine kernels

Measure the flour into a bowl and rub in the butter. Add the ground almonds, grated cheese and seasonings. Beat the egg yolk with a dessertspoonful of water and use to mix all to a stiff paste, adding more water if necessary. Roll out fairly thinly and cut into pretty biscuits. Brush with beaten egg and sprinkle with the chosen finish. Bake in a moderately-heated oven until lightly coloured.

Suggested oven temperature — 375º or " 3 ".

CHEESE STRAWS

3 oz cheese pastry

Roll the cheese pastry into a strip about 3¹/₂ to 4 inches wide. Trim the edges and cut across into narrow straws. Place these on a baking sheet and out of the scraps cut a few rings. Bake in a moderately-heated oven until a light golden colour.

Suggested oven temperature — 375º or " 3 ".

TO SERVE: Place a few straws through each ring and serve freshly baked. Sometimes the tips of the straws are first dipped in paprika pepper.

CHEESE PINWHEELS

3 oz cheese pastry
Marmite

Roll the cheese pastry into a neat rectangular shape. It should be fairly thin. Spread with marmite and roll up. Refrigerate until firm. Cut into slices, turn onto the cut surface and bake in a moderately-heated oven until lightly coloured.

Suggested oven temperature — 375º or " 3 ".

YARMOUTH STICKS

3 oz cheese pastry
anchovy fillets

Roll the cheese pastry into a strip about 3¹/₂ inches wide. Cut into narrow straws. Meanwhile, drain the anchovy fillets free of oil. Lay a fillet on each strip of pastry, pinch the two together at one end, if necessary using a little egg to make them stick. Twist together, pinching the other end lightly. Bake in a moderately-heated oven until crisp and the pastry is a pale golden brown.

Suggested oven temperature — 375º or " 3 ".

CANAPÉS

The word " canapé " literally means " sofa " and consists as a rule of dainty cheese or salt biscuits, or small pieces of toasted or fried bread garnished with savoury morsels in great variety.

If bread is used as the base, the simplest and best way to prepare it is as follows:

Cut the bread into small dainty pieces and butter lavishly. Arrange on a greased baking tray and toast in a hot oven until golden in colour.

Alternatively, the bread may be toasted, cut into shapes and buttered. Such a base is apt to be tough unless it is freshly prepared and, for this reason, is not generally recommended.

The garnishing of the canapés may be done in an endless variety of ways, using any tasty, colourful food. The following are only a few suggestions out of the almost endless possibilities:

CANAPÉS À LA ROSE: Use round cheese biscuits as the base and pile neatly cut dice of tomato on top. Pipe stars of green savoury butter round the edge and sprinkle the tomato with a little chopped parsley.

CREAMED CHEESE CANAPÉS: Combine well-seasoned grated cheese with a little cream, and pile on top of small cheese biscuits. Decorate with sliced pickled gherkin, stuffed olives or nuts. Diced celery is sometimes added to the cheese mixture.

ANCHOVY and SARDINE CANAPÉS: Use square and rectangular cheese biscuits respectively. Place a curled anchovy fillet on each square biscuit and sardines on the rectangular biscuits. Pipe attractively with pink and green savoury butters.

SHRIMP CROWNS: Use square cheese biscuits as the base and pipe the centre with a generous star of butter flavoured with mayonnaise. Arrange shrimps radiating from the centre to each corner, arching them to simulate a crown.

ORANGE and CHEESE CANAPÉS: Prepare bases of toasted bread. Spread with a well-flavoured cream cheese and decorate with two wedges of mandarine orange.

A suitable cheese spread may be made as follows:

Chop 1½-2 oz processed Gruyère cheese and melt in a bowl over hot water. Beat in 3 tablespoonfuls thin cream. Cool, stirring occasionally, and lastly fold in 1 tablespoonful salad cream and season highly. This mixture can be piped attractively.

PEANUT BACON TOAST: Prepare bases of toasted bread and spread thickly with peanut butter. Sprinkle each canapé with crumbled crisply-cooked bacon.

MUSHROOM AND CHEESE TARTLETS

3 oz cheese pastry

Filling:

4 oz mushrooms

1 oz butter or margarine
seasoning

Use the cheese pastry to line boat-shaped patty tins.

Meanwhile, chop the mushrooms finely. Melt the butter and add. Season and divide around the pastry boats. Decorate with a fine trellis cut from the cheese pastry. Bake in a moderately-heated oven for 15-20 minutes.

Suggested oven temperature—400° or "6".

SAUSAGE ROLLS

Sausage rolls may either have closed or open ends and may be large or small, but in any case they should be well filled with meat and the pastry casing should be thin. Sometimes a little finely chopped onion and parsley are incorporated into the sausage meat.

The actual techniques for making them can vary considerably.

6 oz flaky pastry
¾ lb pork sausage meat or sausages (skinned)

Roll the pastry into a strip approximately 6-7 inch wide. Cut in two by the length. Divide the sausage meat and form into two rolls the length of the pastry. Place down the centre of the strips of pastry and brush the edges with a little water. Roll the pastry round the sausage meat arranging the join to the underside. Trim the ends and cut into pieces of equal length. Brush with beaten egg and snip the top of each with scissors. Bake in a hot oven for the first 10 minutes then reduce the heat for 20-30 minutes.

Suggested oven temperature—475° reduced to 425° or "9" reduced to "6".

SAVOURY BOUCHÉES

Roll puff pastry out to approximately a quarter inch in thickness. Cut into rounds with a fluted cutter approximately 2 to 2$^1/_2$ inches across. Turn over and place on a baking tray which has been sprinkled with water. Brush with egg and using a slightly smaller cutter, mark the centres cutting only half-way through the pastry. Roll the pastry trimmings a little thinner and from these cut the lids. Again turn over and arrange on a damp baking-tray. Brush with egg. Since the bouchées and lids require different times for baking, they are best if arranged on different trays. They should also be left aside in a cool place for 15-30 minutes before baking. Bake in a hot oven for approximately 10-15 minutes.

Suggested oven temperature — 475° or " 9 ".

Remove the centre of each bouchée and scoop out any partially-cooked paste. The case is now ready for the chosen filling, which should be piled in the centre. Put on the pastry lid and serve hot or cold.

Suitable fillings include cooked chicken, ham, shrimps moistened with a rich sauce, stewed mushrooms or a stew of steak, kidney and mushrooms.

CHEESE PUFF PASTRY

Roll out a piece of puff pastry in which only half the turns have been made. Brush lightly with oil and sprinkle two-thirds of the strip with seasoned grated cheese. Fold in three, turn and roll out again. Continue in this fashion until the pastry has had its full number of rollings. Allow the dough to rest in the ordinary way between rollings and before use.

Cheese puff may also be made using left over puff pastry trimmings, rolling in as much grated cheese as possible in one or two turns.

CHEESE STRAWS: Roll out the cheese puff pastry into a strip 5 to 6 inches wide. Trim the edges, brush with egg and sprinkle with caraway or poppy seeds. Cut into straws and arrange on a damp baking tray. Bake in a hot oven until crisp and golden.

CHEESE PALMIERS: Roll out a piece of cheese puff pastry with grated cheese and form a strip approximately 14 inches long. Fold in the ends to the middle. Fold in the doubled ends once more, press down lightly and fold in two. Chill. Cut into slices about quarter inch thick and place them on a heavily-greased tray, spacing them well apart. Bake in a fairly hot oven and when half cooked and about fully expanded, turn over and return to the oven to complete the baking.

Suggested oven temperature — 425° or " 6 ".

CHEESE D'ARTOIS

$^1/_4$ *lb puff or rough puff pastry*

Filling:

1 *egg*	*salt, pepper and cayenne*
2 *oz grated cheese*	1 *oz melted butter or margarine*

Roll the pastry thinly and divide equally into two. Beat the egg and add to the grated cheese. Season highly and stir in the melted butter. Spread this mixture on one half of the pastry. Damp the edges and cover with the second piece of pastry. Brush with beaten egg and mark into fingers. Bake in a hot oven for approximately 25 minutes.

Suggested oven temperature — 450° or " 7 ".

Cut into fingers and serve hot.

CHEESE AIGRETTES

1/2 oz butter or	1 oz grated cheese
margarine	*salt, pepper and*
1 gill water	*cayenne*
1 1/2 oz flour	2 small eggs

Put the butter and water into a saucepan and bring to the boil. Quickly add the flour and beat well until it forms a ball. Beat in the grated cheese and season highly. Beat in the eggs a little at a time. Drop the mixture in teaspoonfuls into deep fat which is barely smoking, and fry gently until golden brown. Drain and serve hot, dusted with finely-grated cheese.

CHEESE AND GHERKIN ROLL

1/2 lb grated cheese	1 chopped hard-boiled
2 tablespoonfuls	egg
minced onion	1/2 cupful crushed
1 clove garlic — minced	cracker biscuits
2 tablespoonfuls	1/2 teaspoonful salt
chopped gherkin	pepper
1/2 tablespoonful	1/4 teaspoonful made
chopped pickles	mustard
4 chopped stuffed olives	1/4 cup mayonnaise

Combine the ingredients and shape into a roll. Wrap in paper and chill. Slice as required and serve on cracker biscuits. Alternatively the mixture may be made into balls and rolled in chopped nuts. Serve on cocktail sticks.

DEVILS ON HORSEBACK

5 stewed prunes	5 croûtes of hot
a little chutney	buttered toast
5 small rashers of bacon	or fried bread

Stone the prunes and fill the cavity with a little chutney. Rind the bacon and stretch. Wrap a slice round each prune. Impale on a skewer and bake in a hot oven until the bacon is cooked.

Serve hot on croûtes of buttered toast or fried bread.

SALTED NUTS

2 oz nuts	1 tablespoonful salt
2 tablespoonfuls butter	pepper
or oil	

Blanch and skin the nuts. Heat the butter or oil in a small frying pan and fry the nuts very slowly until they are crisp and golden brown. Mix the salt and pepper on a sheet of soft kitchen paper and toss the nuts in this mixture. If wished, they may be dried off in a cool oven.

TOASTED MUSHROOM ROLLS STARCH-REDUCED

thin slices of starch-reduced bread
butter

Filling:

1 oz butter or	8 oz finely-chopped
margarine	mushrooms
	a little water
	salt and pepper
	1 small tablespoonful flour

Prepare the filling first:

Melt the butter and add the mushrooms. Sweat together for a few minutes until soft. Add sufficient water to cover. Season. Stew gently, for approximately 5 minutes. Then thicken with the flour blended with a little extra water. Cool.

Butter the bread generously. Then spread the unbuttered side thickly' with the mushroom filling. Roll up. If wished, trim the ends, and brown and crisp in a hot oven. Serve hot.

ASPARAGUS CRISPS

thin slices of buttered starch-reduced bread
grated cheese
asparagus tips
melted butter

Sprinkle the slices of buttered bread with grated cheese. Place an asparagus tip at one end — if the asparagus is at all fibrous cut in three or four places. Roll up. Brush with melted butter and brown and crisp in a hot oven. Serve hot.

ANCHOVY AND CHEESE CRISPS

thin slices of buttered starch-reduced bread
grated cheese
anchovy fillets
melted butter

Sprinkle the slices of buttered bread with grated cheese. Place an anchovy fillet at one end and roll up. Brush with melted butter and brown and crisp in a hot oven. Serve hot.

BANANA ROLLS

thin slices of starch-reduced bread
butter
bananas
sugar and ground nutmeg to sprinkle

Butter the bread generously and lay buttered side down on a working surface. Quarter the bananas, dip in sugar and sprinkle with the spice. Lay a piece of fruit on one end of a slice of bread and roll up. Brown and crisp in a hot oven. Serve hot.

SANDWICHES

To be at their best sandwiches must be made from really fresh bread, while the butter and filling should be spread generously. A sharp knife does much to ensure neatness and an attractive appearance.

In the matter of sandwiches, there is a great variety for they may be sweet or savoury, dainty or substantial, plain or toasted, rolled, closed or open and single deck or decker. The fillings are varied too and may either be concocted on the inspiration of the moment from the food which is to hand, or special sandwich spreads prepared. In any case they must be moist, well-seasoned and have a tasty quality.

Sandwich ingenuity need not stop at variety of shapes and filling, but should include the sandwich bread itself, and the changes which can be rung on white, wholemeal, brown, malt and nut bread.

The following are only a few suggestions out of the almost endless possibilities for fillings:

1. HARD-BOILED EGGS — finely chopped or minced and moistened with lightly-whipped cream or salad dressing. This is good combined with garden cress, thinly-sliced cucumber or with chopped walnuts. Other suitable additions include onion juice, chopped herbs such as chives or parsley, curry powder, grated cheese or even shrimps.

2. SCRAMBLED EGGS may be successfully used in decker sandwiches, largely because of their good colour. The other fillings should have contrasting colour, and tomato and watercress make a good choice.

3. BOILED HAM or bacon minced and moistened with a white sauce. The seasoning should include mustard.

Tongue and corned beef may be used in a similar way.

4. MEAT CURRY minced and moistened with curry sauce makes an interesting sandwich filling and proves a good way to use a little left-over curry.

5. CHEESE lends itself to a variety of uses. Either it may be used grated or in the form of a cream cheese and it may be combined with other ingredients such as chopped celery, walnuts, gherkin, hard-boiled eggs or thinly-sliced cucumber.

In all cases it is important to ensure that the filling is moist and cream, mayonnaise, white sauce or a combination may be added for this purpose.

6. SALAD sandwiches may be made from a mixture of salad plants or from one only. Their success lies in the crispness of the lettuce, watercress or celery as the case may be. The salad should be used in conjunction with a good dressing.

7. TOMATOES should be skinned, thinly sliced and well seasoned. As they are apt to make a very moist sandwich it may be necessary to drain them on a nylon sieve before use. They may be used alone, with mayonnaise or combined with chopped herbs such as marjoram or chopped gherkin or other pickle.

Scrambled egg with tomato makes a popular sandwich filling.

8. SWEET FILLINGS for sandwiches can also be made in great variety:

Preserves of all kinds can be used including lemon curd, and it is important that these should be stiff.

Fresh fruits are acceptable, particularly sliced or mashed bananas, or even sliced strawberries with sugar and cream.

Crystallised or preserved fruit can also be utilised, such as finely-chopped ginger combined with cream, or stewed dates or a mixture of date and apple.

SALMON SANDWICHES

A good recipe for use when catering for large numbers. The quantities given will produce about 150 sandwiches.

Filling number 1:
1 *tall tin salmon*
1^1/$_2$ *lb butter*
2 *tablespoonfuls vinegar*
salt and pepper
3 × 2 *lb sliced white loaves*

Filling number 2:
1^1/$_2$ *lb butter*
2 *tablespoonfuls chopped parsley*
1/$_4$ *finely-chopped cucumber or 3 tablespoonfuls chopped gherkins*
1 *tablespoonful grated onion*
2 × 2 *lb sliced brown loaves*

Prepare the fillings first:

Flake the salmon finely and work into the creamed butter. Flavour with the vinegar and seasoning. If necessary, add a little colouring.

Combine the ingredients for the second filling.

To make up the sandwiches:

Spread all the slices from one of the white loaves on a working surface and divide half the salmon filling around. Spread the filling and cover with slices of brown bread. Cover the brown bread with half the second filling. Proceed in this fashion alternating the brown and white bread and the fillings so that decker sandwiches are produced consisting of three slices of white bread and two of brown and with four layers of filling. After pressing, remove the crusts and cut into sandwiches.

BREAD, CAKES AND BISCUITS

THE CHOICE OF FLOURS

To get good results when baking, it is advisable to use the correct kind of flour for the dish being made. Broadly speaking, there are two types available:

One type is referred to as a strong or bread flour. It has a high gluten content, absorbs more water and therefore gives a correspondingly greater bulk. It is the best choice for yeast mixtures, flaky pastries and batters since their success depends on developing a strong elastic dough. If used for steamed puddings, greater bulk is obtained.

The other type of flour is called a soft or cake flour. It contains less gluten and more starch and, therefore, absorbs fat well. It gives a soft dough ideal for cakes, biscuits, soda breads and scones.

There are also various speciality flours to choose such as self-raising soda bread flour and self-raising cake flour. These are always made from flour with a low gluten content.

ULSTER's heritage in the matter of bread, cakes and biscuits is considerable, for her housewives delight in a well-laden tea-table. Pride of place must go to soda bread with its floury, brown crossed crust, spongy farls fresh from the griddle, brown bread with its pleasant rough nuttiness, dark spicy treacle bread, currant bread, seedy bread — the list is long. Apart from these traditional items, home-baked cakes and biscuits are made in great variety.

SODA BREAD

1 *lb flour*
1 *teaspoonful salt* } *or use soda bread*
1 *teaspoonful baking soda* } *self-raising flour*
    approximately $^1/_2$- $^3/_4$ *pint buttermilk*

Sieve the dry ingredients into a bowl. Mix lightly and quickly, adding sufficient buttermilk to give a soft but not sticky dough. Turn onto a well-floured surface and shape into a round cake approximately 1½ inch thick. Transfer to a greased or floured baking sheet or an 8 inch sandwich tin and mark into four farls. Bake in a fairly hot oven for 30-35 minutes.

Suggested oven temperature — 450° or " 7 ".

GRIDDLE SODA BREAD: If the soda bread is to be baked on the griddle, it should be rolled rather thinner than bread for the oven. The griddle should be gently heated prior to mixing the dough. To test the temperature for baking, dust with flour. When correctly heated, the griddle should brown it in 3-4 minutes.

WHEATEN BREAD

³/₄ lb wheaten or whole meal	1 teaspoonful golden syrup (optional)
¹/₄ lb flour	1½-2 oz butter or margarine (optional)
1 teaspoonful salt	approximately ³/₄ pint buttermilk
1 teaspoonful baking soda	

Sieve the flour, salt and baking soda. Add the wheaten meal. Rub in the golden syrup and the butter if these are used. Mix lightly adding sufficient buttermilk to give a soft but not sticky dough. Turn onto a surface sprinkled with wheaten meal and form into a round cake approximately 1½ inch thick. Mark into four farls and bake in a fairly hot oven for 30-35 minutes.

Suggested oven temperature — 450° or " 7 ".

Wheaten bread may also be baked on the griddle.

SULTANA SODA BREAD

1 lb flour	or use 1 lb soda bread self-raising flour
1 teaspoonful salt	
1 teaspoonful baking soda	
	4 oz sultanas
2 oz butter or margarine	2 oz candied peel
	1 oz castor sugar
approximately ³/₄ pint buttermilk	

Sieve the flour, salt and baking soda. Cut and rub in the butter. Add the sultanas, chopped peel and sugar. Make a well in the centre and stir in sufficient buttermilk to make a soft but not sticky dough. Turn onto a well-floured surface and form into a round cake. Mark into four farls and bake in a fairly hot oven for 30-35 minutes.

Suggested oven temperature — 450° or " 7 ".

TREACLE BREAD

1 lb flour	or use 1 lb soda bread self-raising flour
1 teaspoonful salt	
1 teaspoonful baking soda	
	1 oz castor sugar
1 teaspoonful ground ginger (optional)	2 tablespoonfuls treacle buttermilk

Sieve the dry ingredients. Mix the treacle with a little buttermilk and use to mix all to a soft dough, adding more buttermilk as necessary.

Turn on to a floured board and shape into a round cake. Mark into four farls. Bake in a fairly hot oven for 30-35 minutes.

Suggested oven temperature — 450° or " 7 ".

Alternatively, treacle bread may be baked on the griddle.

POTATO CAKE

Potato cake is also spoken of as potato bread or fadge. It is a traditional Irish dish and may be served hot with butter and sugar or fried and eaten with fried bacon, sausages and similar items.

1/2 lb cooked potatoes   *1 oz melted butter or*
1/2 teaspoonful salt   *margarine (optional)*
              approximately 2 oz flour

Potato cake is best made while the potatoes are still hot.

Put the potatoes through a potato ricer. Add the salt and melted butter, then work in enough flour to make a pliable paste. Roll into a circular shape about 1/4 inch thick. Cut into six or eight farls and bake on a hot greased griddle until well browned on both sides.

Alternatively, potato cake may be cut into large rounds with a plain cutter. POTATO OATEN CAKE is made in a similar way to potato cake but using oatmeal instead of flour.

POTATO APPLE CAKE

Make the potato cake as already described and cut in two. Roll each piece to give a circle and cover one with finely-chopped apple. Damp the edge and cover with the second piece. Neaten and seal the edges by pinching with the fingers and thumb. The cake may either be baked on the griddle until brown on both sides or cooked in a fairly hot oven. TO SERVE: Split round the side and turn the top back. Cover the apple with thin slices of butter and dust with sugar. Close again and put all in the oven until the butter and sugar have melted.

SULTANA SCONES

8 oz flour   *1 oz castor sugar*
1/2 teaspoonful salt   *2 oz sultanas*
1 teaspoonful baking   *1/2 oz candied peel*
   powder   *(optional)*

2 oz butter or   *1 egg (optional)*
   margarine
         approximately 3/4 gill milk

Measure the flour, salt and baking powder into a bowl. Cut and rub in the butter. Add the sugar, sultanas and chopped peel. Beat the egg and use with milk as necessary, to mix all to a soft dough. Turn on to a floured surface and roll out 1/2-3/4 inch thick. Cut into scones. Brush with egg or milk and bake in a hot oven for about 15 minutes.

Suggested oven temperature—475° or "9".

WHEATEN SCONES

8 oz wheaten meal   *1/2 teaspoonful cream*
4 oz flour   *of tartar*
3/4 teaspoonful salt   *1 oz butter or margarine*
1/2 teaspoonful baking   *1 dessertspoonful castor*
   soda   *sugar*
              buttermilk

Put the wheaten meal into a bowl and sieve in the flour, salt, baking soda and cream of tartar. Cut and rub in the butter. Add the sugar and mix all to a light dough with the buttermilk. Turn on to a surface sprinkled with wheaten meal. Roll out and cut into scones. Bake in a hot oven for 15 minutes.

Suggested oven temperature—475° or "9".

TREACLE SCONES

1/2 lb flour   *1/2 teaspoonful mixed*
1/2 teaspoonful salt   *spice*
1/2 teaspoonful baking   *1 oz butter or margarine*
   soda   *1 oz castor sugar*
1 teaspoonful cream of   *1 tablespoonful*
   tartar   *treacle*
1/2 teaspoonful ground   *milk to mix*
   cinnamon

Sieve the flour, salt, baking soda, cream of tartar and the spices together. Cut and rub in the butter. Add the sugar. Mix the treacle with a little milk and use to mix all to a soft dough, adding more milk as necessary. Roll out and cut into scones. Bake in a hot oven for 15 minutes.

Suggested oven temperature — 475° or " 9 ".

FRENCH SCONES

10 *oz flour*	3 *oz butter or margarine*
1/2 *teaspoonful salt*	3 *oz castor sugar*
1 *teaspoonful baking powder*	1 *egg*
	milk to mix

Filling: *raspberry jam*

Prepare the scone mixture in the usual way and cut in two. Roll one half to fit a swiss-roll tin. Spread with raspberry jam. Cover with the second half of the scone dough. Brush with egg. Bake in a hot oven for 20-30 minutes. Cut into fingers and dust with icing sugar.

Suggested oven temperature — 450° or " 7 ".

ORANGE SCONES

1/2 *lb flour*	2 *oz butter or margarine*
1/2 *teaspoonful salt*	1 *oz castor sugar*
2 *teaspoonfuls baking powder*	*the grated rind of*
	1 *orange*
approximately 3/4 *cup rich milk*	

To finish the scones:

loaf sugar	*orange juice*

Measure the flour, salt and baking powder into a bowl. Cut and rub in the butter. Add the sugar and the grated rind of the orange and mix all to a soft dough with the milk. Roll out and cut into scones. Dip a lump of sugar into the orange juice and immediately press it gently into the centre of a scone. Repeat the process until each scone is filled. Bake in a hot oven for approximately 15 minutes.

Suggested oven temperature — 475° or " 9 ".

DOUGHNUTS (BAKING POWDER)

6 *oz flour*	2 *oz butter or margarine*
a pinch of salt	1 *oz castor sugar*
1 *small teaspoonful powder*	1 *egg*
	milk to mix

Filling: *raspberry jam*
Coating: *castor sugar and ground cinnamon*

Prepare the scone mixture in the usual way. Roll out 1/4 inch thick. Cut into small circles and put a little raspberry jam on the centre of half of these. Brush the other half with milk and put two together, pressing the edges well together. Fry in a pan of faintly-smoking deep fat for 6-8 minutes, turning when brown on the underside. Serve freshly fried and tossed in sugar flavoured with ground cinnamon.

DROPPED SCONES

4 *oz flour*	1-2 *teaspoonfuls golden*
a pinch of salt	*syrup*
1/2 *teaspoonful baking soda*	*buttermilk to mix*

Sieve the flour, salt and baking soda into a bowl. Add the syrup and enough buttermilk to give a creamy batter. Beat well until glossy and smooth. Drop the mixture from the point of a spoon onto a hot, greased griddle. When brown on one side turn and brown on the other. Cool in the folds of a cloth.

SLIM CAKES

1/2 *lb flour*	4 *oz butter or margarine*
1/2 *teaspoonful salt*	2 *oz castor sugar*
1/4 *teaspoonful baking soda*	2 *oz sultanas (optional)*
a little buttermilk to mix	

Sieve the flour, salt and baking soda. Cut and rub in the butter. Add the sugar and sultanas. Mix to a stiff dough with buttermilk. Roll out $^1/_4$ inch thick. Cut into farls or rounds and bake on a moderately-heated griddle, turning when nicely browned on the underside.

Serve hot with butter.

YEAST MIXTURES

Yeast is a living organism, which, if kept warm and moist, will grow and multiply, creating, as it does so, carbon-dioxide gas. This acts as a raising agent in the dough. Yeast can be killed by too high a temperature, but cold merely retards its growth and keeps the plant in a quiescent state. It follows, therefore, that in working with yeast in the normal way, everything should be warm or at least at average room temperature. However, if it is more convenient, the rising of a yeast dough may be delayed for 12 hours by storing it in a cold larder, or 1-2 days if it is stored in a refrigerator. During this prolonged rising period it should be covered to prevent surface drying. A large polythene bag may be used to envelope the bowl; alternatively, cover with foil and a damp tea-towel.

YEAST BREAD — WHITE

1 *lb strong, plain flour*	$^1/_2$-1 *oz yeast*
1 *teaspoonful salt*	*approximately* $^1/_2$ *pint*
1 *teaspoonful sugar*	*warm water*

Measure the flour, salt and sugar into a bowl. Blend the yeast with the water. Add this yeast liquid to the flour and mix to an elastic dough. Turn onto a floured surface and knead thoroughly. Alternatively, use the dough hook of the electric mixer to mix and knead.

Return the dough to the bowl. Cover with a damp cloth and put to rise in a warm place until double its size — about 1 hour.

Re-knead and shape. Drop into a 2 lb loaf tin. Put in a warm place for another 10-15 minutes or until the yeast begins to work again. Bake in a hot oven for approximately 40 minutes.

Suggested oven temperature — 450° or " 7 ".

On removal from the oven, the loaf is sometimes rubbed with butter paper to give a slight glaze and soften the crust.

YEAST BREAD — BROWN

1 *lb wholemeal*	1 *teaspoonful brown*
$^1/_4$ *lb flour*	*sugar or treacle*
1$^1/_4$ *teaspoonfuls salt*	$^1/_2$-1 *oz yeast*
	approximately $^3/_4$-1 *pint warm water*

Measure the wholemeal, flour, salt and sugar into a bowl. Blend the yeast with the warm water. Use to mix the dry ingredients to an elastic dough. Knead well on a floured surface. Alternatively, use the dough hook of the electric mixer to mix and knead.

Return the dough to the bowl and cover with a damp cloth. Put in a warm place to rise until double its original size — about 1-1$^1/_2$ hours.

Re-knead and shape. Drop into a 2 lb loaf tin and put in a warm place again until the yeast begins to work. Bake in a hot oven for approximately 50 minutes.

A brown yeast loaf has a very wholesome appearance if it is brushed with milk and sprinkled with coarse oatmeal before baking.

YEAST ROLLS

1 *lb flour*	2 *oz butter or margarine*
1 *teaspoonful salt*	$^1/_2$-1 *oz yeast*
1 *teaspoonful sugar*	*approximately* $^1/_2$ *pint warm milk*

Measure the flour, salt and sugar into a bowl. Cut and rub in the butter. Blend the yeast with the warm milk and use to mix the flour into a light elastic dough. Knead or beat thoroughly. Cover with a damp cloth and put in a warm place to rise. When double its original size, turn the dough onto a floured surface, re-knead and shape or cut into rolls. Prove for a further 10-15 minutes. Brush with egg and sprinkle with poppy seeds, if wished. Bake in a hot oven for 15 minutes.

Suggested oven temperature—475° or " 9 ".

BAPS

The Scots breakfast roll.

1 *lb flour*	1 *oz yeast*
1 *teaspoonful salt*	$1/2$ *pint warm milk or milk and water*
1 *teaspoonful sugar*	2 *oz lard*

Measure the flour, salt and sugar into a mixing bowl. Blend the yeast with the warm milk. Add the lard and stir until the fat is melted. Use to mix the flour into a soft elastic dough. Knead thoroughly. Cover with a damp cloth and put in a warm place to rise until double its original bulk—about $3/4$-1 hour.

Re-knead and divide into eight pieces. Knead each into an oval shape and flatten slightly. Place on a greased or floured baking tray and prove again until the yeast begins to work—about 10-15 minutes. Dust with flour and bake in a hot oven for 15 minutes.

Suggested oven temperature—450° or " 7 ".

If wished, the mixture may be refrigerated overnight for baking fresh for breakfast. In this case, the procedure is as follows:

Mix the dough as already described and knead thoroughly. Then without proving, divide into eight pieces. Knead each into an oval shape and flatten slightly. Place on a greased tray, brush the tops with oil and place inside a polythene bag. Put in the refrigerator overnight. In the morning, flour the surface of each bap and place the tray on the top shelf of a cold oven. Switch to 450° or " 7 " and bake for 30 minutes.

CROISSANTS

$1/2$ *lb flour*	$1/2$ *oz yeast*
$1/2$ *teaspoonful salt*	*approximately* $1/4$ *pint*
1 *teaspoonful sugar*	*warm milk*
4 *oz butter or margarine*	

Measure the flour, salt and sugar into a bowl. Blend the yeast with the warm milk and use to mix all to a soft dough. Work until smooth. Rest in the refrigerator. Roll the dough into an oblong. Cover half the strip with the butter as in making flaky pastry. Fold in two. Give a half turn and re-roll. Fold in three and repeat, giving in all 3 or 4 turns. It is advisable to return the dough to the refrigerator between rollings to rest and firm.

If convenient, leave overnight in the refrigerator wrapped in polythene.

To shape the croissants roll to a wide strip about $1/4$ inch thick. Cut into triangles. Roll from the base to the tip, touching the tip with egg to prevent unrolling. Curve into a horse-shoe shape and prove for 10-15 minutes. Brush with egg and bake in a hot oven for 15-20 minutes.

Suggested oven temperature—450° or " 7 ".

161

CLOVERLEAF ROLLS

8 *fluid oz milk*
2 *dessertspoonfuls castor sugar*
1/2 *teaspoonful salt*
1 *oz butter or margarine*

1 *oz yeast*
2 *fluid oz warm water*
2 *eggs*
1 *lb warm flour*

Put the milk, sugar, salt and butter into a saucepan and warm enough to melt the fat and sugar. Turn into a mixing bowl.

Dissolve the yeast in the warm water and add to the milk mixture. Break in the eggs and whisk all together. Gradually beat in the warm flour. Beat well. Brush the dough with melted margarine. Cover and leave in a warm place to rise until it doubles its size. This will take approximately one hour.

Melt some butter in a small saucepan and use to keep the hands greased. Take a portion of the dough and, using both hands, work to a smooth surface. Squeeze a small ball of the dough between the finger and thumb, break off with the other hand and place in a greased muffin or patty tin, three to each tin. Leave in a warm place to rise to double the size again. Bake in a hot oven for approximately 10 minutes.

Suggested oven temperature—475° or "9".

GRIZANI ROLLS

1/2 *lb flour*
1/2 *teaspoonful salt*
1 *teaspoonful sugar*

1 *oz butter or margarine*
1/2 *oz yeast*
1 *gill warm milk*
1 *egg*

Warm the flour and add the salt and sugar. Cut and rub in the butter. Cream the yeast with the warm milk. Beat the egg and add. Use to mix all to a soft dough. Knead well. Shape

into 10-12 rolls and arrange on a greased baking tray. Leave in a warm place until they double in size. Brush with egg and bake in a hot oven for 10-15 minutes.

Suggested oven temperature — 475° or "9".

CREAM COOKIES

1/2 *lb flour*
1/2 *teaspoonful salt*
1 *oz butter or margarine*

1 *oz castor sugar*
1/2 *oz yeast*
1/4 *pint milk (approximately)*

1 *egg*
raspberry jam and whipped cream to fill

Put the flour and salt into a bowl and rub in the butter. Add the sugar. Cream the yeast with the warm milk. Beat the egg and add. Use these to mix all to a soft dough. Beat well using the dough hook of the mixing machine, a wooden spoon or the hand. Cover and put in a warm place to rise until double its original bulk — about 3/4-1 hour. Re-knead and divide into 10 pieces. Shape each into a ball and place on a greased tray. Prove again until the yeast begins to work. Bake in a hot oven for 15 minutes.

Suggested oven temperature — 475° or "9".

When cold, make a diagonal cut with scissors. Spread the opening with raspberry jam and fill with whipped cream. Dust with icing sugar.

CHELSEA BUNS

1/2 *lb flour*
1/2 *teaspoonful salt*
1 *oz butter or margarine*

1 *oz castor sugar*
1/2 *oz yeast*
approximately 1/4 *pint warm milk*

Filling:

2 oz sultanas

2 oz currants

2 oz candied peel

$^1/_2$ teaspoonful mixed spice

2 oz melted butter or margarine

2 oz castor sugar

Make the yeast dough in the usual way. Combine the ingredients for the filling. Roll the dough into a rectangular shape and scatter the filling evenly over it. Roll up and cut into $1^1/_2$ inch pieces. Turn onto the cut surface and place fairly close together on a greased tray. Prove for a further 10-15 minutes. Bake in a hot oven for 20-30 minutes.

Suggested oven temperature — 450° or " 7 ".

When cooked, these buns may be brushed with a heavy syrup of sugar and water or iced with water icing.

DOUGHNUTS (YEAST)

$^1/_2$ lb flour

$^1/_2$ teaspoonful salt

1 oz butter or margarine

1 oz castor sugar

$^1/_2$ oz yeast

approximately $^1/_4$ pint warm milk

To finish: raspberry jam and granulated sugar for tossing

Measure the flour and salt into a bowl and rub in the butter. Add the sugar. Cream the yeast with the warm milk. Use to mix the flour to a soft dough, adding more milk as necessary. Beat well. Cover the bowl with a damp cloth and put in a warm place to rise — about $^3/_4$-1 hour. Re-knead and divide into 10 portions. Shape into round buns and prove for a further 10-15 minutes. Fry in deep fat heated to just under haze point, turning in the fat as necessary. Drain and make a diagonal cut in each with scissors. Spread the opening with raspberry jam and toss in granulated sugar.

GINGERBREAD

$^1/_2$ lb flour

a pinch of salt

1 teaspoonful ground cinnamon

1 teaspoonful ground ginger

1 teaspoonful mixed spice

4 oz castor sugar

4 oz butter or margarine

1 teacupful milk

2 tablespoonfuls treacle or syrup

1 egg

1 teaspoonful baking soda

Measure the first six items into a bowl. Melt the butter, add the milk and treacle and stir well together. Beat the egg and add together with the baking soda. Use to mix the dry ingredients to a thick pouring consistency. Pour into a prepared swiss-roll tin and bake in a moderately-heated oven for approximately 40-45 minutes.

Suggested oven temperature — 375° or " 3 ".

Serve cut into squares.

DATE AND WALNUT LOAF

4 oz dates

1 tablespoonful syrup

1 tablespoonful treacle

5 oz wheaten meal

5 oz flour

$^1/_2$ teaspoonful salt

$^1/_2$ teaspoonful baking soda

2 oz walnuts

buttermilk

Chop the dates and cover with boiling water. Add the syrup and treacle and leave until cold. Combine the dry ingredients. Chop the walnuts and add. Add the date mixture and sufficient buttermilk to mix all to a soft consistency. Turn into a greased 2 lb loaf tin and bake in a hot oven for 1 hour.

Suggested oven temperature — 425° or " 6 ".

BOILED FRUIT CAKE

1 breakfast cupful water	1 breakfast cupful sultanas
4 oz butter or margarine	3 teaspoonfuls mixed spice
1 breakfast cupful soft brown sugar	2 breakfast cupfuls flour
1 breakfast cupful currants	1 teaspoonful baking soda
1 beaten egg	

Put the water, butter, sugar, fruit and spice into a saucepan and simmer for 20 minutes. Cool. Then stir in the flour, baking soda and beaten egg. Turn into a prepared 7 inch cake tin and bake in a moderate oven for approximately 1½ hours.

Suggested oven temperature — 350° or " 3 ".

LUNCHEON CAKE

1 lb flour	4 oz sultanas
1 teaspoonful salt	4 oz currants
2 teaspoonfuls baking powder	2 oz candied peel
2 teaspoonfuls mixed spice	1 dessertspoonful treacle
6 oz butter a margarine	2 eggs
6 oz castor sugar	approximately ½ pint milk

Measure the flour, salt, baking powder and spice into a bowl. Cut and rub in the butter. Add the sugar, fruit and chopped candied peel. Combine the treacle with the beaten eggs and the greater part of the milk. Use to mix all to a soft consistency, adding more milk as necessary. Turn into an 8 inch cake tin and bake in a fairly hot oven for approximately 1½ hours.

Suggested oven temperature — 350° or " 3 ".

ROCK BUNS

½ lb flour	3-4 oz castor sugar
a pinch of salt	3-4 oz currants or sultanas
1 teaspoonful baking powder	1 egg
3-4 oz butter or margarine	milk

Measure the flour, salt and baking powder into a bowl. Cut and rub in the butter. Add the sugar and fruit. Beat the egg and use together with a little milk, to mix all to a very stiff paste.

Put out in small rough heaps on to a greased baking tray. Bake in a hot oven for approximately 15 minutes.

Suggested oven temperature — 450° or " 7 ".

RASPBERRY BUNS

5 oz flour	2-3 oz butter or margarine
3 oz ground rice	3 oz castor sugar
a pinch of salt	2 eggs
1 teaspoonful baking powder	milk
raspberry jam	

Measure the flour, ground rice, salt and baking powder into a bowl. Cut and rub in the butter. Add the sugar. Beat the eggs and use together with a little milk, to mix all to a very stiff paste. Turn onto a floured surface and divide into 18-24 pieces. Shape each into a ball, make a hole in the centre and insert a little jam. Close up the opening, turn over and place on a greased tray. Brush with egg and bake in a hot oven for 15 minutes or according to size.

Suggested oven temperature — 450° or " 7 ".

COCO-NUT BUNS

½ lb flour	3 oz castor sugar
a pinch of salt	2 oz coco-nut

1 *teaspoonful baking powder*   2-4 *oz butter or margarine*
1 *egg and a little milk*

Measure the flour, salt and baking powder into a bowl. Cut and rub in the butter. Add the sugar and coco-nut. Beat the egg and use, together with milk as required to mix all to a very stiff paste. Put out in small rough heaps onto a greased tray. Bake in a hot oven for approximately 15 minutes.

Suggested oven temperature — 450° or " 7 ".

N.B. These coco-nut buns may be split diagonally and filled with a vanilla-flavoured butter icing made from 1¹/₂ oz butter. Serve dusted with icing sugar.

LITTLE APPLE CAKES

8 *oz flour*   4 *oz butter or margarine*
a pinch of salt   4 *oz castor sugar*
¹/₂ *teaspoonful baking soda*   1 *teaspoonful cream of tartar*
1 *egg and a little milk*

Filling: *approximately* 1 *cupful stewed apple*

Sieve the flour, salt, baking soda and cream of tartar together. Cut and rub in the butter. Add the castor sugar. Beat the egg and use to mix all to a stiff paste, adding a little milk if necessary. Roll out rather less than ¹/₄ inch thick and cut into rounds. Use half of these to line patty tins. Fill with the stewed apples and cover with the remainder of the rounds of paste. It is not necessary to damp the edges. Bake in a hot oven for 15 minutes. Serve warm dusted with icing sugar.

This quantity should make 18 small cakes.

Suggested oven temperature — 425° or " 6 ".

QUEEN CAKES

2 *oz butter or margarine*   ¹/₄ *teaspoonful baking powder*
2 *oz castor sugar*   *the rind of* ¹/₂ *lemon*
1 *egg*   *a little milk if necessary*
2-4 *oz flour*   4 *oz currants*

Cream the butter and sugar thoroughly. Beat in the lightly-whisked egg gradually. With the last of the egg, add the flour and a little milk if necessary. Finally, add the lemon rind and fruit. Two-thirds fill greased patty tins and bake in a fairly hot oven for 15 minutes.

Suggested oven temperature — 425° or " 6 ".

CUP CAKES

2 *oz butter or margarine*   1 *egg*
2 *oz castor sugar*   2 *oz flour*
¹/₄ *teaspoonful baking powder*

To finish: *raspberry jam and whipped cream*

Cream the butter and sugar. Beat in the lightly-whisked egg, adding it in small amounts. With the last of the egg add the flour and baking powder. Two-thirds fill paper baking cases or greased patty tins. Bake in a fairly hot oven for 15 minutes.

Suggested oven temperature — 425° or " 6 ".

Cup cakes may be finished by various methods:

BUTTERFLY CAKES: Cut a thin slice from the top of each cake. Cut this piece in two again. Spread the cake with jam and pipe with a star of cream. Replace the two half slices of cake butterfly fashion. Dust with icing sugar.

BASKET CAKES: Remove a slice from the top of each cake. Spread the cake with jam and pipe with whipped cream. Replace the slice of cake at an angle to show off the cream. Dust with icing sugar.

CORK CAKES: Using a ¹/₂ inch cutter, remove a cork-shaped piece from the centre of each cake. Fill the bottom of the cavity with jam. Pipe with a star of cream and place the cork-shaped piece of cake lightly on top. Dust with icing sugar.

ICED CUP CAKES: Ice the top of each cake with water icing in various colours and flavours. Decorate simply with cherry, angelica, walnuts or silver balls.

COBURG CAKES

3 oz butter or margarine	1 teaspoonful treacle
2 oz castor sugar	5 oz flour
1 egg	¹/₂ teaspoonful baking powder
1 teaspoonful golden syrup	1 teaspoonful ground ginger
a few split almonds	

Cream the butter and the sugar. Beat in the lightly-whisked egg adding it gradually. Add the syrup and treacle. Lastly stir in the dry ingredients. Put a split almond in the bottom of each greased patty tin and two-thirds fill with the mixture. Bake in a fairly hot oven for 15 minutes.

Suggested oven temperature — 425° or " 6 ".

ONE EGG SANDWICH CAKE

4 oz butter or margarine	¹/₄ pint milk
4 oz castor sugar	7 oz flour
1 egg	1 teaspoonful baking powder

Filling: *raspberry jam*

Cream the butter and sugar thoroughly. Gradually beat in the lightly-whisked egg. Lastly add the milk and the dry ingredients alternately. Divide the mix-

ture between two prepared sandwich tins. Bake in a moderate oven for 20 minutes.

Suggested oven temperature — 400° or " 5 ".

Sandwich with raspberry jam or as wished.

VICTORIA SANDWICH

Victoria sandwich may also be spoken of as a butter sponge.

5 oz butter or margarine	3 eggs
	6 oz flour
5 oz castor sugar	
1 teaspoonful baking powder	

Cream the butter and sugar thoroughly. Gradually beat in the lightly-whisked eggs. With the last of the egg add the flour and baking powder. Divide the mixture between two prepared sandwich tins and bake in a moderate oven for 25-30 minutes.

Suggested oven temperature — 400° or " 6 ".

When cool, sandwich with raspberry jam or lemon curd and dust the top with sugar.

COFFEE AND WALNUT SANDWICH

5 oz butter or margarine	5 oz flour
5 oz castor sugar	1 teaspoonful baking powder
3 eggs	1 oz instant coffee
2 oz chopped walnuts	

Filling:

2 oz butter or margarine	1 dessertspoonful coffee essence
3 oz icing sugar	1 oz chopped walnuts

Cream the butter and sugar thoroughly. Gradually beat in the lightly-whisked eggs. With the last of the egg add the flour, baking powder and instant coffee.

Finally, add the chopped nuts and divide the mixture between two prepared sandwich tins. Bake in a moderate oven for 30 minutes.

Suggested oven temperature—400° or " 6 ".

Filling: Cream the butter and gradually beat in the sieved icing sugar. Flavour with coffee essence and add the chopped nuts. Use to sandwich the cake.

The top of the cake may be iced with coffee-flavoured water icing made using 4 oz icing sugar.

CHOCOLATE SANDWICH CAKE (1)

4 oz butter or margarine	5 oz flour
4 oz castor sugar	1 teaspoonful baking powder
3 eggs	4 oz sweetened chocolate powder

¹/₂ teaspoonful vanilla flavouring

Filling:

1¹/₂ oz butter or margarine	2 oz sweetened chocolate powder
3 oz icing sugar	1 oz chopped walnuts

Cream the butter and sugar. Gradually beat in the lightly-whisked eggs. With the last of the egg add the flour, baking powder, chocolate powder and vanilla flavouring. Divide the mixture between two prepared sandwich tins and bake in a moderately-heated oven for 30 minutes.

Suggested oven temperature—400° or " 6 ".

Filling: Cream the butter and gradually beat in the sieved icing sugar. Moisten the chocolate powder with a little boiling water and add together with the chopped walnuts. Use to sandwich the cake.

The top of the cake may be iced with chocolate-flavoured water icing made using 4 oz icing sugar.

CHOCOLATE SANDWICH CAKE (2)

3 oz butter or margarine	1 oz cocoa
3 oz castor sugar	small ¹/₂ teaspoonful baking soda
5 oz flour	1 teaspoonful baking powder
1 egg	vanilla flavouring
1 tablespoonful golden syrup	rather more than 1 gill buttermilk

Cream the butter and sugar. Beat in the golden syrup and the lightly-whisked egg. Add the dry ingredients alternately with the buttermilk keeping the mixture slack. Divide between two small sandwich tins and bake in a moderately-heated oven for approximately 20-25 minutes.

Suggested oven temperature—400° or " 6 ".

Fill and ice as desired.

WALNUT CAKE

3 oz butter or margarine	6 oz flour
4 oz castor sugar	¹/₂ teaspoonful cream of tartar
2 eggs	¹/₄ teaspoonful baking soda
¹/₂ gill milk	

1 oz walnuts
¹/₂ teaspoonful vanilla flavouring

Filling:

1¹/₂ oz butter or margarine	a little vanilla flavouring
3 oz icing sugar	1 tablespoonful cream

1 oz chopped walnuts

Cream the butter and the sugar. Gradually beat in the lightly-whisked eggs. Add the milk alternately with the dry ingredients. Lastly, add the chopped walnuts and the vanilla flavouring. Divide the mixture between two prepared sandwich tins and bake in a moderate oven for 20-25 minutes.

Suggested oven temperature—400° or " 6 ".

Filling: Cream the butter and gradually beat in the sieved icing sugar. Add the vanilla flavouring, cream and chopped walnuts. Use to sandwich the cake.

The cake may also be iced with white water icing or American icing if wished and decorated with walnuts.

RUSSIAN CAKE

4 oz butter or	4¹/₂ oz flour
margarine	1 teaspoonful baking
4 oz castor sugar	powder
2 eggs	pink colouring

Filling: *apricot jam*
Almond paste:

6 oz ground almonds	4 oz icing sugar
2 oz castor sugar	egg to bind
a little almond essence	

Cream the butter and sugar thoroughly. Gradually beat in the lightly-whisked eggs. With the last of the egg add the flour and baking powder. Spread half the mixture in one side of a prepared Russian cake tin. Colour the remainder of the cake mixture pink and spread in the other side of the cake tin. Bake in a moderate oven for approximately 30 minutes.

Suggested oven temperature — 400° or " 6 ".

Cut the two strips of cake into four long pieces. Spread with apricot jam and re-assemble to give a chess-board effect.

Prepare the almond paste in the usual way and roll to a rectangular shape equal to the dimensions of the cake. Spread with the apricot jam and place the cake in the centre. Carefully envelope it in the marzipan, pinching away the join with the fingers. Lastly decorate the four edges by pinching with the fingers as in making shortbread, and trim the two ends.

MADEIRA CAKE

¹/₂ lb butter or	a pinch of ground
margarine	cinnamon
10 oz castor sugar	12 oz flour
the grated rind of	1 teaspoonful baking
¹/₂ lemon	powder
5 eggs	³/₄ gill milk
2 slices of candied citron peel	

Cream the butter with the sugar, grated lemon rind and cinnamon. Beat in the eggs adding them one at a time. Add the flour and baking powder alternately with the milk. Turn the mixture into a prepared 8 inch cake tin and bake in a moderate oven for approximately 1¹/₂ hours. After the first half-hour, when the cake is beginning to set, place the slices of peel on top.

Suggested oven temperature — 350° or " 3 ".

DUNDEE CAKE

¹/₂ lb butter or	1 teaspoonful baking
margarine	powder
¹/₂ lb castor sugar	¹/₂ lb currants
the grated rind of	¹/₂ lb sultanas
1 lemon	3 oz candied peel
4 eggs	2 oz ground almonds
10 oz flour	2 tablespoonfuls milk
a few split almonds	

Cream the butter with the sugar and grated lemon rind. Beat in the eggs one at a time. With the last of the egg start adding the flour and baking powder. Lastly, add the fruit, shredded peel and ground almonds and correct the consistency as required, with milk. Turn the mixture into a prepared 8 inch cake tin, scatter the split almonds over the top and bake in a moderate oven for 2-2¹/₄ hours.

Suggested oven temperature — 350° or " 3 ".

CHERRY CAKE

6 oz butter or margarine	1/2 teaspoonful baking powder
6 oz castor sugar	4-8 oz glacé cherries
3 eggs	a little milk
8 oz flour	a little vanilla flavour-
1 oz ground rice	ing or a little grated lemon rind

Cream the butter and sugar. Add the beaten eggs gradually. With the last of the egg, start adding the dry ingredients. Add the cherries and flavouring. Turn the mixture into a prepared 7 inch tin and bake in a moderate oven for 1-1¼ hours.

Suggested oven temperature — 350° or " 3 ".

WHITE GINGER CAKE

6 oz butter or margarine	3 eggs
5 oz sugar	8 oz flour
the grated rind of 1/2 lemon	1 teaspoonful baking powder
1/4 teaspoonful ground ginger	6 oz preserved ginger
	1 tablespoonful ginger syrup
White water icing:	8 oz icing sugar
	a little ginger syrup
	boiling water
Decoration:	slices of preserved ginger.

Cream the butter with the sugar, grated lemon rind and the ground ginger. Whisk the eggs and add them gradually to the mixture, beating well between each addition. With the last of the egg add the flour and baking powder adding them in roughly three amounts. Add the chopped preserved ginger and the ginger syrup. Turn the mixture into a prepared 7 inch cake tin and bake in a moderate oven for 1-1½ hours.

Suggested oven temperature — 350° or " 3 ".

When cold, cover the ginger cake with water icing and decorate with slices of ginger. Alternatively, the cake may be spread with a little apricot jam glaze, chopped ginger scattered on top and the white water icing used to cover all.

DARK GINGER CAKE

4 oz butter or margarine	2 eggs
4 oz castor sugar	8 oz flour
1 dessertspoonful golden syrup	1/2 teaspoonful baking powder
1 tablespoonful treacle	1/2 teaspoonful ground ginger
4 oz preserved ginger	

Cream the butter with the sugar. Add the syrup and treacle and beat in well. Drop in the eggs one at a time and beat thoroughly. Add a little flour after beating in each egg.

Finally, add the remainder of the flour, the baking powder and ground ginger and, with the last of these, add the chopped ginger. Turn the mixture into a prepared 7 inch cake tin and bake in a moderate oven for 1-1¼ hours.

Suggested oven temperature — 350° or " 3 ".

GENOA CAKE

1/2 lb butter or margarine	1/2 lb currants
1/2 lb castor sugar	1/2 lb sultanas
6 eggs	1/2 lb raisins
10 oz flour	1/4 lb candied lemon peel
the grated rind and juice of 1 lemon	a few flaked almonds

Cream the butter and sugar. Beat in the eggs and flour gradually and alternately. Lastly, add the grated rind and juice of the lemon together with the fruit and shredded peel. Turn the mixture into a prepared 8 inch cake tin, sprinkle with the flaked almonds and bake in a moderate oven for 2¹/₂ hours.

Suggested oven temperature — 350° or " 3 ".

SPONGE SANDWICH CAKE

3 *eggs*   3 *oz castor sugar*
                3¹/₂ *oz flour*

There are at least three accepted methods of making a sponge mixture:
1. Separate the yolks from the egg whites and whisk the latter until stiff. Gradually beat in the yolks and the sugar, adding these alternately and beating well between each addition. Continue whisking until the mixture is thick and creamy in colour. Sift the flour onto the egg mixture and fold it in lightly.
2. Combine the eggs and sugar in a bowl and beat together until they are thick and creamy in colour. The process is sometimes hastened if the basin is placed over a pan of hot water. Sift the flour onto the egg mixture and fold it in lightly.
3. Separate the yolks from the egg whites. Add the sugar to the former and whisk together until thick and creamy. Whisk the egg whites until stiff and fold into the yolk mixture. Sift the flour onto the sponge and fold it in lightly.

Divide the mixture between two prepared sandwich tins and bake in a moderate oven for 20-25 minutes.

Suggested oven temperature — 400° or " 6 ".

Sandwich with jam, lemon curd, cream or as required.

SWISS-ROLL — JAM FILLING

3 *eggs*   3 *oz flour*
4¹/₂ *oz castor sugar*   ¹/₂ *teaspoonful baking*
                                    powder
                1 *tablespoonful cold water*

hot jam or lemon curd to fill

Separate the yolks from the egg whites and whisk the latter until stiff. Gradually beat in the sugar and yolks adding each alternately and beating well between each addition. Continue beating until the mixture is light and thick. Fold in the sifted flour and baking powder, together with the water. Spread the mixture in a lined and greased swiss-roll tin and bake in a hot oven for approximately 12 minutes.

Suggested oven temperature — 475° or " 7 ".

Turn out onto a sugared paper. Spread quickly with the hot jam and roll up tightly. Trim the ends and dust with sugar.

SWISS-ROLL — CREAM FILLING

4 *oz castor sugar*   3 *eggs*
                2¹/₂ *oz flour*
whipped cream to fill

Measure the sugar on to a sheet of paper and heat for six minutes in an oven set at 475° or " 7 ". Add to the eggs and beat together until thick and creamy in colour. Fold in the sieved flour and spread in a lined and greased tin measuring 10 inches by 14 inches. Bake in a hot oven for 10-12 minutes.

Suggested oven temperature — 475° or " 7 ".

Turn out on to a piece of paper dusted with flour. Cool. Trim the two long edges. Spread lightly with whipped cream and roll up.

DEVONSHIRE CREAMS

2 *eggs*   3 *oz flour*
3 *oz castor*   ¹/₄ *teaspoonful baking*
sugar   *powder*
whipped cream and raspberry jam to fill

Separate the yolks from the egg whites. Whisk the latter until stiff. Gradually and alternately, whisk in the sugar and yolks. Continue beating until thick and a creamy colour. Sift and fold in the flour and baking powder. Drop the sponge mixture out into spoonfuls on-to a greased and floured tray. Dust with castor sugar and bake in a hot oven for 5-7 minutes.

Suggested oven temperature — 475° or " 7 ".

When cold, sandwich with raspberry jam and whipped cream. Dust with icing sugar.

GENOESE PASTRY

4 *eggs*   3 *oz flour*
4 *oz castor*   3 *oz butter or*
sugar   *margarine*

Break the eggs into a bowl. Add the castor sugar and beat together over hot water until thick. Meanwhile, measure the flour into a sieve, and oil the butter over gentle heat.

Remove the egg mixture from the heat and continue beating until cool. Sieve half the flour on top of the eggs and lightly fold into the mixture, at the same time adding the melted butter gradually. Repeat, being careful not to over-stir the mixture as this will cause it to fall. Pour into a prepared swiss-roll tin and bake in a moderate oven for 25 minutes. Alternatively, the mixture may be baked in a 7 inch cake tin for 40-45 minutes.

Suggested oven temperature — 375° or " 4 ".

ALMOND CARAMEL CAKE

a three egg sponge sandwich cake
Caramel:

4 *oz granulated sugar*   *a little water*
a pinch of cream of tartar

2 *oz toasted flaked almonds*
Butter icing:

3 *oz butter or*   1 *tablespoonful*
margarine   *cream*
6 *oz icing sugar*   *a little lemon juice*
a little vanilla flavouring

Put the sugar for the caramel into a small, strong saucepan. Add a little water and stir over gentle heat until dissolved. Stir in the cream of tartar and remove the spoon. Bring to the boil and boil gently until a rich golden brown. Pour immediately onto a greased tin. When cold crush with a rolling pin and mix with the toasted flaked almonds.

Prepare the butter icing in the usual way and use to sandwich the cake.

Spread over the sides of the cake and roll it in the caramel mixture. Finally spread the top of the cake with the icing and sprinkle with caramel and almonds.

PINEAPPLE CAKE

a three egg sponge sandwich or a four egg Genoese.
Candied pineapple:

1 *small tin of sliced*   2 *oz granulated sugar*
pineapple
Crème au beurre:

1 *oz granulated sugar*   1 *egg yolk*
2 *tablespoonfuls*   3 *oz butter or*
water   *margarine*
White icing:

10 *oz icing sugar*   *pineapple juice*
Prepare the candied pineapple first:

Cut each circle of pineapple in two horizontally. Put half the juice and the sugar into a frying-pan and, when dissolved, add the fruit. Cook quietly until transparent and a rich colour. Remove from the syrup and put aside to cool and dry.

Prepare the crème au beurre and into

it beat the syrup from the pan and any untidy pieces of candied pineapple. Use to sandwich the cake.

Arrange the rings of candied pineapple on the top of the cake overlapping them neatly. Coat the top and sides with the white pineapple water icing.

GRIESTORTE

4 eggs
7 oz castor sugar
3¹/₂ oz ground almonds
rind and juice of ¹/₂ lemon
3¹/₂ oz fine semolina

Filling: *apricot jam*
Icing:
4 oz icing sugar   *a little lemon juice*
boiling water

Separate the yolks from the egg whites. Add the sugar to the former and beat together until thick and light. Stir in the ground almonds, lemon rind and juice and put aside for 3 minutes. Whisk the egg whites until stiff and fold into the yolk mixture together with the semolina. Turn the mixture into a prepared 9 inch cake tin and bake in a moderate oven for approximately 35 minutes.

Suggested oven temperature — 375° or " 5 ".

When cold, split and fill with the apricot jam. Coat the top of the cake with the lemon-flavoured icing.

COFFEE MERINGUE CAKE

Meringue;
4 egg whites   8¹/₂ oz castor sugar
a pinch of salt
Coffee crème au beurre:
3 oz granulated sugar   3 egg yolks
6 tablespoonfuls water   8 oz butter
coffee essence
To decorate. 6 oz toasted flaked almonds or
toasted coco-nut.

Line four baking sheets with greaseproof paper and draw a circle on each, using a round sandwich tin as a guide. Grease.

Add the salt to the egg whites and whisk until very stiff. Whisk in four teaspoonfuls of sugar, adding each separately and beating well between each addition. Fold in the remainder. Divide the meringue out onto the prepared trays and spread neatly to give a layer between ¹/₄ and ¹/₂ inch thick. Dust with castor sugar and bake in a very moderate oven until golden and dry—about 1 hour.

Suggested oven temperature — 300°-200° or " ¹/₂ " to " ¹/₄ ".

Prepare the crème au beurre in the usual way and flavour with coffee essence. Use to sandwich the four layers of meringue together. Trim the sides of the cake as necessary and spread with the icing. Roll in the toasted nuts. Cover the top of the cake with the icing and sprinkle with nuts.

To decorate: Cut four or five strips of greaseproof paper about 1 inch wide and lay neatly across the cake. Dust over these with a generous shower of icing sugar. Remove the paper carefully.

ALMOND CHEESE CAKES

4 oz rich short crust or flaky pastry
a little apricot or raspberry jam

Filling:
1 egg white   a little almond essence
1¹/₂ oz ground almonds   a pinch each of baking
3 oz castor sugar   soda and cream of
1 teaspoonful semolina   tartar

Use the pastry to line approximately 2 dozen patty tins. Put a little jam in each.

Filling: Whisk the egg white lightly and fold in the remainder of the ingredients. Divide around the prepared patty tins and bake in a moderate oven for approximately 20 minutes.

Suggested oven temperature — 400° or " 6 ".

PASTRY CASES

4 oz butter or   1 dessertspoonful
  margarine   milk
1½ oz castor sugar   6 oz flour

Cream the butter and sugar together. Add the milk and gradually work in the flour. Roll out and use to line patty tins. Prick and bake in a moderate oven until a light biscuit colour.

Suggested oven temperature — 375° or " 3 ".

Suggested fillings are as follows:

APPLE CREAMS: Fill each pastry case with stewed apple and pipe with a star of whipped cream. Sprinkle the cream with a little green cake decoration.

PINEAPPLE CREAMS: Two-thirds fill each pastry case with crushed pineapple. Level with whipped cream and then spread the top of each cake with yellow-coloured water icing made using the boiled pineapple juice. Decorate with a sprinkling of green cake decoration.

DESSERT CAKES

6 oz butter or   1½ oz icing sugar
  margarine   6 oz flour
Filling: *black or green grapes and a little hot sieved apricot jam*

Cream the butter with the sieved icing sugar until very soft. Gradually work in the flour. Transfer the mixture to a forcing bag fitted with a large size star icing tube. Pipe into patty tins in a spiral starting in the centre. Finish with a circle of stars round the edge. Put aside in a cool place to firm. Then

bake in a moderte oven until a light biscuit colour.

Suggested oven temperature — 375° or " 3 ".

Cut the grapes in two and remove the seeds. Add to the hot sieved apricot jam and stir lightly until they are coated. Arrange in a pyramid shape in the pastry cases.

VIENNESE TARTLETS

8 oz butter or   2 oz icing sugar
  margarine   8 oz flour
a little raspberry jam or red-currant jelly for
  decorating

Cream the butter with the sieved icing sugar until very soft. Gradually work in the flour. Transfer the mixture to a forcing bag fitted with a large star pipe and pipe into patty tins using a circular motion to give a swirl slightly hollow in the centre. Put aside in a cool place to firm. Bake in a moderate oven until a light biscuit colour.

Suggested oven temperature — 375° or " 3 ".

Pipe the centre with a bead of raspberry jam.

CURRANT SQUARES

Pastry:
½ lb flour   1 teaspoonful baking
1 dessertspoonful   powder
  cornflour   6 oz butter or margarine
½ teaspoonful salt   cold water
Filling:
½ lb currants   2 oz granulated sugar
½ lb sultanas   1½ oz cornflour
¼ lb raisins   1 chopped cooking apple
1 teaspoonful mixed   ¼ pint water
  spice

Prepare the filling first:

Combine the ingredients in a saucepan

and stew together until the apple is tender. Put aside to cool.

Next prepare the pastry:

Measure the dry ingredients into a bowl and cut and rub in the butter. Mix to a stiff paste with water. Turn onto a floured surface and cut in two. Use one half to line a swiss-roll tin. Spread with the filling and cover with the remaining piece of pastry. Bake in a moderate oven for approximately 40 minutes.

Suggested oven temperature — 425° or "6".

Cut into squares and serve dusted with icing sugar.

ECCLES CAKES

¹/₂ lb rough puff or flaky pastry

Filling:

1 oz butter or margarine	1 oz soft brown sugar
4 oz currants	a little grated nutmeg
1 oz chopped candied peel	a little mixed spice

Melt the butter and stir in the other ingredients. Put aside to cool.

Roll the pastry out and cut into circles of approximately 3-4 inches in diameter. Divide the filling around these, damp the edges, then gather together to seal. Pinch securely to prevent the filling oozing out. Turn over and roll lightly to produce a round flat cake with the currants just beginning to show. Mark criss-cross with the back of a knife. Brush with water and dust with sugar. Bake in a hot oven for 15-20 minutes.

Suggested oven temperature — 475° or "9".

MILLE FEUILLES

Puff pastry trimmings

Filling: *raspberry jam and whipped cream*

Roll the trimmings of puff pastry into 3 or 4 rectangular pieces to fit swiss-roll tins. Place on the wet trays, prick well and put aside in a cool place to rest before baking. Bake in a fairly hot oven and when half cooked, turn each piece over on the tray and return to the oven to complete the cooking. The pastry, when ready, should be lightly brown, crisp but not risen a great deal.

Suggested oven temperature — 450° or "7".

When cold, sandwich together with a light spreading of raspberry jam and whipped cream. Press well, if necessary, under a board.

Cut into fingers and dust thickly with icing sugar.

Alternatively, Mille Feuilles may be spread with white water icing and feathered with chocolate and pink water icing before cutting into fingers.

SNOWBALLS

choux pastry
whipped cream to fill
icing sugar to dust

Put the choux pastry out on to a greased tray in rough teaspoonfuls. Alternatively, pipe out in "bulbs" using a forcing bag fitted with an éclair pipe. Bake in a moderately hot oven for 20-30 minutes.

Suggested oven temperature — 425° or "6".

Fill with whipped cream and served thickly dusted with icing sugar.

ÉCLAIRS

choux pastry
whipped cream to fill
chocolate water icing made using
3 oz icing sugar

Put the choux pastry into a forcing

CHRISTMAS CAKE

8 oz butter

8 oz soft brown sugar

4-5 eggs

8 oz flour

1 lb currants

8 oz sultanas

4 oz raisins

4 oz candied peel (mixed peel)

4 oz glacé cherries

2 oz ground almonds

1 teaspoonful ground ginger

½ "   "   "   ground mixed spice

½ "   "   "   ground cinnamon

½ "   "   "   ground cloves

¼ "   "   "   ground coriander seed

⅛th pint brandy (OR) whisky (OR) rum

METHOD

Wash and dry the FRUIT
Halve or quarter the CHERRIES
Chop the PEEL.
Line an 8" CAKE TIN

Cream the _butter_ and _sugar_.
Gradually beat in the _eggs_ alternately
with the _flour_ and _spices_ -
Lastly, add the prepared _fruit_.

Turn the _mixture_ into a lined tin.
Bake in a moderate oven for
     approx 3 hours
Temp 325°-300° a 3-2 Gasmark
When cooked baste with spirits while
     still hot.

bag fitted with an éclair pipe. Pipe it out into finger lengths onto a greased baking sheet. Bake in a moderately hot oven for approximately 25 minutes.

Suggested oven temperature—425º or " 6 ".

When cold, fill with whipped cream and coat the tops with chocolate water icing. Alternatively, coffee-flavoured icing may be used.

MERINGUES

3 egg whites   a pinch of salt
      6 oz castor sugar
Filling: whipped cream

Add the salt to the egg whites and whisk until very stiff. Then beat in a teaspoonful sugar to each white, adding each separately and beating well between each addition. Fold in the remainder of the sugar.

If the electric mixer is being used, the procedure is as follows:

Using the balloon whisk beat the egg whites and salt until very stiff. Then beat in 3 teaspoonfuls sugar as before. Turn the speed of the machine back to " slow " and shoot in the remainder of the sugar from a piece of paper. Quickly turn the speed up to " high " and then " off " immediately.

Shape the meringues by using two spoons or by piping onto a greased and floured tray. Dust with castor sugar and bake in a very moderate oven until a light golden colour and quite dry. This may take 2-3 hours according to size.

Suggested oven temperature — 300º-200º or " ¹/₄ ".

When required for use, sandwich two together with whipped cream.

BRANDY SNAPS

2 oz butter or   2 oz flour
   margarine   the juice of ¹/₄ lemon
2 oz castor sugar   1 small teaspoonful
2 oz golden syrup   ground ginger
      whipped cream to fill

Put the butter, sugar and syrup into a small saucepan and place over a gentle heat to melt. The mixture should not become more than lukewarm. Stir in the flour, lemon juice and ground ginger. The mixture may be used immediately or refrigerated before proceeding:

Put the mixture out in small teaspoonfuls, allowing two to each well-greased baking sheet. Bake in a moderate oven until a rich brown colour.

Suggested oven temperature — 400º or " 6 ".

Remove from the oven and cool for a moment. Then lift from the tray using a sharp pliable knife and quickly roll up — either round a greased horn mould or the greased handle of a wooden spoon.

Serve filled with whipped cream.

JAPANESE CAKES

Macaroon mixture:
3 egg whites   6 oz ground almonds
      6 oz castor sugar
Coffee butter icing:
2 oz butter or   3 oz icing
   margarine   sugar
     coffee essence to flavour
Pink water icing to decorate:
1 tablespoonful icing   pink colouring
  sugar   boiling water

Whip the egg whites until light but not stiff and fold in the castor sugar and the ground almonds. Spread evenly in a lined and greased swiss-roll tin. The knife may be dipped in water if necessary. Bake in a moderate oven until it is golden and just set.

Suggested oven temperature — 375° or " 4 ".

Cut into small rounds using a 1¼-1½ inch plain cutter. Break the scraps into small pieces and return to the oven to crisp out. Then crush with a rolling-pin.

Prepare the coffee butter icing in the usual way.

Use it to sandwich two circles of the macaroon mixture together. Spread the butter icing on the sides and roll in the crumbs; cover the top also and again toss in the crumbs.

Prepare the pink water icing in a cup and pipe a small bead of it in the centre of each cake.

TRUFFLE CAKES

6 oz cake-crumbs   2 oz ground almonds
4 oz castor sugar   a little sherry to flavour
         apricot jam to bind

To finish:
some melted cake coating chocolate
chocolate vermicelli
diamonds of angelica

Measure the finely-sieved cake crumbs, the sugar and ground almonds into a bowl. Flavour with sherry and bind into a stiff paste using apricot jam. Form into small balls. Dip into the melted chocolate and then toss in the chocolate vermicelli. Decorate with a diamond of angelica. Dust with icing sugar and serve in small paper cases.

Note: If preferred, a little grated orange rind and some juice may be used instead of sherry to flavour these cakes.

ALMOND MACAROONS

2 oz almonds   1 teaspoonful rice flour
4 oz castor sugar   a little almond essence
½ oz ground almonds   1-1½ egg whites

Blanch and chop the almonds finely. Combine with the other dry ingredients and flavour lightly with almond essence. Whip the egg whites to a froth and add to the almond mixture. The consistency should be fairly stiff. Put out with a teaspoon onto a tray lined with rice paper.

Decorate with cherry and a sprinkling of flaked almonds. Bake in a very moderately-heated oven for approximately 30-40 minutes.

Suggested oven temperature — 325° or " 3 ".

ALMOND PETITS FOURS

1½ egg whites   4 oz ground almonds
2 oz castor sugar   almond essence
Decoration. flaked almonds, cherries and angelica

Whisk the egg whites until frothy and stir in the sugar, ground almonds and almond essence. The consistency should be fairly stiff. Beat well and transfer to a forcing bag fitted with a meringue star pipe. Pipe out onto rice paper in the form of stars, fingers, whirls and " S " and " C " scrolls. Decorate prettily with the flaked almonds, small pieces of cherry and diamonds of angelica. Put aside for a while before baking — perhaps even overnight. Brush lightly with egg and toast quickly in a hot oven.

Suggested oven temperature — 450° or " 7 ".

OATCAKE — PLAIN

1 teacupful oatmeal   1 teaspoonful bacon fat
a pinch of salt   or dripping
a pinch of baking soda   boiling water

Put the oatmeal and salt into a mixing bowl. Crush the lumps from the baking soda and add. Melt the bacon fat in

Glaze: *approximately 2 tablespoonfuls hot apricot jam*

Icing:

3 *oz icing sugar*   *boiling orange juice*

Cream the butter and sieved icing sugar together until very soft. Add the grated orange rind and gradually work in the flour. Put the mixture into a forcing bag fitted with a large star pipe and pipe into finger shapes. Put aside in a cool place to firm. Bake in a moderately-heated oven for approximately 15-20 minutes.

Suggested oven temperature — 375° or " 4 ".

Meanwhile, heat the apricot jam and make the orange icing. When the biscuits are a golden brown, remove from the oven and brush with the apricot jam. Then brush with the icing and return all to the oven for about one minute to set the icing.

When cold, trim neatly. The ends of the biscuits may be dipped in melted cake-covering chocolate if wished.

AUSTRALIAN GINGERBREAD

4 *oz butter or*   4 *oz flour*
margarine   1/4 *teaspoonful baking*
2 *oz castor sugar*   *powder*
          1 *teaspoonful ground ginger*

Icing:

4 *tablespoonfuls*   3 *teaspoonfuls golden*
sugar   *syrup*
1 *teaspoonful ground*   2 *oz butter or*
ginger   *margarine*

Cream the butter and sugar together. Work in the flour, baking powder and ground ginger. Spread or press into a swiss-roll tin and bake in a moderately-heated oven for approximately 20 minutes.

Suggested oven temperature — 375° or " 4 ".

Place all the ingredients for the icing in a saucepan and stir over a gentle heat until melted. Use to ice the ginger slab while both are warm. Cool and cut into fingers.

ANZAC BISCUITS

3 *oz butter or*   1 *teacupful*
margarine   *oatmeal*
3 *oz castor*   1 *teaspoonful baking*
sugar   *soda*
1 *tablespoonful*   1 *teaspoonful ground*
golden syrup   *ginger*
1 *teacupful flour*   2 *tablespoonfuls water*

Cream the butter with the sugar and beat in the golden syrup. Gradually work in the remainder of the ingredients. Shape into small balls, flatten slightly and bake in a moderately-heated oven for approximately 15-20 minutes.

Suggested oven temperature — 375° or " 4 ".

DUTCH BISCUITS

4¹/₂ *oz butter or*   1 *oz semolina or*
margarine   *ground almonds*
3 *oz soft brown*   ¹/₄ *teaspoonful baking*
sugar   *powder*
6 *oz flour*   *almond or vanilla*
                         flavouring

To finish: *demerara sugar*

Cream the butter with the sugar and gradually work in the dry ingredients. Form into a log shape and roll in demerara sugar. Chill. When firm, cut into slices and bake in a moderately-heated oven for approximately 20 minutes.

Suggested oven temperature — 375° or " 4 ".

NAPOLEON BISCUITS

4 *oz flour*   1 *oz castor sugar*
3 *oz butter or*   1 *oz ground almonds*
margarine   1 *egg yolk*
          raspberry jam

179

Measure the flour into a bowl and cut and rub in the butter. Add the castor sugar and the ground almonds and mix to a stiff paste with the egg yolk. Chill if necessary.

Then roll to fit a swiss-roll tin. Bake in a moderately-heated oven until pale brown.

Suggested oven temperature — 375º or " 4 ".

Cut in two and spread one half with raspberry jam. Lay the other half on top and cut into fingers. Dust thickly with icing sugar.

Suitable for immediate use only.

IMPERIAL BISCUITS

4 oz butter or margarine	1/2 teaspoonful baking powder
4 oz castor sugar	1 teaspoonful ground cinnamon
8 oz flour	1 small egg

Filling: *raspberry jam*

Icing:

6 oz icing sugar	boiling water

Decoration: *small pieces of cherry*

Cream the butter with the sugar and gradually work in the dry ingredients with the egg. Chill if necessary. Roll out thinly and cut into biscuits. Bake in a moderately-heated oven for approximately 15-20 minutes.

Suggested oven temperature — 375º or " 4 ".

Sandwich two together with raspberry jam and ice the top with a teaspoonful of water icing. Decorate with a small piece of cherry.

ALMOND TUILES

2 egg whites	1/2 teaspoonful vanilla flavouring
4 oz castor sugar	
2 oz flour	2 oz flaked almonds
2 oz melted butter or margarine	

Whisk the egg whites until stiff. Beat in the sugar and fold in the other ingredients. Put the mixture out in teaspoonfuls onto a greased tray allowing two to a tray. Using two forks pull the mixture apart until wafer thin. Bake in a moderately-heated oven until a delicate golden brown.

Suggested oven temperature — 375º or " 4 ".

Carefully lift the biscuits off the tray and cool over a rolling pin.

Almond tuiles are a suitable accompaniment for many cold puddings and ices.

DUTCH FANS

9 oz flour	2 1/4 oz castor sugar
6 3/4 oz butter or margarine	1/2 egg white

Rub the butter into the flour. Add the sugar and mix all to a stiff paste with the beaten egg white. Roll out thinly and cut into large circles with a fluted flan ring. Cut each circle into four fan shapes and bake in a moderate oven until a delicate golden brown.

Suggested oven temperature — 375º or " 4 ".

Dust with castor sugar while still warm.

Dutch fans are suitable to serve as an accompaniment to many cold puddings and ices.

ICINGS AND FILLINGS

ALMOND ICING OR PASTE

8 oz ground almonds	1-2 eggs
4 oz castor sugar	1 tablespoonful sherry
4 oz sieved icing sugar	a little almond essence
a little vanilla flavouring	

Put the ground almonds, castor and icing sugars into a bowl. Add the flavourings and mix in with the tips of the fingers. Whisk the egg and use to mix all to a stiff consistency. Work with the hand until smooth.

AMERICAN OR MOUNTAIN ICING (1)

1 *lb granulated*   *a pinch of cream of*
  sugar   *tartar*
1 *gill water*   2 *egg whites*

Put the sugar and water into a strong saucepan and stir over gentle heat until the sugar is dissolved. Stir in the cream of tartar, remove the spoon and bring to the boil. Boil briskly until a little, when tested in cold water, will give a " soft ball " or until 115.5° C or 240° F is reached. Meanwhile, whisk the egg whites until stiff. Once the syrup is ready, pour it gently onto the whites, beating all the time. Continue whisking until the mixture thickens and shows signs of holding its shape. Use quickly.

AMERICAN OR MOUNTAIN ICING (2)

This recipe is probably easier than the first recipe and the result is suitable to use on a walnut cake or other light mixture.

12 *oz icing sugar*   ¹/₄ *teaspoonful cream of*
3 *tablespoonfuls water*   *tartar*
        2 *egg whites*

Put the ingredients into a bowl and place over a pan of boiling water. Stir until dissolved. Then whisk until the mixture will stand in peaks. Remove from the heat and continue beating until the icing cools and is thick enough for spreading.

ROYAL ICING (1)

A very hard icing suitable for tier cakes.

1 *lb icing*   1 *teaspoonful lemon*
  sugar   *juice*

approximately 2 *egg*   ¹/₂ *teaspoonful*
  whites   *glycerine*

Sieve the icing sugar through a nylon or hair sieve. Whisk the egg whites until frothy and add the icing sugar gradually until the required consistency. Add the lemon juice and glycerine and beat thoroughly before use.

ROYAL ICING (2)

A softer icing suitable for one tier cakes.

1 *lb icing sugar*   4 *tablespoonfuls boiling*
1 *egg white*   *water*
juice of ¹/₂ *lemon*   ¹/₄ *teaspoonful cream of*
                           tartar

Sieve the icing sugar into a bowl and add the other ingredients. Beat thoroughly for 10-15 minutes before use.

Royal icing is most successful made using the electric mixer and using the flat beater.

BUTTER ICING

4 *oz icing sugar*
2 *oz butter (unsalted by preference)*
flavouring and colouring

Sieve the icing sugar passing it through a nylon or hair sieve. Cream the butter and gradually beat in the icing sugar. Beat thoroughly adding flavouring and colouring as required. Suggested flavourings include:

  (a) 2 oz melted chocolate
  (b) 1¹/₂ dessertspoonfuls coffee essence
  (c) 1 tablespoonful lemon curd
  (d) ¹/₂ glass sherry

The addition of a little cream is also an improvement.

FRENCH BUTTER ICING OR CRÈME AU BEURRE (1)

1 *oz granulated sugar*   1 *egg yolk*
2 *tablespoonfuls*   3 *oz butter (unsalted by*
  water   *preference)*

Dissolve the sugar in the water and bring to the boil. Boil gently, without stirring until a little, when tested in cold water, will form a " thread " between the finger and thumb. Pour this syrup gradually onto the whisked egg yolk and continue beating until thick and light. Cream the butter and gradually beat in the egg mixture. Add flavouring as required.

FRENCH BUTTER ICING OR CRÈME AU BEURRE (2)

2 *egg whites*   4 *oz icing sugar*
        8 *oz butter (unsalted by preference)*

Whisk the egg whites. Place the bowl over a pan of hot water and gradually beat in the sieved icing sugar. Continue beating until stiff.

Cream the butter and gradually beat in the cooked meringue. Flavour and colour as required.

WATER ICING

$^1/_2$ *lb icing sugar*
2-3 *tablespoonfuls boiling water or fruit juice such as orange or pineapple*

Sieve the icing sugar into a bowl and gradually beat in sufficient boiling water or fruit juice to give a spreading consistency. Beat well before use.

Water icing may also be flavoured with coffee essence, the syrup from a jar of ginger or sherry.

CHOCOLATE WATER ICING

6 *oz icing sugar*   *a speck of butter*
3 *oz melted chocolate   vanilla flavouring*
        1-2 *tablespoonfuls boiling water*

Sieve the icing sugar into a bowl. Add the chocolate, butter and vanilla and lastly beat in sufficient boiling water

to give a spreading consistency. Beat well before use.

LEMON CURD

1 *lemon*   1 *egg*
4 *oz granulated*   1 *oz butter or*
  sugar   *margarine*

Grate the lemon and squeeze the juice. Put in a small saucepan with the sugar, beaten egg and butter. Cook over a gentle heat until it thickens. There is no danger of curdling.

ORANGE FILLING

1 *oz butter*   1 *oz ground almonds*
1$^1/_2$ *oz icing sugar   the rind of 1 orange*
1 *yolk of a   a little orange*
  hard-boiled egg   juice
      1 *tablespoonful whipped cream*

Cream the butter with the sieved icing sugar. Sieve the egg yolk and beat into the butter mixture. Gradually add the other ingredients, adding sufficient orange juice to give a spreading consistency.

CREAM SUBSTITUTE

4 *oz butter*   2 *tablespoonfuls*
2 *oz castor sugar*   *cornflour*
                         1 *gill milk*
            vanilla flavouring

Cream the butter and sugar thoroughly. Blend the cornflour with the milk and cook together in the usual way. Cover and cool. Gradually beat into the butter mixture while still lukewarm. Lastly add the vanilla flavouring.

WHITE PRALINE

A useful finish for iced cakes.
6 *oz granulated sugar* $^1/_2$ *gill water*
        3 *oz ground almonds*

Put the sugar and water into a saucepan and stir over a gentle heat until dissolved. Remove the spoon and wash down the sides of the saucepan. Bring to the boil and boil until 120°C or 248°F or until a little will form a hard ball when tested in water. Remove from the heat and add the ground almonds. Stir until the mixture grains. Sieve and store for use as required.

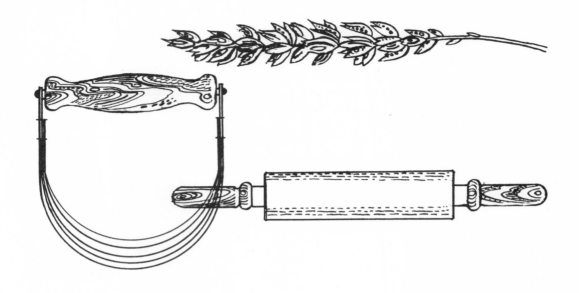

PASTRY

SUET PASTRY

8 *oz flour*
1 *teaspoonful baking powder*
$^1/_2$ *teaspoonful salt*
3-4 *oz finely-chopped kidney suet or shredded suet*
approximately 1 gill water

Measure the flour, baking powder and salt into a bowl. Add the prepared suet and mix all to an elastic consistency with water. Turn onto a floured surface and toss lightly to form a smooth ball.

Suet pastry is generally boiled or steamed, but may also be baked.

A small proportion of flour may be replaced by an equal weight of breadcrumbs to make a lighter pastry.

SHORT CRUST PASTRY

8 *oz flour*   *a pinch of salt*
4 *oz fat — butter, margarine or equal quantities of margarine and lard*
water

Measure the flour and salt into a bowl, cut and rub the fat into it, using the tips of the fingers, until it resembles fine breadcrumbs. Mix with water, added gradually until small lumps of dough are formed. Draw these together with the fingers to form a firm paste.

If the pastry is to be used for a sweet dish 1 oz sugar may be added to 8 oz flour. It should be added after the fat has been rubbed into the flour.

RICH SHORT CRUST PASTRY (1)

8 *oz flour*
a pinch of salt
5 *oz butter or margarine*
1 *dessertspoonful castor sugar*
1 *egg yolk or* $^1/_2$ *egg approximately*
1 *tablespoonful water*

Mix flour and salt in a bowl, cut and rub in the fat until the mixture resembles breadcrumbs. Add the sugar and mix to a stiff paste with egg and water.

RICH SHORT CRUST PASTRY (2)

A rich recipe suitable for use with an electric mixing machine.

12 *oz flour*	8 *oz butter or*
pinch of salt	*margarine*
2 *oz castor sugar*	1 *egg*

Measure flour, salt, sugar and fat into the bowl of the mixing machine. If the fat is firm it should be cut into pieces of about one ounce. Break in the egg, use the flat beater, switch to a moderate speed and mix to a stiff paste.

FRENCH FLAN PASTRY OR PÂTÉ SUCRÉE

4 *oz flour*	2 *oz caston sugar*
pinch of salt	2 *yolks or* 1 *yolk and*
2 *oz butter or*	1 *dessertspoonful*
margarine	*water*

Measure the flour and salt onto a suitable surface, make a bay in the centre and place the fat, sugar and liquid in it. Use the fingertips of one hand to blend these together and then gradually draw in the flour and knead gently to form a smooth paste.

Leave it aside in a cool place for at least 30 minutes before rolling out.

CHEESE PASTRY

3 *oz flour*	3 *oz grated cheese (if*
salt, pepper, cayenne	*possible use a propor-*
and mustard	*tion of Parmesan)*
1½ *oz butter or*	1 *yolk of egg*
margarine	*little water if necessary*

Add the seasonings to the flour, cut and rub in the fat. Add the grated cheese and mix all to a stiff paste with egg and water if necessary.

HOT WATER CRUST

¾ *lb flour*	1 *gill milk or water*
¾ *teaspoonful salt*	4 *oz lard*

Measure the flour and salt into a bowl, bring the milk or water and lard to the boil in a saucepan. Pour the boiling mixture into the flour and knead until smooth. Leave aside in a warm place for a short time until it is a consistency for moulding. The pastry must be handled quickly or it becomes too firm for manipulation. It is used for mutton, pork and veal and ham pies.

ROUGH PUFF PASTRY

8 *oz flour*	5-6 *oz butter, margarine*
½ *teaspoonful salt*	*or a mixture of*
approximately 1 *gill*	*margarine and lard*
water	*blended together.*

Measure the flour and salt into a bowl, cut the fat into pieces the size of a walnut and mix them through the flour keeping the lumps separate. Mix to an elastic consistency with water, turn onto a floured surface and knead lightly. Roll into a strip about three times as long as broad. Dust lightly with flour, damp the edges and fold in three. Seal on three sides by pressing with the rolling-pin; give the pastry a half turn so that the open ends are back and front. Distribute the air by marking into ridges with the rolling pin. Roll out again and repeat until it has been rolled and folded in all three or four times. If possible leave in a cool place for a short time in between rollings. When it is ready for use the fat should be evenly distributed through the dough. Use for sweet or savoury dishes.

FLAKY PASTRY

8 *oz flour*	6 *oz butter, margarine*
½ *teaspoonful*	*or a mixture of*
salt	*margarine and lard*
	blended together
approximately 1 *gill water*	

Measure the flour and salt into a bowl. Work the fat on a plate until the consistency is pliable, form into a neat pat and divide into four. Add one quarter to the flour and cut and rub in with the fingers. Add sufficient water to mix all to an elastic dough. Turn onto a floured surface, knead lightly and roll out into a long strip approximately five or six inches wide. Cover two-thirds of the strip with small pieces of fat cut from the second quarter. Dust lightly with flour, damp the edges and fold in three. Give a half turn so that the open ends are now back and front. Roll out, repeating the process with the third and fourth quarters of the fat. A final rolling may still be necessary if the pastry is still streaky with fat.

The pastry should be put in a cool place to firm between rollings, or as found necessary.

Use for sweet and savoury dishes.

PUFF PASTRY (1)

8 oz flour   8 oz butter or margarine
1/2 teaspoonful salt   cold water to mix

Measure the flour and salt into a bowl and rub in a small piece of the fat. Mix to an elastic dough with water. Turn onto a floured surface and knead lightly. Put aside to relax while preparing the fat.

The fat should be firm but pliable for rolling; it may be necessary to work it a little.

Roll the dough out into a square.

Shape the fat into a square also, but a size smaller. This is most conveniently done between two pieces of greaseproof paper.

Arrange the fat diamond fashion on the dough and fold in the four corners,

envelope shape. Roll out into a long strip. Flour lightly, damp the edges and fold in three. Give a half turn, so that the open ends are to and from one-self. Seal with the rolling pin and roll out again, repeating the process so that in all the pastry is rolled seven times.

Between rollings, or as found necessary, the puff pastry should be put aside to relax and firm.

Use for sweet and savoury dishes.

PUFF PASTRY (2)

8 oz flour   8 oz butter or margarine
1/2 teaspoonful salt   water to mix

Measure the flour and salt onto a marble slab and divide it roughly into two parts of approximately one-third and two-thirds. Put the smaller portion into a bowl. Add the fat and work the two together to form a firm paste. Put aside in a cool place.

Meanwhile mix the larger portion of the flour into an elastic dough with the cold water. Knead until smooth.

Pat and roll the butter and flour mixture into a long strip and roll the dough so that it is equal in size to half the strip of fat and flour. Place it on one end of the long strip and fold this over so that the dough is neatly enclosed in a casing of butter.

Give the pastry a half turn, so that the open ends are back and front and roll into a long strip. Give a double fold. To do this:

Fold the two ends into the centre of the strip and then fold in two. This should give a total of four layers. Seal with the rolling pin and again give a half turn.

Repeat the rolling and folding in all four times, allowing a rest between the second and third rollings, or more frequently, if the pastry is difficult to handle.

Use for sweet and savoury dishes.

CHOUX PASTRY

2 oz lard   2¹/₄ oz flour
1 gill water   a pinch of salt
2 small eggs

Put the lard and water into a medium-sized saucepan and bring to the boil. Immediately boiling point is reached shoot in the flour and salt from a piece of paper. Draw the pan to the side of the heat and beat until smooth using a wooden spoon. Then return to the heat and cook for three minutes, beating thoroughly. Cool it slightly before continuing. Whisk the eggs and gradually beat into the mixture in the saucepan. While adding the last of the egg it is important to watch the consistency of the mixture. If correct it should be soft, but still capable of holding its shape.

Use as required.

BAKING TEMPERATURES FOR PASTRIES

Type of Pastry	Electricity	Gas
Suet	400°-425°	6-7
Short Crust	450°	7
Rich Short Crust No. 1	425°	6
Rich Short Crust No. 2	400°	5
French Flan Pastry	400°	5
Hot Water Crust	400°	6
Rough Puff ⎫		
Flaky ⎬	475°	9
Puff ⎭		
Choux	450°	7

These temperatures should only be taken as an approximate guide. In practice the type of dish for which the pastry is used will be a controlling factor. As a general rule small items such as patties are baked in a rather hotter oven than a large item such as a vol-au-vent.

JAMS AND JELLIES

APPLE GINGER

6 lb apples
2 pints water
the rind and juice
  of 4 lemons

2 teaspoonfuls ground
  ginger
6 lb preserving sugar
$^1/_2$ lb crystallised ginger

Peel, core and slice the apples and put in a pan with the water, lemon rind and juice, and the ground ginger. Tie the peel and cores in muslin and hang them in the pan. Bring slowly to the boil and simmer until tender. Remove the bag of peel after squeezing out the juice. Add the heated sugar and chopped crystallised ginger. Stir until the sugar is dissolved. Bring to the boil and boil rapidly until a little will set when tested.

Yield approximately 10-11 lb.

APRICOT JAM

2 lb dried apricots
6 pints water

the juice of two lemons
6 lb preserving sugar

4-6 oz almonds if wished

Wash the apricots and soak in the water for at least 24 hours. Bring slowly to the boil and simmer gently for $^1/_2$ hour. Add the lemon juice, heated sugar and the blanched, shredded almonds. Stir until the sugar has dissolved. Bring to the boil and boil rapidly until the jam sets when a little is tested on a plate.

Yield approximately 10 lb.

APRICOT AND PINEAPPLE JAM

1 lb dried
  apricots
3 pints water and
  pineapple juice

the rind and juice of
  3 lemons
$^3/_4$ lb drained crushed
  pineapple

4 lb preserving sugar

Wash the apricots and soak for 24 hours in the water and pineapple juice. Add the lemon juice and simmer until tender. Add the lemon rind, the crushed pineapple and the heated sugar. Stir until the sugar is dissolved, then bring to the boil. Boil briskly until a little shows signs of setting when tested on a plate.

BLACKCURRANT JAM

4 lb blackcurrants   3 pints water
6 lb preserving sugar

Remove the stems from the fruit, wash and put in a preserving pan with the water.

Simmer gently until the fruit is completely tender and the bulk reduced considerably. Add the heated sugar and stir until dissolved. Bring to the boil and boil briskly until a little will set when tested on a plate.

Yield approximately 10 lb.

DAMSON OR PLUM JAM

4 lb damsons or plums 1³/₄ pints water
5 lb preserving sugar

Wash the fruit and stew in the water until well broken down. Add the heated sugar, stir until dissolved, then boil briskly for about 10 minutes, removing as many stones as possible as they rise to the surface. Test on a cold plate for setting.

Pot and seal immediately.

Yield approximately 8-9 lb.

DAMSON CHEESE

3 lb damsons   ¹/₂ pint water
1 lb preserving sugar to each lb of fruit pulp

Wash the damsons and stew them in the water until tender. Rub through a coarse sieve. Weigh the pulp obtained, return to the pan and add an equal weight of warm sugar. Stir until dissolved, then bring to the boil. Simmer until a little, when tested on a plate, shows signs of setting.

GOOSEBERRY JAM

4¹/₂ lb gooseberries   1¹/₂ pints water
6 lb preserving sugar

Wash, top and tail the gooseberries and stew in the water until well broken down. Add the heated sugar, bring to the boil, and boil briskly until a little will set on a plate.

MARROW AND GINGER JAM

5 lb prepared marrow   3³/₄ lb preserving sugar
the rind and juice of   5 oz crystallised
5 lemons   ginger
1 chilli pod

Put the prepared marrow and the rind and juice of the lemons into a strong pan. Cover with a lid and cook gently until quite tender. This will take approximately 1 hour. Add the heated sugar and stir until dissolved. Add the chopped ginger and the chilli pod and bring to the boil. Continue boiling until thick. Skim if necessary and remove the chilli pod before potting and sealing in the usual way.

RASPBERRY JAM

6 lb raspberries   6 lb preserving sugar

Put the raspberries into a preserving pan and place over a very gentle heat until some juice has been extracted. Then simmer gently until the fruit is tender. Add the heated sugar, stir until dissolved and boiling point is reached. Boil briskly until a little will set when tested on a plate.

RHUBARB AND GINGER JAM

2¹/₂ lb rhubarb   1 oz root ginger
2¹/₂ lb preserving   4 oz crystallised
sugar   ginger

Wash the rhubarb, split the stems if necessary and cut into inch pieces. Put in a basin layered with the sugar. Cover and leave overnight. Next day transfer to a preserving pan and add the bruised root ginger tied in muslin. Bring to the boil and boil briskly for 15 minutes. Add the chopped crystallised ginger and continue boiling until the rhubarb is clear and the jam shows signs of thickening. Remove the bag of root ginger after squeezing out the juice and pot and cover in the usual way.

STRAWBERRY JAM

7 lb strawberries   6 lb preserving sugar
the juice of 4 lemons or 2 teaspoonfuls tartaric acid

Hull the strawberries and wash if necessary.

Put the fruit, sugar and lemon juice or tartaric acid into a preserving pan and heat gently, stirring all the time until the sugar is dissolved. Bring to the boil and boil briskly until a little will set when tested on a plate. Skim and cool well before potting.

Yield approximately 10 lb.

BLACKBERRY JELLY

6 lb blackberries   3 pints water
2¹/₄ lb apples   1 lb sugar to each pint of blackberry juice

Put the blackberries into a preserving pan. Wash and quarter the apples and add together with the water. Simmer gently until the fruit is well broken down. Strain through a scalded jelly bag. Measure the fruit juice and sugar. Return the juice to the preserving pan and bring to the boil. Add the heated sugar and boil briskly until a little will set when tested on a plate.

CRAB APPLE JELLY

6 lb crab apples   3 teaspoonfuls cloves
3 pints water   1 lb sugar to each pint apple juice

Wash the crab apples and put into a preserving pan with the water and cloves. Simmer gently for about 1-1¹/₂ hours or until tender. Strain through a scalded jelly bag and measure the juice. Weigh and warm the sugar. Return the juice to the preserving pan and bring to the boil. Add the heated sugar and boil rapidly until setting point is reached. Skim and pour into small heated jars. Cover immediately.

APPLE JELLY may be made in a similar way.

GOOSEBERRY AND ELDERFLOWER JELLY

gooseberries   1 lb sugar to each pint
water to barely   fruit juice
cover   3-4 elderflowers to each pint juice

Wash the gooseberries, but do not top or tail. Place in a preserving pan and barely cover with water. Simmer gently until the fruit is thoroughly pulped. Strain through a scalded jelly bag and measure the juice. Weigh and warm the sugar. Bring the juice to the boil and add the heated sugar. Boil rapidly until beginning to show signs of setting. Tie the elderflowers in muslin and put into the jelly at this stage. After 3-4 minutes taste, and then remove the flowers if the flavour is pleasing. When setting point is reached, skim and pot in the usual way.

RED-CURRANT JELLY

6 lb red-currants   1¹/₄ lb sugar to each pint juice

Wash the fruit, remove the leaves but not necessarily the stalks and put into a preserving pan. Heat gently to draw the juice and then simmer very slowly until the fruit is completely mashed. The time required is about ³/₄-1 hour. Strain through a scalded jelly bag. Measure the juice and bring to the boil. Add the heated sugar and bring to the boil again. Boil briskly for approximately 1 minute or until setting point is reached. As soon as it shows signs of setting, skim and pot in small heated jars.

Red-currant jelly is used as an accompaniment for roast mutton and other meats and on this account it is more satisfactory if the jelly is firm.

SLOE JELLY

equal quantities of ripe sloes and crab or cooking apples
water to barely cover   *1 lb sugar to each pint juice*

Wash the sloes and crab apples and put into a preserving pan. Barely cover with water and simmer gently until the fruit is thoroughly broken down. The time required is about 1½ hours. Strain through a scalded jelly bag. Measure the juice and bring to the boil. Add the heated sugar and boil rapidly until a little will set when tested on a plate.

This jelly has a piquant flavour quite its own and is delicious served with roast mutton, hare or venison.

THICK MARMALADE

2 lb Seville oranges   *1 lemon*
2 sweet oranges   *6 pints water*
           6 lb preserving sugar

Wash the fruit and cut in two. Squeeze the juice, collect the pips and tie in muslin. Slice the peel finely. Put the sliced fruit, juice, pips and water into a bowl and leave overnight. Next day, transfer to a preserving pan and simmer gently until the peel is quite soft. The time required is approximately 2 hours. Remove the bag of pips, squeezing out the juice and add the

heated sugar. Stir until dissolved, then bring to the boil and boil rapidly until setting point is reached. Skim and cool well before pouring into heated jars.

Approximate yield 10 lb.

JELLY MARMALADE

3 lb Seville oranges   *7 pints water*
½ oz citric or   *5 lb preserving*
   tartaric acid   *sugar*

Wash the oranges and peel off the golden rind very thinly. Cut approximately 6 oz of this into fine shreds. Soak overnight covered with some of the measured water. Cut up roughly the remains of the orange and soak in another bowl with the acid and the greater part of the water.

Next day, put the shreds of orange and the water into a saucepan and simmer gently for 1½ hours or until tender. Simmer the orange separately in a preserving pan. The time required is approximately 2 hours. Strain the liquid from the shreds into the larger pan and then strain all through a jelly bag. Bring the juice to the boil. Add the heated sugar, stir until dissolved then boil briskly until setting point is reached. Skim and add the shreds of orange peel. Cool a little before pouring into heated jam jars.

Approximate yield 8 lb.

GRAPEFRUIT MARMALADE

4 large grapefruit   *7 pints water*
½ oz citric or   *7 lb preserving*
   tartaric acid   *sugar*

Cut the grapefruit in two, squeeze the juice and collect the pips. Tie the latter in muslin. Cut the peel of the fruit into fine shreds. Put the sliced fruit, juice, pips, acid and water into a bowl and leave to steep overnight. Next day bring to the boil and simmer gently for 2 hours or until the peel is quite soft. Remove the pips and add the heated sugar. Stir until dissolved, then boil rapidly until a little will set when tested on a plate. Skim and cool before pouring into heated jam jars.

Approximate yield 10-11 lb.

LEMON MARMALADE

6 *large lemons*   6 *pints water*
preserving sugar

Wash the lemons and cut in two. Squeeze the juice and slice the peel finely. Put the sliced fruit, the juice and water into a bowl and leave to steep overnight. Next day, bring gently to the boil and simmer for 2 hours or until the peel is completely tender. Weigh the contents of the pan and add an equal weight of heated sugar. Stir until dissolved, bring to boiling point and boil rapidly until a little will set when tested. Skim and cool before pouring into heated jam jars.

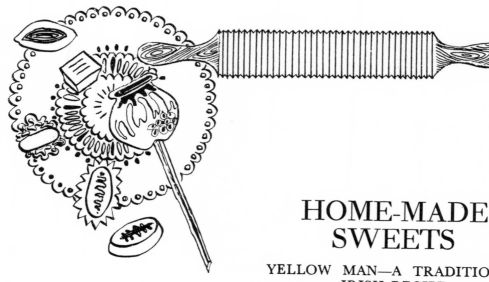

HOME-MADE SWEETS

YELLOW MAN—A TRADITIONAL IRISH RECIPE

1 oz butter	1/2 lb brown sugar
2 tablespoonful water	1 small teaspoonful
1 lb golden syrup	baking soda

Choose a strong, roomy saucepan and melt the butter in it. Then add the water, syrup and sugar. Stir over a gentle heat until the sugar is dissolved. Boil without stirring until a little when tested in cold water is crisp. Stir in the baking soda and pour onto a greased marble slab or large dish. Turn in the edges to the centre and commence to pull as soon as it is sufficiently cool. Pull until it is a light colour. Traditionally, it is left in one large cake to be broken up as required.

HONEYCOMB TOFFEE

1 oz margarine	1 dessertspoonful
8 oz golden syrup	vinegar
4 oz demerara	1/4 teaspoonful baking
sugar	soda

Melt the margarine in a strong medium-sized saucepan. Add the golden syrup, sugar and vinegar. Stir over a gentle heat until the sugar is dissolved. Bring to the boil and boil briskly without

SUGAR BOILING DEGREES

The solution of sugar in water begins to boil at 101.5° C or 215° F and increases in temperature to 157°C or 315°F without burning. In sweet-making there are special names for different temperatures: The THREAD or 107-110°C or 225-230°F: the syrup when tested between the finger and thumb forms a fine thread.

The SOFT BALL or 115.5-118.5°C or 240-245°F: the syrup when tested in cold water forms a soft ball.

The HARD BALL or 120-124°C or 248-255°F: the syrup when tested in cold water gives a firm ball.

The CRACK or 138-149°C or 280-300°F: the syrup when tested in cold water forms a crisp piece of toffee.

CARAMEL or 154.5-177°C or 310-350°F: the syrup changes after this temperature and becomes golden brown. If boiling is continued it will become darker and eventually burn.

stirring until a little when tested in cold water is crisp. Remove from the heat and when the bubbles have subsided stir in the baking soda. Quickly pour into a greased tin. One measuring 6 by 9 inches is suitable. Break into pieces for serving, or, if preferred, mark into squares before it is cold.

TOFFEE

1¹/₄ gills water	¹/₄ teaspoonful cream
1 lb demerara sugar	of tartar
2 oz butter or	1 neat tablespoonful
margarine	golden syrup
1 dessertspoonful vinegar	

Put the water into a strong medium-sized saucepan and add the sugar. Stir over a gentle heat until the sugar is dissolved. Then stir in the remainder of the ingredients and boil briskly, without stirring, until the mixture reaches 138ºC or 280ºF or the CRACK. Remove from the heat and when the bubbles have subsided pour into an oiled tin; one measuring 6 by 9 inches is suitable for the purpose. Mark into squares while still warm. Finish by wrapping each toffee in waxed paper or store in an airtight tin.

3 oz chopped nuts may be added before moulding if wished.

BUTTERSCOTCH

1 lb granulated sugar	3 oz butter
1¹/₄ gills water	¹/₂ teaspoonful vanilla
¹/₄ teaspoonful cream	flavouring
of tartar	

Put the sugar and water into a strong medium-sized saucepan and dissolve over a gentle heat. Stir in the cream of tartar, remove the spoon and boil briskly until 115.5ºC or 240ºF is reached. Add the butter cut into thin slices and continue boiling until 138ºC or 280ºF is reached.

Allow the bubbles to subside and pour into a greased tin making the toffee about ¹/₄ inch thick. Mark deeply into squares before it cools and store in an airtight tin.

FUDGE

¹/₄-¹/₂ lb butter or	1 tall tin unsweetened
margarine	evaporated milk
1 tablespoonful golden	2 lb granulated
syrup	sugar
	flavouring

Melt the butter or margarine into a strong roomy saucepan and add the syrup, tinned milk and sugar. Stir over a gentle heat until the sugar is dissolved. Bring to the boil, then, stirring all the time, boil until a little when tested in cold water will give a soft ball. Remove from the heat and allow the bubbles to subside. Stir in the chosen flavouring and beat until beginning to thicken. Quickly pour into an oiled tin. One measuring 8 inches square is suitable. When firm, but before the mixture is cold; turn out and cut into squares.

Suggested flavourings include:
  (a) the grated rind of an orange
  (b) ¹/₄ lb chopped preserved ginger
  (c) 2 tablespoonfuls coffee essence
  (d) 4-8 oz chopped walnuts
  (e) 4-8 oz dark chocolate
  (f) vanilla essence or rum.

ORANGE BARBADOS FUDGE

¹/₄ pint milk	4 oz walnuts
3 oz butter	1 oz candied orange peel
1 lb Barbados	the grated rind of
sugar	1 large orange

Put the milk and butter into a strong saucepan and stir over a gentle heat until the butter is melted. Add the sugar and stir until dissolved. Boil gently stirring constantly to 115.5ºC or 240ºF or until a soft ball is formed when a little is tested in cold water. Remove from the heat and allow the bubbles to subside. Add the chopped walnuts, orange peel and the grated rind of the orange. Beat until beginning to thicken. Quickly pour into a 6½ inch square sandwich tin. Turn out and cut into squares before the fudge is quite cold.

FRUIT CREAM FUDGE

¼ pint cream	1 oz preserved ginger
2 oz butter	1 oz glacé pineapple
1 lb granulated sugar	1 oz glacé cherries
a little vanilla flavouring	2 oz orange and lemon slices

Put the cream and butter into a strong saucepan and stir over a gentle heat until the butter is melted. Add the sugar and stir until dissolved. Bring to the boil and boil gently until a little when tested will give a soft ball. Stir constantly with a wooden spoon. Remove from the heat and, after the bubbles have subsided, add the vanilla essence and chopped fruit. Beat until beginning to thicken, then pour into a 6½ inch square sandwich tin. Turn out and cut into squares before the mixture is quite cold.

RUM TRUFFLES

3 oz dark chocolate	1 oz butter
1 yolk of egg	rum to flavour
chocolate vermicelli for finishing	

Break the chocolate into pieces and melt carefully by placing in a bowl over a pan of hot water. Stir in the yolk of egg, the butter and rum. Put aside until firm enough to handle then shape into balls and roll each in chocolate vermicelli. This quantity should give approximately twelve sweets. Serve in crinkled paper cases.

CHESTNUT TRUFFLES

1 lb chestnuts	1 yolk of egg
2 oz butter	6 oz icing sugar
rum to flavour	
powdered chocolate for coating	

Make a cut in each chestnut and put in a saucepan with water to cover. Bring to the boil and boil for 10 minutes. Take the chestnuts from the water one at a time and remove both the outer and inner skins.

Stew the prepared chestnuts in a little milk until tender. Avoid overcooking. Drain well and sieve.

Cream the butter and beat in the yolk of egg. Gradually work in the chestnuts and the sieved icing sugar. Flavour with rum. If necessary put in a cool place to firm. Shape into balls and roll in the powdered chocolate. Serve in paper cases.

Suitable alternative coatings for truffles include flaked drinking chocolate or cocoa and icing sugar used in equal quantities.

MARSHMALLOWS

10 oz granulated sugar	¾ oz gelatine
¼ pint water	¼ pint water
¼ teaspoonful cream of tartar	2 egg whites
vanilla flavouring or colouring and flavouring to taste	

Dissolve the sugar in the first quarter pint of water and stir in the cream of tartar. Remove the spoon and bring to the boil. Boil briskly until 128°C or 260°F is reached.

Meanwhile dissolve the gelatine in the second quarter pint of water. Pour the syrup onto the gelatine solution, then pour both gradually onto the stiffly-beaten egg whites. Add the vanilla flavouring, or colouring and flavouring as wished, and continue beating until thick. Pour into a tin which has been lightly oiled and dusted with icing sugar. Put aside to set.

When firm loosen round the edges with a knife and turn out onto sieved icing sugar. Cut into squares using scissors. Toss the pieces of marshmallow in a mixture of cornflour and icing sugar used in the proportion of half cornflour to sugar. Finally, leave exposed in a warm atmosphere to dry.

TURKISH DELIGHT

1 *lb granulated sugar*	3 *oz cornflour*
1 *gill water*	7 *oz icing sugar*
$1/_4$ *teaspoonful*	5 *gills water*
tartaric acid	2 *oz honey*

flavouring as wished, e.g. lemon rind or the grated rind of a tangerine orange
pink colouring

Put the sugar with one gill of water into a saucepan and dissolve over a gentle heat. Stir in the tartaric acid. Remove the spoon and bring to the boil. Boil steadily until 115.5°C or 240°F is reached.

Meanwhile, combine the cornflour with the icing sugar and blend with a proportion of the 5 gills of water. Bring the remainder of the water to the boil and pour onto the cornflour mixture. Return all to the pan and bring to the boil, stirring vigorously and cook until clear and thick. Remove from the heat and beat in the syrup gradually. Continue to boil this mixture for 20-30 minutes. This time must not be shortened as it is essential to change the character of the starch. When ready the mixture should be a pale straw colour and transparent. At this stage add the honey and flavouring and pour half into a buttered tin. Colour the remainder pink and pour it on top of the mixture already in the tin. Put aside to cool and set.

When firm, loosen round the edges with a knife and turn out onto sieved icing sugar. Cut into neat pieces using scissors and toss in icing sugar.

CREME-DE-MENTHE

Creme-de-menthe may be made using the above recipe colouring the mixture green and flavouring it with oil of peppermint.

FONDANT

2 *lb granulated sugar*	1 *tablespoonful glucose*
	or
$2^1/_2$ *gills water*	$1/_4$ *teaspoonful cream of tartar*

Put the sugar and water into a strong saucepan and dissolve slowly and thoroughly over a gentle heat. Stir in the glucose or cream of tartar, then remove the spoon and wash down the sides of the pan with a pastry brush dipped in water. Bring the syrup to the boil and boil gently until 115.5°C or 240°F and keeping the sides of the saucepan washed down as required.

Meanwhile sprinkle a marble slab or large dish with water. When the syrup is ready allow the bubbles to subside and pour it gently onto the prepared surface. Sprinkle the surface also with cold water to prevent a crust forming. Allow it to cool until it can be turned up at the sides with a wooden spatula. If worked while it is too hot it will grain. Now gather it up with a sugar scraper working from the edges to the centre and keeping it together as much as possible. Finally, when sufficiently cool knead with the hand until the fondant is white and perfectly smooth like a piece of putty.

The fondant is now ready to be flavoured and coloured for use as required. STORING OF FONDANT: fondant is at its best for use after it has mellowed for an hour or so. While mellowing cover it with a damp cloth. It will keep for some weeks, but if exposed to the air it will become dry and hard. Store in a cool place.

FONDANT CREAMS

The prepared fondant may be flavoured in a wide variety of ways and coloured appropriately. Suitable flavourings include lemon, orange or tangerine rind, fine coco-nut, vanilla, coffee, violet, rose or pineap-ple-flavoured essences or oil of peppermint.

The flavourings and colourings should be gradually worked into the fondant which should then be rolled out and cut into rounds or other shapes as desired

PEPPERMINT CREAMS (UNCOOKED)

1/4 pint white sauce of a coating consistency and without seasoning
approximately 1 1/2 lb sieved icing sugar
oil of peppermint to flavour

Put the cold sauce into a bowl and gradually work in sufficient sieved icing sugar to give a stiff paste. Flavour with the oil of peppermint and work until smooth, using the hands. Turn out onto a board dusted with icing sugar and roll out about quarter of an inch thick. Cut into rounds with a small plain cutter and leave exposed for a time to dry.

This mixture may be flavoured in a variety of ways as recommended for the fondant creams.

COCO-NUT ICE (UNCOOKED)

6 tablespoonfuls unsweetened condensed milk
3/4 lb icing sugar
3 oz fine coco-nut
vanilla flavouring and pink colouring

Put the condensed milk into a bowl and flavour with the vanilla.

Combine the sieved icing sugar with the coco-nut and gradually work into the milk. The mixture should be very stiff. Divide in two and roll one half to fit a 6 inch square tin. Colour the second half pink, roll out and press firmly on top of the white layer. Put aside in a cool place to firm, if possible until the next day, then cut into pieces.

PEPPERMINT ICE

1 lb granulated sugar   *2 tablespoonfuls cream*
1 1/4 gills water   *a little oil of*
1/4 teaspoonful cream   *peppermint*
of tartar   *green colouring*
2 oz fine coco-nut

Put the sugar and water into a saucepan and stir over a gentle heat until the sugar is dissolved. Stir in the cream of tartar, remove the spoon and bring to the boil. Boil gently until 115.5°C or 240°F. Remove from the heat and allow the bubbles to subside. Now stir gently until cloudy. Add the cream, flavouring, colouring and coco-nut and continue stirring until creamy and beginning to thicken. Pour into a greased tin; one 6 by 9 inches is suitable. Turn out and cut into pieces before it is quite cold.

COOKED MARZIPAN

1 lb granulated   *2 egg whites*
sugar   *2-4 tablespoonfuls*
1 1/4 gills water   *icing sugar*
3/4 lb ground   *a little almond and*
almonds   *vanilla flavouring*

Put the sugar and water into a saucepan and stir over a gentle heat until the sugar is dissolved. Remove the spoon and bring to the boil. Boil gently until 115.5ºC or 240ºF. Remove from the heat and when the bubbles have subsided stir gently to grain slightly, then stir in the ground almonds. Half whip the whites of egg and add. Return to the heat and cook for a few minutes. Add the flavouring and turn the mixture out onto a board or slab already dusted with icing sugar. Allow to cool a little, then knead until smooth, working in the sieved icing sugar at the same time. STORING OF MARZIPAN: Colour before storing if necessary, then wrap each piece in waxed paper, wrap in a dry towel and store in an airtight tin. It will keep for 3-4 weeks.

MARZIPAN DATES

dessert dates
marzipan — coloured pink, green and natural
caramel ·
    8 oz granulated sugar
    ³/₄ gill water
    a pinch of cream of tartar

Stone the fruit neatly. Shape the marzipan into oval pieces and use for stuffing the dates. Now impale on skewers or cocktail sticks and prepare the caramel:

Put the sugar and water into a small saucepan and heat gently until the sugar is dissolved. Stir in the cream of tartar, remove the spoon and bring to the boil. Boil gently until 149ºC or 300ºF or until a light straw colour. Remove from the heat and allow the bubbles to subside. Then quickly dip each stuffed date, put to cool and harden on a greased surface. When firm remove the sticks and serve in little paper cases. These sweets must be stored in an air-tight tin otherwise they go sticky.

Alternatively, the stuffed dates may be finished more simply by tossing in castor sugar.

CARAMEL WALNUTS

walnuts
marzipan — coloured pink, green and natural
caramel:
    8 oz granulated sugar
    ³/₄ gill water
    a pinch of cream of tartar

Use choice walnuts and if necessary freshen by putting in the oven for a few minutes.

Form the marzipan into balls and place half walnuts on either side, pressing gently. Impale on skewers or cocktail sticks and prepare the caramel:

Put the sugar and water into a small saucepan and stir over a gentle heat until the sugar is dissolved. Stir in the cream of tartar, remove the spoon and bring to the boil. Boil gently until a light straw colour. Remove from the heat, allow the bubbles to subside, then quickly dip each sweet. Put to cool and set on a greased surface. When hard remove the sticks and serve in little paper cases. Store in an air-tight tin.

Alternatively, the stuffed walnuts may be finished more simply by tossing in castor sugar.

POPCORN

TO POP CORN: Use a special popping corn and begin by covering the bottom of a medium-sized saucepan with a little olive oil or melted butter or margarine. Sprinkle in a layer of corn, cover with a lid and place over a gentle heat. When the corn begins to pop, increase the heat a little and shake the pan until all the grains are cooked. The popcorn may be eaten as it is, salted, or made into sweets as follows:

POPCORN CANDY

1 *lb granulated*   2 *oz butter or*
  sugar   *margarine*
1 *gill water*   *approximately* 1$^1/_2$
                      pints popped corn

Put the sugar, water and butter into a saucepan and place over a gentle heat until the sugar is dissolved. Remove the spoon and bring to the boil. Boil gently until 115.5°C or 240°F or a soft ball. Remove from the heat, allow the bubbles to subside. Stir to grain lightly, then stir in the popcorn. Drop from a teaspoon onto a greased tin.

POPCORN BALLS

Vanilla syrup:
$^1/_2$ *lb granulated sugar*
$^3/_4$ *gill water*
a little vanilla flavouring

Put the sugar and water into a small saucepan and stir over a gentle heat until the sugar is dissolved. Remove the spoon, bring to the boil and boil gently until 115.5°C or 240°F or a soft ball. Then add a little vanilla flavouring.

Meanwhile, have some corn popped and warm in a warm bowl. Sprinkle a little of the syrup over it, stirring lightly to coat each piece and until the whole becomes sticky. Then shape into balls with the hands. Wrap each ball in waxed paper.

APPENDIX

THE COMPARATIVE COOKING TEMPERATURES OF ELECTRIC AND GAS OVENS

Dish	Electric oven — thermostatic control	Gas — number
Scones	475°	9
Puff		
Rough Puff } Pastries	475°	9
Flaky		
Short Crust Pastry	450°	7
Rich Short Crust Pastry	425°	6
Bread	450°	7
Small Cakes	425°	6
Sponge Sandwich	400°	6
Butter Sandwich	400°	5
Biscuits	375°	5
Shortbread	375-350°	3
Large Cakes (plain or fruit)	350°	3-2
Christmas Cakes	325-300°	2-1
Meringues	300° reduced to 200°	$1/_2$-$1/_4$
Meat	425°	6
Poultry	400°	7-6
Complete Meals	400-450°	6-7
Fruit Bottling	300°	1-2

These temperature comparisons are approximate; in using them it should be remembered that ovens vary slightly in the readings they give.

BRITISH AND AMERICAN MEASURES

British measurements by the spoonful are taken as rounded spoonfuls.

American measurements by the spoonful are always level.

A British tablespoonful = 4 teaspoonfuls.

An American tablespoonful = 3 teaspoonfuls.

A British pint = 20 fluid oz

An American pint = 16 fluid oz

An American measuring cup = 8 fluid oz, and will hold approximately 4-4$^1/_2$ oz flour, 7 oz sugar and 7 oz butter or margarine. Flour should be sifted before being measured.

HANDY MEASURES

1 oz flour = 1 fully rounded tablespoonful

1 oz castor, granulated or demerara sugar = 1 rounded tablespoonful

2 oz golden syrup or treacle = 1 rounded tablespoonful

1 oz coco-nut or dried fruit = 1 rounded tablespoonful

1 teacupful of liquid = fully 1 gill
1 breakfast-cupful of liquid = fully $^1/_2$ pint

These measurements are approximate, a great deal depending on the care with which the individual does the measuring.

201

BIBLIOGRAPHY

DAVID, ELIZABETH, *Italian Food*, London, MacDonald, 1959, 335 pp.

DAVID, ELIZABETH, *French Country Cooking*, London, MacDonald, 1958, 207 pp.

DRUMMOND, SIR JACK C. and WILBRAHAM, ANNE, *The Englishman's Food: A History of Five Centuries of English Diet*, London, Cape, 1958, new rev. ed., 482 pp.

EVANS, E. ESTYN, *Irish Heritage*, Dundalk, Dundalgan, 1952, 6th ed., 190 pp.

EVANS, E. ESTYN, *Irish Folk Ways*, London, Routledge & Kegan Paul, 1961, 324 pp.

HARTLEY, DOROTHY, *Food in England*, London, MacDonald, 1962, 675 pp.

IRWIN, FLORENCE, *Cookin' Woman: Irish Country Recipes*, London, Oliver & Boyd, 1949, 229 pp.

JACK, FLORENCE B., *Cookery for Every Household*, London, Nelson, 1938, 711 pp.

Larousse Gastronomique: The Encyclopaedia of Food, Wine and Cooking, (originally published in French), London, Hamlyn, 1961, 1098 pp.

McNEILL, F. MARIAN, *The Scots Kitchen: Its Traditions and Lore, with Old-Time Recipes*, London, Blackie, 1963, 282 pp.

SALAMAN, REDCLIFFE N., *The History and Social Influence of the Potato*, London, C.U.P., 1949, 685 pp.

SENN, CHARLES H., *Dictionary of Foods and Culinary Encyclopaedia*, London, Ward-Lock, 7th ed., 188 pp.

SIMON, ANDRE L., *A Concise Encyclopaedia of Gastronomy*, London, Collins, 9 vols., 1948.

SPRY, CONSTANCE and HUME, ROSEMARY, *The Constance Spry Cookery Book*, London, Dent, 1961, 1235 pp.

WOODHAM-SMITH CECIL, *The Great Hunger*, London, Hamish Hamilton, 1962, 510 pp.

GLOSSARY

Aigrette Small cheese fritter.

Allspice Or Jamaica pepper, so called because its flavour is similar to a mixture of clove, nutmeg and cinnamon.

Allumette Matchstick.

Au gratin Refers to food coated with a sauce; sprinkled with breadcrumbs or grated cheese; flaked with butter and browned in the oven or under the grill.

Baba A small light yeast cake, usually containing currants, which is soaked in a syrup flavoured with rum.

Bake To cook by dry heat usually, but not necessarily in an oven.

Baste To spoon liquid or melted fat over food to keep it moist.

Batter A combination of flour, other ingredients and a liquid well beaten together such as a cake batter or frying batter.

Beat To mix with a quick rotary movement.

Biscuit A dry crisp cake. The word is of French origin and the literal meaning is " twice cooked ". In America, the word is used to denote a scone, while biscuits are referred to as cookies.

Bisque A thick cream soup usually made with shellfish.

Blanch (a) To put in cold water and bring to the boil with the object of removing the skin, e.g. almonds.
(b) To put in cold water and bring to the boil in order to whiten, e.g. in the preparation of rabbit
(c) Certain vegetables are

blanched to reduce their pungency, e.g. onions, or to kill the enzymes as in the preparation of peas for deep-freezing.

(d) Other foods, e.g. sweetbreads, are blanched to whiten and make them firm before cooking.

Blend   To combine by stirring to a smooth consistency.

Boil   To cook in a liquid in which bubbles rise to the surface and break.

Bouchées   Small patties of puff pastry of a size that they make a traditional " mouthful ".

Bouillon   The French term for stock or broth.

Boulangère — à la   A French term describing a dish left with the baker to be cooked in his oven after the bread has been baked.

Bouquet garni   A bouquet of herbs — usually parsley stalks, thyme and bay-leaf used to flavour savoury dishes.

Boxty   Either pancakes or dumplings made in parts of Ireland notably Co. Tyrone, Fermanagh, Cavan and Leitrim. Grated raw potato and potato starch are necessary ingredients.

Braise   A method of cooking which is a combination of roasting and stewing.

Bran   The inner husks of wheat or oats sifted away in the manufacture of flour.

Brotchen   In Ireland, the word indicates a broth, but in the Highlands of Scotland, it is commonly used for porridge.

Buttermilk The milk that remains after the butter has been separated by churning. Sour milk may be used as a substitute for buttermilk.

Carrageen moss   An Irish seaweed found on the rocks at low tide. It is gathered in April and May and dried and bleached. It is used for making a hot bed-time drink or a type of blancmange.

Champ   An Irish form of creamed potatoes to which a vegetable such as chives, scallions or peas are added at the same time as the hot milk. It is served with a hollow in the centre of each portion into which a lump of butter is put.

Charcuterier   A purveyor of dressed, cooked meats — particularly pork and various sausages.

Clam   A bivalvular shell fish. Around the coast of Ireland scallops are sometimes referred to as clams by the fishermen.

Colcannon A Scotch dish of mashed potatoes and boiled cabbage.

Compôte   Fruit stewed in syrup.

Coriander A sweet, aromatic seed. It is sometimes used in curries.

Court-bouillon Stock in which fish is cooked.

Croûte A piece of fried bread upon which entrées are served.

Croûtons Dice or fancy shapes of toasted or fried bread used to garnish some soups and savoury dishes.

Daube A name referring to braised meat or poultry.

Decant To pour a liquid from one vessel into another, leaving the sediment in the original receptacle.

Dish ring Generally made of highly ornamented silver and used in Ireland for serving boiled potatoes. The ring surrounds a wooden bowl, alternatively, a napkin was used under the potatoes.

Dripping The fat from roasted meat.

Elderflower The flowers of the elder tree used for flavouring, particularly in association with gooseberries.

Elvers Young eels.

Fadge Another name for the traditional potato cake of Ireland.

Farce Forcemeat or stuffing.

Farls A term used in Irish and Scottish baking referring to the traditional shape of the bread. The circular cake is marked with a cross so that it can be readily broken into quarters or farls after baking.

Flakemeal Flaked porridge oats.

Forcemeat Stuffing for meat or birds. It does not necessarily contain meat.

Friandises "Dainties" or "dainty bits"—a name for small decorative cakes frequently served with ices and cold sweets. They are uncooked.

Garnish Edible decoration added to a dish to improve the appearance and flavour. Often a dish is named after the garnish used.

Griddle or girdle A round plate of cast-iron with a semicircular handle. It is properly used over an open turf fire. In Scotland, the word girdle is used instead of griddle as in Ireland.

Gigot d'agneau Leg of lamb. The word "gigot" is used both in French and Scottish cooking.

Gigot de mouton Leg of mutton.

Grand'mère —à la A French term describing a dish cooked in the old style.

Harnen stand A traditional Irish cooking utensil used as a toaster or bread stand for "harning" or hardening bread, particularly oatcake after it has been baked on the griddle. It is generally of wrought

	iron and is often very ornamental.
Hors-d'oeuvre	A light, appetising course served at the beginning of a meal.
Infuse	To steep in liquid without boiling as in making tea.
Julienne	Food, particularly vegetables, cut into fine shreds.
Liaison	The thickening for soups, sauces and creams.
Ling	A common fish round the coast of Ireland. It is frequently salted and dried over the hedges in summer.
Mace	A spice which forms the leafy network which envelopes the nutmeg.
Macédoine	(a) Vegetables cut in even-sized dice, or cooked and combined with mayonnaise for an hors-d'oeuvre. (b) Fruit evenly divided for fruit salad or fruit set in jelly.
Mandoline	A French cooking utensil used for slicing vegetables, particularly potatoes. It may be plain or fluted.
Marinade	A seasoned liquid, often wine or vinegar, in which meat and fish are steeped. Its purpose is to increase the flavour of the food and make it more tender.
Mille feuilles	Translated literally the word means "a thousand leaves". It refers to a cake made with several layers of puff pastry sandwiched with jam and cream.
Nutmeg	Is an aromatic spice and is the seed of the nutmeg tree.
Oatmeal	The grain obtained from oats when dried and ground. There are three types — coarse or pinhead, medium and fine.
Pamphrey	The name used in Ireland for spring greens.
Panada	A thick sauce used for binding ingredients together for croquettes and similar dishes. It is also used in the making of hot soufflés.
Pasta	The general name covering the countless Italian varieties of macaroni, vermicelli and noodles.
Patty	A small round pie made with puff pastry and filled with a savoury mixture.
Pectin	A natural gum-like product from the cell-walls of fruit — particularly when underripe. It is essential in obtaining a good set when jam making.
Petits fours	A name covering many kinds of small fancy cakes or biscuits. They are always baked as the name indicates, " four " meaning " oven ".
Pistachio	A small nut valued on account of its flavour and pretty green colour.
Poach	To cook in liquid under boiling point.
Pork fillet	The undercut or fillet of

the pig which is obtained when bacon is being prepared for curing.

Pork griskin Meaty trimmings obtained when bacon is being prepared for curing.

Potato A well-known and valued vegetable, which played an important part in the social history of Ireland. Locally, it is also spoken of as taties, praties, Murphies or spuds.

Potato oaten A form of potato cake made with oatmeal instead of flour.

Potato ricer A kitchen untensil used for pressing potatoes to give a result similar to sieving.

Potato ring See dish ring.

Pot oven A kind of Dutch oven used in traditional Irish kitchens. It may either be suspended over the turf fire or rested on a trivet. The lid is shaped so that live turfs may be placed on top.

Poundies A word used in parts of Ireland for creamed potatoes.

Purée A smooth pulp obtained by sieving.

Ragoût A rich stew of meat.

Rennet A liquid obtained from the inner membrane of a calf's stomach. It is used to make milk clot as in making junket.

Roasting Originally roasting meant cooking by radiated heat, but it has come to mean the baking of meat in the oven.

Roux A combination of melted butter and flour used to thicken sauces and soups. It may be white, fawn or brown.

Sablé A shortcake or biscuit.

Saffron Prepared from the dried stamens of the saffron or autumn crocus. Used in cooking for flavouring and colouring savoury dishes and cake.

Sauter To toss in hot fat over the heat. The process may either be done quickly without a lid, or more slowly in a covered pan until the food has absorbed the fat.

Savarin A spongy yeast cake baked in a ring mould and soaked in a syrup flavoured with rum. It is named after Brillat-Savarin a French gastronome.

Scallions The name used in Ireland for spring onions.

Schnitzel A thin slice of meat, generally veal.

Seasoning A substance which is added to food to give it greater relish such as salt. the word is often used to include forcemeat and stuffing. It also defines the act of seasoning a dish.

Shortening Any kind of fat used in baking.

Shred	(a) To cut vegetables with a knife or shredder into fine matchstick pieces. (b) To tear or scrape meat or fish.
Simmer	To cook in liquid which is boiling so gently that the bubbles only form slowly at the side of the pan.
Sippets	Triangles or crescents of fried or toasted bread used for garnishing.
Sloes	The fruit of the black thorn.
Sloke	An edible seaweed found around the coasts of Ireland and Wales. It is very similar to spinach in flavour and is, therefore, often spoken of as sea-spinach.
Stew	To cook gently in liquid in a covered pan.
Thump	A word used in parts of Ireland for creamed potatoes.
Truffles	Highly esteemed fungi which grow underground. They are primarily valued on account of their aroma, but the colour of the black truffle is also useful decoratively. Black truffles are found in France, particularly in Perigord. White truffles are found in northern Italy. Truffle cakes are small cakes made in imitation of black truffle.
Truss	To tie a bird with string in order to keep it a good shape while it is being cooked.
Vol-au-vent	A large round or oval case of puff pastry. The literal translation is " a puff of wind ".
Wheaten meal	Meal made by grinding wheat. It is coarser and more flaky with the inner husk than wholemeal.
Whole meal	A brown flour ground from the whole wheat grain.
Yellow man	A traditional sweet or toffee made in Ireland. It is often sold at country fairs.
Yellow meal	A meal ground from maize used to make porridge, bread and scones. In traditional Irish cooking, it is sometimes known as Golden Drop.
Zest	The outer skin of citrus fruits valued for its flavour.

INDEX

217